WORKING TOGETHER FOR CHILDREN,
YOUNG PEOPLE AND THEIR FAMILIES

SERIES EDITOR

Child Welfare in the United Kingdom

1948–1998

Edited by

Olive Stevenson

**Blackwell
Science**

© 1999 by
Blackwell Science Ltd
Editorial Offices:
Osney Mead, Oxford OX2 0EL
25 John Street, London WC1N 2BL
23 Ainslie Place, Edinburgh EH3 6AJ
350 Main Street, Malden
  MA 02148 5018, USA
54 University Street, Carlton
  Victoria 3053, Australia
10, rue Casimir Delavigne
  75006 Paris, France

Other Editorial Offices:

Blackwell Wissenschafts-Verlag GmbH
Kurfürstendamm 57
10707 Berlin, Germany

Blackwell Science KK
MG Kodenmacho Building
7–10 Kodenmacho Nihombashi
Chuo-ku, Tokyo 104, Japan

The right of the Author to be identified as
the Author of this Work has been asserted
in accordance with the Copyright, Designs
and Patents Act 1988

First published 1999

Set in 10/12 pt Sabon
by DP Photosetting, Aylesbury, Bucks
Printed and bound in Great Britain by
MPG Books Ltd, Bodmin, Cornwall

The Blackwell Science logo is a trade mark
of Blackwell Science Ltd, registered at the
United Kingdom Trade Marks Registry

DISTRIBUTORS

Marston Book Services Ltd
PO Box 269
Abingdon
Oxon OX14 4YN
(Orders: Tel: 01235 465500
          Fax: 01235 465555)

USA
Blackwell Science, Inc.
Commerce Place
350 Main Street
Malden, MA 02148 5018
(Orders: Tel: 800 759 6102
               781 388 8250
          Fax: 781 388 8255)

Canada
Login Brothers Book Company
324 Saulteaux Crescent
Winnipeg, Manitoba R3J 3T2
(Orders: Tel: 204 837 2987
          Fax: 204 837 3116)

Australia
Blackwell Science Pty Ltd
54 University Street
Carlton, Victoria 3053
(Orders: Tel: 03 9347 0300
          Fax: 03 9347 5001)

A catalogue record for this title
is available from the British Library

ISBN 0-632-04993-6

Library of Congress
Cataloging-in-Publication Data

Child welfare in the United Kingdom,
  1948–1998 / edited by Olive Stevenson.
      p. cm. – (Working together for
  children, young people, and their
  families)
      Includes bibliographical references
  and index.
      ISBN 0-632-04993-6
      1. Child welfare – Great Britain.
  2. Children – Services for – Great
  Britain.   3. Children – Government
  policy – Great Britain.   4. Social work
  with children – Great Britain.
  I. Stevenson, Olive.   II. Series.
  HV751.A6C385 1998
  362.7′0941 – dc21   98-25920
                                     CIP

For further information on Blackwell
Science, visit our website:
www.blackwell-science.com

Contents

List of Contributors

Stewart Asquith MA(Hons), DipSocAdmin, PhD   St. Kentigern Professor for the Child, Centre for the Child and Society, University of Glasgow

Keith Bilton MA (Cantab), DipPub & SocAdmin   Child Welfare Consultant

Roger Bullock MA, PhD   Director of the Dartington Social Research Unit, Bristol University

Pauline Hardiker BA, MA   Senior Lecturer (Associate), School of Social Work, University of Leicester

Lorraine Harding BA, MA   Senior Lecturer in Social Policy, Department of Sociology and Social Policy, University of Leeds

Nigel Parton BA, CQSW, MA   Professor in Child Care, Centre for Applied Childhood Studies, School of Human and Health Sciences, University of Huddersfield

Mike Stein BA, MPhil   Professor of Social Work, Department of Social Policy and Social Work, and Co-Director of the Social Work Research and Development Unit, University of York

Olive Stevenson CBE, MA(Oxon), DLitt, LittD(Hon)   Professor Emeritus of Social Work Studies, University of Nottingham

June Thoburn MSW, LittD, DipP & SocAdmin   Professor of Social Work, School of Social Work, University of East Anglia, Norwich

Introduction
by Professor Olive Stevenson

This book was an ambitious enterprise, which sprang from a growing conviction that the post-war history of child welfare had been neglected. The fundamental issues, which are of as much concern today as they were in 1948, are rarely placed in the context of those 50 years, from which there is much to learn. It seemed timely to stand back and reflect on the achievements and failures of the period but also to look forward to the next phase of this demanding work. There can be no more worthwhile activity than the search to improve the quality of life for deprived children and there is an honourable record in Britain of commitment to that task. There are also disturbing examples of the failure to protect children and to offer them 'a good enough' life in care.

We have learnt that it is very, very difficult to act as a 'corporate' good parent for children who are separated from their parents, or to offer effective protection and support to them in their own homes.

The book explores a wide range of issues which are central to child welfare practice and I have been fortunate in securing contributions from highly respected authors. Part I puts the practice debates in a wider context of social policy. These four chapters remind us that the well-being of children is crucially dependent on many factors outside the personal social services, whether these be social, political and economic, or related to other essential social services.

Part II considers the complex, sensitive work required in caring, or arranging care, for children in need, and the influences, forces and fashions which have pulled it in various directions. It was predictable that the authors' views of history would vary to some extent and those readers who have themselves knowledge and experience of the years under review may find themselves saying 'I don't see it like that'. It may be particularly difficult for those who are or were in practice if their own contribution to child welfare seems insufficiently valued within the general picture. But there can never be a definitive version of the past and this book makes no such claim. I hope it will stimulate an informed debate and offer students and new practitioners a framework within which to put their current and (as always) pressing concerns.

Olive Stevenson
Professor Emeritus of Social Work Studies
University of Nottingham

Acknowledgements

Many people have been patient in the preparation of this book. The contributing authors and their secretaries have, without exception, been good tempered and patient. Friends, especially Sara Glennie, have put up with my musings and Sarah Jones has borne up bravely with muddles over discs and last minute frenzies. Thanks to all.

This book acknowledges with gratitude the pioneers of post-war child welfare whose compassion and commitment was powerful and from whom so much has been learnt. Some of what they taught us, directly and indirectly, was lost for a while but is beginning to be rediscovered.

Part I

The Wider Context of Child Welfare

Chapter 1

Ideology, Politics and Policy

Nigel Parton

Introduction

The focus of this chapter is to provide a critical analysis of the key social, economic and political factors which have influenced child welfare policy and practice in England and Wales since the Second World War. It will attempt to locate developments in child welfare in the context of the more wide-ranging changes and transformations in social welfare during the period, for in many respects child welfare policies and practices reflect their time and place, particularly the changing relationship between the family, the market and the State. A central part of the analysis, therefore, will be concerned with examining how the balance of responsibilities and relationships between the family, the market and the State have been reconfigured and refashioned during the period and to consider the impact and implications for child welfare policy.

A key element of the argument is that local authority child care has increasingly become the subject of public and political concern and debate in a way which was not evident at the start of the period and that these concerns and debates have become increasingly contested. In the process, the very nature of policy and practice has changed. As Jean Packman has argued (1981, 1993), from the moment of their inception following the Children Act 1948, the development of local authority Children's Departments through to their incorporation in Social Services Departments in 1971 could be characterised as:

'idealistic, acutely critical of both their ancestors and contemporary figures (especially medical ones); optimistic and pushy about their own capacities to do good and ambitious to do more.'

(Packman, 1993: p. 183)

However, by the late 1970s this positive and optimistic stance had been superseded by a much gloomier and harsher reality. Not only was there considerable disillusionment amongst practitioners and managers but this disillusionment seemed to be shared by the wider public and politicians (Packman, 1993: p. 190). I will suggest that while these elements have continued to pervade the field throughout the 1980s and 1990s, there is an increasing recognition of the complexities, uncertainties and risks involved which in themselves seem to capture some of the emerging characteristics of the political and cultural climate of the time (Parton, 1998a, 1998b).

For the purposes of the analysis I will consider the post-war era in terms of three historical periods. From 1945 to the mid-1960s, from the mid-1960s to the late 1970s and from the late 1970s to the current time. I will examine how the different institutions of the family, the market and the State have been coordinated and balanced and how this has changed across the three periods. Although I will be concerned with the shifting balance between the three institutions, I will give particular attention to the changing role of the State. This is not because the State plays the primary role in providing welfare, certainly not in child welfare where the family is central, but because the State is the crucial organiser in establishing the mix, relationships and boundaries between the institutions. It is therefore important to identify the political decisions, settlements and changes which have shaped and modified the balance and composition of the three institutions. I am particularly concerned to make explicit embedded assumptions, often unstated, about the role of the family, the position of women and the nature of social citizenship, all of which are key to understanding the changing nature and role of child welfare policy and practice.

The Children Act 1948 and the post-war settlement

The Children Act 1948, which established local authority Children's Departments, received little political or public attention at the time. Neither of the major historical accounts of the 1945–51 Labour Government (Morgan, 1984; Pelling, 1984) mentions the Children Act and a recent comprehensive history of British social policy suggests the legislation owed 'more to accident and necessity' and 'there appears to have been little ideological input from any quarter' (Laybourn, 1995: p. 226). As Hill (1993) suggests, the legislation and the introduction of Children's Departments was politically uncontroversial.

However, although uncontroversial, the establishment of Children's Departments was a significant development which provided the framework and essential principles for developments over the next 25 years. The new departments tried to lay to rest the Poor Law and embodied the revolutionary principle that the new agencies should seek the *best* development of children deprived of a *normal* home life. Under section 15 of the Poor Law Act 1930 it was the duty of the local authority to:

'set to work and put out as apprentices all children whose parents are not, in the opinion of the council, able to keep and maintain their children.'

The influence of the 1601 and 1834 Poor Law Acts is explicit and there is no reference to any duties to educate, compensate or care for the children involved. However, the responsibilities in section 12 of the Children Act 1948 are much more generous and state that:

(1) Where a child is in the care of the local authority, it shall be the duty of that authority to exercise their powers with respect to him so as to further his best interests and to afford him opportunity for the proper development of his character and abilities.
(2) In providing for a child in their care, a local authority shall make such use of facilities and services available for children in the care of their own parents, as appears to the local authority reasonable in his case.

As Jean Packman (1981) has argued, children 'in care' were in future to be treated as individuals and not as an undifferentiated category of youngsters and should have access to the same range of facilities as any other children.

The new departments should be staffed by an entirely new kind of personnel who were professionally trained in the psychosocial sciences and who had a thorough understanding of human relationships and needs. Child care officers were not drawn in any significant numbers either from Poor Law staff or the pre-war voluntary agencies. The groundwork for such an approach had been laid in the inter-war period, in particular the development of child guidance clinics and the growth and influence of psychologists who emphasised the importance of the family, particularly the relationships between mother and child (Rose, 1989; Holman, 1996). Furthermore, the Second World War, particularly the policy of evacuation, provided a new visibility for children separated from their parents and provided the proponents of psychodynamic and psychosocial approaches to mother–child relations with an opportunity to research and thereby demonstrate the importance of a *normal* family life to ensure that children developed appropriately and were well-adjusted. Much of the pioneering groundwork of people like John Bowlby and others at the Tavistock Clinic, which was to prove so crucial in informing the philosophy and approach of the new Children's Departments, was developed at this time. Not only was the experience of war significant in influencing the nature and form of the post-war economic and social reconstruction but also the family was seen to play a central role in it. It is not surprising therefore that the Children Act 1948 and the introduction of Children's Departments was politically uncontroversial; it was thoroughly consistent with the central principles and approaches of that reconstruction. To understand such developments, however, it is important to draw out the assumptions which underpinned such developments and how these related to these more wide-ranging political, social and economic reconfigurations.

Like other Western nations, Britain faced major tasks of social and economic reconstruction at the end of the war which were reinforced by popular demands that there should not be a 'return to the 1930s' and the importance of creating 'a land fit for heroes'. The issue for an essentially capitalist society was how to combine a commitment to a free market economy with maintaining social harmony. It was further evident that Britain's position as a world power was considerably weakened and was subordinated to the 'Western alliance' under the leadership of the USA, an alliance whose defining characteristics were increasingly determined by the opposition to the Eastern communist bloc and the growing cold war. The creation of what came to be called 'the welfare state' was to play an important role in enhancing national prestige both at home and abroad and compensating for this loss of prestige to the USA and imperial decline (Clark & Langan, 1993).

The establishment of the welfare state or 'welfarism', as Rose & Miller (1992) refer to it, is best understood not simply in terms of the growth of the interventionist state but as a particular form of government. The key innovations of welfarism lay in the attempts to link the fiscal and economic capacities of the State to the government of social life. As a political rationality, welfarism was structured by the wish to encourage national growth and well-being through the promotion of *social* responsibility and the mutuality of *social* risk, and was premised on the notion of *social* solidarity (Donzelot, 1988). Post-war welfarism rested on the twin and interrelated approaches derived from Keynes and Beveridge.

The Keynesian element stood for an increase in government in terms of attempts to manage economic demand in a market economy through judicious state intervention, particularly by increased public expenditure during a recession, with the aim of maximising production and maintaining full employment. The depression of the inter-war years had demonstrated that, left to itself, the capitalist market economy could not function effectively. It led to a drastic fall in production and mass unemployment and fed social and political unrest. The Keynesian approach stood for state intervention from the demand side of the economy in order to ensure high levels of economic activity and full employment.

While Keynesian theory provided the economic component of postwar welfarism, ideas derived from Beveridge formed the social component and were based on the idea of insurance, in its widest sense, against the hazards of the market economy. Unlike the Keynesian economic argument, the social argument for welfarism was not new.

Since the days of Bismarck in Germany and Lloyd George in Britain, most Western capitalist countries had developed forms of social protection underwritten and coordinated by the State. What was new in the post-war period was that the principle of state intervention was made explicit, and the institutional framework which would make State responsibility for maintaining minimum standards became a reality.

A number of assumptions characterised the development of welfarism in the 25 years after the Second World War. The institutional framework of universal state welfare services, particularly in health, education and social security, was seen as the best way of maximising welfare and that the State worked for the whole society and was the best way of coordinating this. The social services were instituted for benevolent purposes meeting 'social needs', compensating socially caused 'diswelfares' and promoting 'social justice'. Their underlying functions were ameliorative, integrative and redistributive. Social progress would be achieved through the agency of the social democratic State and professional interventions. Increased public expenditure, the cumulative extension of statutory welfare provision and the proliferation of government regulations backed by expert administration represented the main guarantors of equity and efficiency. Similarly, certain social scientific knowledge was seen as helpful in informing and ordering the approach of the emerging professions which were seen as having a significant contribution to developing individual and social welfare.

As Michael Sullivan (1992) has concluded from his review of the literature and research on the post-war period, there is widespread agreement amongst political analysts and commentators that there was a considerable political consensus on the essential principles and parameters of the mixed economy, full employment and the welfare state. More particularly he argues that:

> 'there is clear agreement that consensus politics were, in some sense, the pivot of the discourse and craft of UK national politics in the pre-Thatcher post-war period. Keynesian economic management and Beveridge's social philosophy had acted as midwives to a relatively durable form of welfare capitalism.'

> (Sullivan, 1992: p. 11)

The post-war reconstruction of welfare in Britain thus involved the elaboration of a new set of relationships between the State, the market and the family. However, whilst most attention in histories and analyses of social policy has usually been given to the expansion of State provision during this period, this expansion was premised on the assumption that most welfare needs would be satisfied by the family and the market. Only in education and health was it the State's role to be the primary agency of provision and even here private provision was allowed to continue. As already noted, Britain's relationship with the USA provided a constraint on the structure, levels and funding of welfare spending but perhaps more significantly the structural inequalities of individual income and wealth exercised a significant influence on access to social welfare. As Richard Titmuss (1958) noted, the social relations of the market-place permeated the new systems, creating a 'social division of welfare' which both reflected and reinforced, in a slightly modified form, the deep-rooted class divisions and inequalities of British society.

Apart from health and education, it was quite clear that the role of the State was to support the institutions of the market and the family. It was assumed that needs would be met primarily through male waged work in the market and the services and care of mothers in the family. For example, the national insurance social security system was premised on the notion of the male breadwinner in employment paying insurance contributions and providing for wives and children. Anyone who did not fit the model was excluded and had to call on the means-tested national assistance scheme.

The post-war welfare services were thus based on a particular model of the economy and the family. Not only did it assume full male employment, it also assumed a traditional role for the patri-archal nuclear family (Pascall, 1986; Williams, 1989). The notion of the 'family wage' was central, linking the labour market to the dis-tribution of social roles and dependency by age and gender within the family. Within the family, women were to trade housework, childbirth and child-rearing and physical and emotional caring as 'labours of love' in return for economic support (Finch & Groves, 1983). In practice, therefore, much 'welfare work' was expected to be undertaken within the family either using the family wage to buy goods and services or by women caring for children and other depen-dants. The provision of state welfare was intended to support the patriarchal nuclear family which was seen as central, positive and beneficent. Such a model was key to the newly-formed Children's Departments which were explicitly designed to provide a residual ser-vice for children deprived of a 'normal family life'. Clearly, however, it would be subject to a whole series of tensions and difficulties if any of the underlying assumptions were seriously questioned or if there were to be significant changes in the key institutions which provided the framework for its work, whether this be the labour market, the patriarchal nuclear family or the other more universal social services – particularly health, education and social security. Beyond this, fur-ther stresses would be created if the political consensus which under-pinned the post-war welfare changes was itself put under strain thereby questioning the politically uncontroversial nature of child care services. All these issues are closely interrelated.

Expansion, modernisation and re-organisation

By the mid 1960s local authority child care services were expanding their operations and reframing their responses in at least three directions: preventive work with families; diversionary and remedial work with young offenders; and, to a lesser extent, investigative and rescue work with neglected and abused children (Packman, 1981; 1993). During the 1960s there was an increasing conviction supported by senior civil servants at the Home Office, sections of the Labour Party, some key academics as well as the emerging profession of social work itself (Hall, 1976; Clarke, 1980; Cooper, 1983), that better services could be provided by means of reorganisation, redrawing the boundaries between services and aiming to provide a rationalised and explicit *family* service. Such developments were particularly informed by the more wide-ranging reappraisal that was taking place at the time of the full range of welfare services introduced in the post-war period. The introduction of Social Services Departments in 1971 was a key element of this more overall reappraisal. However, these changes did not attempt to fundamentally change the principles and underlying assumptions of the post-war settlement. They are better understood as an attempt to modernise and update in the context of important social changes and new challenges. There was still a considerable optimism and consensus that social work and welfarism more generally was a social good for all concerned.

The international post-war economic boom allowed a considerable expansion in the scope of welfare services throughout the West well into the 1970s. However, as I will suggest later, the welfare state in Britain increasingly came to occupy a distinctive political position because, while the British economy grew consistently at an average of 3% a year, it was falling behind its major industrial competitors, whose average rates of growth were around 5% a year. Between 1950 and 1975 the share of gross national product (GNP) taken by public expenditure increased steadily and it was spending on welfare services which accounted for the largest part of the growth. Spending on welfare services rose from a share of 11.3% in 1939, to 16.3% in 1955 and 28% in 1975 (Gough, 1979; Sleeman, 1979). This expansion resulted primarily from changing patterns of need, changing costs of welfare and changing state priorities.

In terms of need there were important demographic changes particularly with regard to the increased proportion of the population not just over retirement age but aged 75 and beyond. Because of the increased incidence of illness, infirmity, disability and social isolation associated with old age, there was increased demand placed upon the social security, health and social care services. This increased dependency in the population was thrown into sharp relief when put alongside the increase in social and geographical mobility and the changing role of women and the nature of the family as I will discuss later. It was also evident by the mid-1960s with the 'rediscovery of poverty' that the assumption that the severe and widespread social deprivations of the inter-war period had been overcome by the welfare reforms was considerably exaggerated (Abel-Smith & Townsend, 1965).

Not only had improvements in technology and expertise in effect created new needs, particularly in terms of demands for health services, it also seems that the proportionate increase in welfare expenditure was caused by the labour-intensive nature of the services which could not be substituted by new technology as in the manufacturing industry. The relative costs of providing welfare services rose faster than the national rate of inflation (Gough, 1979).

The response of the State to this complex and changing network of needs, costs and priorities was to try to modernise the organisational structures through which welfare was provided. Between the early 1960s and the mid-1970s the British welfare state underwent a series of restructurings and reorganisations affecting central and local government and the National Health Service. All were aimed at improving integration and efficiency via better coordination, management and cost-effectiveness.

The role outlined for the new Social Services Department was not just in providing a range of services, including social work, but of coordinating aspects of other welfare services and thereby making services more responsive to need. This included trying to improve the functioning of certain families who were seen as causing a disproportionate amount of demand particularly in terms of delinquency, child neglect, mental illness, etc. – characteristics often associated at the time with 'the problem family' (see, for example, Philp & Timms, 1962). Social Services Departments were established as the 'fifth social service' (Townsend, 1970) with the family as its focus and they would provide the personalised, humanistic dimension to the welfare state, the primary tool being the professional worker's personality and understanding of human relationships. This perhaps marked the high point of the optimism and confidence of social work which primarily had been built upon the development and creativity of the Children's Departments and its key advocates.

However by the early 1970s it was also clear that the notion of the family which lay, not just at the core of the reorganised Social Services Department but also at the heart of the post-war welfare state, was considerably more complex than previously assumed and was changing in important ways. These developments included: a significant increase in married women's paid employment, though much of this was part-time and casual in nature; the growing number of lone-parent families; the growing number of illegitimate births; and the increasing number of older people dependent upon public rather than familial care (Fox-Harding, 1996).

There seemed to be a growing gulf between the ideal and the reality of family life and this put added pressures on social policy and welfare services. Not only had the provision of state welfare been developed on the assumption that it would support the family and it would primarily be the family that would care for its members except in exceptional circumstances, but increasingly it was being suggested that the development of more extensive state services had contributed to the deviations from the ideal. The State had inappropriately taken over responsibilities previously carried out by the traditional patriarchal nuclear family. Such concerns were particularly expressed in relation to the growth in lone-parent families which grew from 570 000 in 1971 to 1 150 000 in 1989 (Burghes, 1993). When these developments were combined with dramatic changes in the labour market and the growth in unemployment and inflation in the 1970s we can see that the role and nature of both the family and the market were shifting in ways which posed fundamental questions for the State and the underlying principles and framework of the post-war reconstruction.

As the pace of economic expansion began to falter in the late 1960s and was replaced by recession in the early 1970s, the difficulties of sustaining the pattern of state welfare in its post-war form became a central focus of public and political debate. In effect just at the point, in the early 1970s, when the reorganised social services became a central and potentially expanded element of the modernised post-war welfare state, the welfare state and the political settlement and consensus on which it was based was being subject to severe questioning and increasing political scepticism and criticism.

Child welfare and 'advanced liberalism'

The oil price rise of 1973 triggered the first worldwide recession since the 1930s and brought the return of mass unemployment throughout the West, eroding what had been one of the main supporting pillars of post-war welfarism. The combination of slowing growth and rising prices – 'stagflation' – produced pressures to curtail public expenditure and wages at a time of growing job losses and increasing poverty. As the problems of economic recession intensified during the 1980s, the pressures on public provision of welfare provoked widespread rethinking about the State's role in welfare and about the restructuring of welfare states throughout the advanced capitalist world. Such developments in the economic sphere were reinforced in the social sphere. It was increasingly recognised that the welfare reforms had not resolved poverty and deprivation, and might in fact have acted to encourage them. Similarly there was also a growth in the crime figures and other indices of social indiscipline more generally; a decline in individual responsibility and, as we have seen, decline in attachments to the traditional nuclear family; an emerging view that the growth in the number of professional social experts had not delivered the social good that had been hoped for.

The 1974–79 Labour Government's attempt to reconcile the conflicting economic demands through the corporatist mechanisms of the social contract were generally judged a failure, provoking trade union militancy in the 'winter of discontent' of 1978/9. The period proved crucial for laying the groundwork whereby welfarism could be supplanted by a new rationality of government informed by the New Right, often associated in the UK with the rise and dominance of Thatcherism (Levitas, 1986; Gamble, 1994; Evans & Taylor, 1996). For the New Right the central principles and rationale of the post-war reconstruction which underpinned the welfarist project were seen as a central part of the problem. Rather than modify and reform, nothing less than fundamental change was required.

The Conservative Party was in power from May 1979 to May 1997, initially headed by Margaret Thatcher and from 1990 by John Major. The political project announced at the beginning of the Thatcher years was to do away with consensus and replace it with conviction politics, to rehabilitate neo-liberal economic principles and re-establish traditional conservatism in the social sphere. As Gamble has argued, what gave the New Right its unity and distinguished it from other right-wing political variants was the combination of a traditional liberal defence of the free economy with a traditional conservative defence of State authority – the free economy and the strong State (Gamble, 1994).

Deakin (1994) has summarised the approach to welfare of the Conservative Government as falling within three distinct but linked enterprises. First, a more efficient management of the existing system of welfare as exemplified by more effective use of public funds and improved standard of the services provided. Second, the introduction of new machinery intended as a means towards these ends, modelled on market provision, using a variety of market-based devices and altering the basic relationship between the State and the recipient of welfare through a change in the way in which welfare is provided, particularly via the introduction of the quasi-market (Le Grand, 1990a; Le Grand & Bartlett, 1993). Third, a moral mission to achieve a basic change in attitudes to welfare by remoralising the recipients of welfare and restoring a sense of personal responsibility, through the substitution of market attitudes towards welfare and increased attachments to the traditional nuclear family.

In the early years the Government was primarily concerned with the economic sphere and a restructuring of both public and private industry via its monetary policy and serious attempts to reduce the power of the trades unions. While this clearly changed the economic context in which social policies operated, the political project proceeded much more cautiously in the welfare sphere. It implemented its agenda gradually, in a piecemeal way and began where political resistance was likely to be at its weakest – in public housing and the social security system. Only after the 1987 election did the Government seriously begin to extend 'market reforms' into those areas with stronger public, professional and political support – health, education and community care, and the personal social services. As Le Grand has pointed out:

'one of the striking features of the first eight years of Mrs Thatcher's government was how little it affected the welfare state.'

(Le Grand, 1990b: p. 351)

We should not forget, however, that there was also a series of changes which attempted to reduce and control the resources available to local government and limit and centralise its powers throughout the period. These changes made a real impact on the work of local authority social services.

Even so, analyses of the patterns of public expenditure on welfare show that it remained very stable:

'Over the thirteen years from 1974 to 1987, welfare policy success-fully weathered an economic hurricane in the mid-1970s and an ideological blizzard in the 1980s.'

(Le Grand, 1990b: p. 350)

However, within this overall pattern, the proportion taken up by health and particularly social security increased in response to growing demand prompted by changing demography and increased unem-ployment.

Spending on the personal social services, starting from a very low initial base, grew by 63.4% between 1970/1 and 1974/5. As Ferlie & Judge have commented, 'the golden age for spending on the personal social services was quite clearly the first half of the 1970s' (Ferlie & Judge, 1981: pp. 313–14). Growth subsequently slowed significantly following the establishment of a 2% annual growth target intended to take account of demographic changes. While resources allocated to the personal social services were maintained at fairly constant levels through the 1980s, it is also clear that the resources were quite insuf-ficient for the tasks at hand. Even in the years when the 2% growth target was more than met, the personal social services failed to maintain absolute, let alone per capita, service levels across the board. Resources were quite insufficient to prevent a decline in the level of service pro-vision (Webb & Wistow, 1987).

However, although the economic and resource elements for the work of the personal social services are important in order to understand its changing role and functions, this is perhaps not the most significant factor during this period. From the early/mid-1970s, social work, particularly in the newly-created Social Services Departments, became publicly and politically controversial in a way which was quite unknown in the post-war period. More particularly a series of child abuse inquiries thrust it into the public arena via the media (Aldridge, 1994) and had an impact well beyond the more specific concerns at the way the cases were handled. It was as if the child abuse tragedies were emblematic of all that was wrong with the post-war welfare state and that therefore social workers took on a symbolic significance and focus for more wide-ranging debates and arguments about the nature and future of welfarism itself.

While there was evidence of an increasing set of concerns about the nature and interventions of social workers from various quarters (Clarke, 1993), it was child abuse inquiries that provided the major catalyst for venting major criticisms of the policies and practices of social workers particularly in local authority Social Services child care. While these criticisms were in evidence from 1973 onwards, following the death of Maria Colwell (Secretary of State, 1974; Parton, 1985), they gained a new level of intensity during the 1980s via the inquiries into the deaths of Jasmine Beckford (London Borough of Brent, 1985), Kimberley Carlile (London Borough of Greenwich, 1987) and Tyra Henry (London Borough of Lambeth, 1987). The 30 or more inquiries published between 1973 and 1987 were all concerned with the deaths of children at the hands of their parents or carers. All the children had died as a result of physical abuse and neglect, and many had suffered emotional neglect and failure to thrive. The emphasis in public inquiry recommendations was to encourage social workers to use their legal mandate to intervene in families to protect children, and to improve practitioners' knowledge of the signs and symptoms of child abuse (DHSS, 1982; DoH, 1991).

However events in Cleveland in the early summer of 1987 and the subsequent inquiry (Secretary of State, 1988) pointed to a new and potentially contradictory set of concerns. This time it seemed that professionals – paediatricians as well as social workers – had failed to recognise the rights of parents and had intervened prematurely in families where there were concerns about sexual abuse. Thus, during 1987 and 1988, it seemed that the fine balance between family autonomy and State intervention had been lost and that both child welfare policy and the practices of professionals was out of touch and out of control. Social workers seemed to be intervening both too little too late and too much too early, or, as it was projected in the media, as both 'fools and wimps' and 'villains and bullies' (Franklin & Parton, 1991). Social workers, seen through the image of child abuse inquiries, seemed to represent all that was wrong with post-war welfarism and were thus extremely vulnerable to public, political and media pillory.

This public opprobrium coincided with the third term of Margaret Thatcher's administration from 1987 which was more centrally concerned with reforming key sectors of welfare provision, particularly in education, health and community care and the approach was thoroughly consistent with its central aims and principles.

However, while the Children Act 1989 can be seen as the culmination of a 15-year period in which child welfare policy and practice had become a major political concern and an ideological battleground of media attention, public outrage, rival pressure groups and experts, it did not, unlike other welfare legislation at the time, bear the clear hallmarks of Thatcherism or the New Right (Packman & Jordan, 1991). Deakin characterises it as an example of 'consensus legislation' (Deakin, 1994: p. 222). The Act was informed not just by child abuse public inquiries, but by research and a series of respected official reports during the 1980s, particularly the Short Report (Social Services Committee, 1984) and the Review of Child Care Law (DHSS, 1985) and was subject to careful civil service drafting and management and exhaustive consultation with a wide range of professional groups and interested parties (Parton, 1991).

The central principles and rationale of the Act seemed almost social democratic or even collectivist in inspiration. It stressed an approach based on negotiation, involving parents and children in agreed plans, and the accompanying guidance encouraged professionals to work in partnership with all concerned. The Act strongly encouraged the role of the State in supporting families with children in need and the keeping of court proceedings and emergency interventions to a minimum.

However, the legislation was being introduced in a very hostile climate – economically, socially and politically. Not only were its intentions compromised by the changes being introduced elsewhere in health, housing, social security, education and community care, but the economy was experiencing a major recession in the early 1990s. This considerably increased unemployment, poverty and social inequality, which led to considerable growth in social exclusion (Walker & Walker, 1997) and to increasing social divisions (Barclay, 1995; Hills, 1995) which had a particular impact on children and families (Holterman, 1995; Utting, 1995). Using 50% of average income after housing costs as a definition of poverty, government figures show that in 1992–93 there were 4.3 million children living in poverty (a third of all children), compared to 1.4 million (10%) in 1979 (DSS, 1995) – an increase considerably greater than for the population as a whole. This growth in social exclusion and social inequality was not simply an unfortunate consequence of economic and social change but formed an important element of the Thatcherite political strategy (Walker, 1990).

While John Major, who succeeded Margaret Thatcher as Conservative leader and Prime Minister in 1990, initially suggested that his Government might become more conciliatory and more sympathetic to One Nation Conservatism, if anything the welfare changes introduced in the Thatcher third term were furthered and consolidated. As the

Government became more embattled and divided, it became even more committed to the introduction of market principles (Deakin, 1994; Evans & Taylor, 1996). What is perhaps most evident is that the bureau/professional model of welfare organisation (Parry *et al.*, 1970) was being superseded by a model where the role and practices of managers became key. Managers, as opposed to professionals, have become the key brokers in the new welfare network which attempts to change the role of the State from a relationship of provider–user to a quasi-market relationship between suppliers and customers (Clarke *et al.*, 1994; Cutler & Waine, 1994; Clarke & Newman, 1997).

In the child welfare field, it has become evident that many social workers have been concerned almost exclusively with the investigation of child abuse and the investigation of risk (Parton *et al.*, 1997; Parton, 1998b). Similarly, by the mid-1990s there was considerable evidence that child welfare policy and practice was failing to develop the policy of family support which was the aspiration of the Children Act 1989 (Aldgate & Tunstill, 1995; Colton *et al.*, 1995). In the light of the publication of an Audit Commission Report (1994) and a major research programme on child protection (DoH, 1995), there has emerged a major debate on the future shape of child welfare services. This is particularly concerned with the relationship and balance between child protection and family support and is discussed in terms of 'the refocusing of children's services' (Parton, 1997).

Conclusions

When the summary of the child protection research (DoH, 1995) was published, it certainly seemed that the complexities and issues were being discussed with a sensitivity which had not been evident in the previous 20 years. Perhaps for the first time it seemed that politicians, and to a lesser extent the media, were appreciative of the real issues at stake in this highly sensitive area, as was evidenced by the Foreword to *Messages from Research* (DoH, 1995) by John Bowis MP, the Parliamentary Under Secretary of State. This was at a time when there continued to be a series of tragedies and scandals in the child abuse field – including the abuse of children and young people in residential care.

However, in the build-up to the General Election of 1997 from mid-1996 onwards, it also seemed that the Conservative Government was preparing a major assault on the personal social services including child welfare. Amidst the sleaze and political infighting, particularly over Europe, which characterised the Major Government from 1993 onwards, there was very little that seemed to hold the parliamentary party together and on which it could safely claim to agree. Again, it seemed that local authority social workers and their clients were a soft target for further critical appraisal. One of the last government acts before the dissolution of parliament in March 1997 was the publication of a White Paper (DoH & Welsh Office, 1997). In the event, the White Paper stopped short of introducing market principles for children's services, which might have dismembered the local authority's child care responsibilities.

In the election, however, the Conservative Party made specific comment on its intentions in relation to local authority child care services (Conservative Party, 1997), claiming it would introduce legislation based on the White Paper to:

(1) provide new guidance 'to ensure social workers properly reflect the values of the community ... and minimising unnecessary interference';
(2) provide social workers working with children with extra special training;
(3) ensure 'unnecessary barriers' to adoption would be removed;
(4) monitor and perhaps amend the Children Act to balance the rights and responsibilities of children and parents;
(5) introduce a parental control order for Courts to impose on parents of children who offend or are at risk of offending; and
(6) introduce a range of tough sanctions for young offenders.

In contrast, the other two main political parties were largely silent on issues of specific relevance to local authority child care services, except for brief references to young offenders.

While it is difficult to identify the detail of future child welfare policy, a number of these policies which are likely to be key are already clear in the early months of the New Labour Government. First, the political context for the resolution of welfare issues and claims is strongly influenced by international economic and political forces. The 'golden age' of welfare states (Esping-Anderson, 1996) is past, and nation states must now compete with each other for transnational investment and trade. Partly as a consequence of these global changes, all First World countries have experienced polarisation of life chances and economic outcomes among their citizens, signalled by the growth of unemployment, poverty and social exclusion. Second, the response of New Labour to these developments has much in common with that of the previous Conservative Government, in part arising from repositioning itself with new political constituencies. It has maximised its political advantage by aligning itself with the aspirations of the upwardly mobile and trading on their insecurities and fears of the 'underclass'. The consequence seems to be a politics of enforcement which is promoting policies of 'welfare to work' reducing the level and eligibility for Social Security benefits, legitimating the limits on welfare spending, and toughening policies on law and order (Jordan, 1998). More specifically, this new orthodoxy argues that national prosperity is crucially related to the skills of the workforce so that education and training have become the key policy instruments for its social programme. The principle of reciprocity applies to civic obligations so that rights imply responsibilities and benefits entail contributions. Welfare-to-work measures are thus morally justified because they apply conditions to benefits which are appropriate and welfare-enhancing (Blair, 1997; Brown, 1997).

This new orthodoxy is also communitarian in its principles for social provision and emphasises family values, self-help, voluntary associations and civic responsibility in an 'age of giving' (Blair, 1997). Such a form of communitarianism which is authoritarian in many of its precepts for social policy (Etzioni, 1993) sits uneasily with the pluralism of present-day cultures and diverse multi-ethnic communities. While it encourages women to care for dependent children, it drives women into the formal labour market.

A number of statements from the Department of Health suggest that Ministers are keen to broaden the current refocusing initiative beyond family support and child protection to embrace a much wider concern with parenting and regenerating the community more generally. This is not just to be the responsibility of the Social Services Department but a key role for local authorities and implies a repositioning of voluntary child care agencies. One consequence could be that the softer family support developments become a prime responsibility of Education and Early Years Services together with both national and local voluntary child care agencies while Social Services Departments become the narrowly defined, child protection agency (Parton, 1997: Chapter 1). The way these arrangements are developed locally is through the Children's Services Planning process. Thus, while concerns about prevention and family support have again come to the fore in the context of the new political realities, Social Services Departments and social work are repositioned in ways which are fundamentally different to the way this work was envisioned when Social Service Departments were introduced in 1971. At a minimum we can say we are living through interesting times which are likely to have significant implications for the way child care social work develops in the new millennium.

References

Abel-Smith, B. & Townsend, P. (1965) *The Poor and the Poorest.* Bell & Hyman, London.

Aldgate, J. & Tunstill, J. (1995) *Making Sense of Section 17: Implementing Services for Children in Need within the 1989 Children Act.* HMSO, London.

Aldridge, M. (1994) *Making Social Work News.* Routledge, London.

Audit Commission (1994) *Seen but not Heard: Coordinating Community Child Health and Social Services for Children in Need.* HMSO, London.

Barclay, P. (1995) *Joseph Rowntree Foundation Inquiry into Income and Wealth*, Vol. 1. Joseph Rowntree Foundation, York.

Blair, T. (1997) Address to the Labour Party Conference. *The Guardian*, 11 October.

Brown, G. (1997) Pre-Budget Report. *The Guardian*, 26 November.

Burghes, L. (1993) *One Parent Families: Policy Options for the 1990's*. Joseph Rowntree Foundation, York.

Clarke, J. (1980) Social Democratic delinquents and Fabian families: a background to the 1969 Children and Young Persons Act. In *Permissiveness and Control; The Fate of the Sixties Legislation* (ed. the National Deviancy Conference), pp. 72–95. Macmillan, London.

Clarke, J. (1993) *A Crisis in Care? Challenges to Social Work*. Sage, London.

Clarke, J., Cochrane, A. & McLaughlin, E. (1994) *Managing Social Policy*. Sage, London.

Clarke, J. & Langan, M. (1993) The British Welfare State: foundation and modernisation. In *Comparing Welfare States: Britain in International Context* (eds A. Cochrane & J. Clarke), pp. 19–48. Sage, London.

Clarke, J. & Newman, J. (1997) *The Managerial State*. Sage, London.

Colton, M., Drury, C. & Williams, M. (1995) *Children in Need: Family Support under the Children Act 1989*. Avebury, Aldershot.

Cooper, J. (1983) *The Creation of the British Personal Social Services 1962–74*. Heinemann, London.

Conservative Party (1997) The Conservative Manifesto 1997: *You Can Only be Sure with the Conservatives*. The Conservative Party, London.

Cutler, T. & Waine, B. (1994) *Managing the Welfare State: The Politics of Public Sector Management*. Berg, Oxford.

Deakin, N. (1994) *The Politics of Welfare: Continuities and Change*, 2nd edn. Harvester Wheatsheaf, Hemel Hempstead.

Department of Health (1991) *Child Abuse: A Study of Inquiry Reports 1980–1989*. HMSO, London.

Department of Health (1995) *Child Protection; Messages from Research*. HMSO, London.

Department of Health and Social Security (1982) *Child Abuse: A Study of Inquiry Reports 1973–1981*. HMSO, London.

Department of Health and Social Security (1985) *Review of Child Care Law; Report to Ministers of an Interdepartmental Working Party*. HMSO, London.

Department of Health & the Welsh Office (1997) *Social Services: Achievement and Challenge*. HMSO, London.

Department of Social Security (1995) *Households Below Average Income: A Statistical Analysis 1979–1992/3 and revised edition*. HMSO, London.

Donzelot J. (1988) The promotion of the social. *Economy and Society*, **17** (3), 395–427.

Esping-Anderson, G. (1996) After the Golden Age. In *Welfare States in Transition: National Adaptations to Global Economies* (ed. G. Esping-Anderson). Sage, London.

Etzioni, A. (1993) *The Spirit of Community*. Free Press, New York.

Evans, B. & Taylor, B. (1996) *From Salisbury to Major: Continuity and Change in Conservative Politics*. Manchester University Press, Manchester.

Ferlie, E. & Judge, K. (1981) Retrenchment and rationality in the personal social services. *Policy and Politics*, **9** (3), 311–30.

Finch, J. & Groves, D. (1983) *A Labour of Love*. Routledge & Kegan Paul, London.

Fox-Harding, L. (1996) *Family, State and Social Policy*. Macmillan, London.

Franklin, B. & Parton, N. (1991) *Social Work, the Media and Public Relations*. Routledge, London.

Gamble, A. (1994) *The Free Economy and the Strong State: The Politics of Thatcherism*, 2nd edn. Macmillan, London.

Gough, I. (1979) *The Political Economy of the Welfare State*. Macmillan, London.

Hall, P. (1976) *Reforming the Welfare*. Heinemann, London.

Hill, M. (1993) *The Welfare State in Britain: A Political History since 1945*. Edward Elgar, Aldershot.

Hills, J. (1995) *Joseph Rowntree Foundation Inquiry into Income and Wealth*, Vol. 2. Joseph Rowntree Foundation, York.

Holman, B. (1996) Fifty years ago: the Curtis and Clyde reports. *Children & Society*, **10** (3), 197–209.

Holterman, S. (1995) *All Our Futures: The Impact of Public Expenditure and Fiscal Policies on Britain's Children and Young People*. Barnados, Ilford.

Jordan, B. (1998) *Social Justice and the Politics of Welfare*. Sage, London.

Labour Party (1997) *New Labour: Because Britain Deserves Better*. The Labour Party, London.

Laybourn, K. (1995) *The Evolution of British Social Policy and the Welfare State*. Keele University Press, Keele.

Le Grand, J. (1990a) *Quasi-markets and social policy*. School for Advanced Urban Studies, University of Bristol, Bristol.

Le Grand, J. (1990b) The state of welfare. In *The State of Welfare: the Welfare State in Britain since 1974* (ed. J. Hills), pp. 338–62. Oxford University Press, London.

Le Grand, J. & Bartlett, W. (1993) *Quasi-Markets and Social Policy*. Macmillan, London.

Levitas, R. (1986) *The Ideology of the New Right*. Polity Press, Cambridge.

Liberal Democrat Party (1997) *The Liberal Democrat Manifesto 1997: Make the Difference*. The Liberal Democrat Party, London.

London Borough of Brent (1985) *A child in trust: report of the Panel of Inquiry investigating the circumstances surrounding the death of Jasmine Beckford*. London Borough of Brent, London.

London Borough of Greenwich (1987) *A child in mind: protection of children in a responsible society: report of the Commision of Inquiry into the circumstances surrounding the death of Kimberley Carlile*. London Borough of Greenwich, London.

London Borough of Lambeth (1987) *Whose child? The report of the panel appointed to inquire into the death of Tyra Henry*. London Borough of Lambeth, London.

Morgan, K.O. (1984) *Labour Party in Power 1945–51*. Oxford University Press, Oxford.

Packman, J. (1981) *The Child's Generation*, 2nd edn. Basil Blackwell and Martin Robertson, Oxford.

Packman, J. (1993) From prevention to partnership: child welfare services across three decades. *Childen & Society*, 7 (2), 183–95.

Packman, J. & Jordon, B. (1991) The Children Act: looking forward, looking back. *British Journal of Social Work,* **21** (2), 315–27.

Parry, N., Rustin, M. & Satyamurti, C. (1970) *Social Work, Welfare and the State.* Edward Arnold, London.

Parton, N. (1985) *The Politics of Child Abuse.* Macmillan, London.

Parton, N. (1991) *Governing the Family; Child Care, Child Protection and the State.* Macmillan, London.

Parton, N. (1997) *Child Protection and Family Support: Tensions, Contradictions and Possibilities.* Routledge, London.

Parton, N. (1998a in press) Advanced liberalism, (post)modernity and social work: some emerging social configurations. *Social Thought* (USA).

Parton, N. (1998b) Risk, advanced liberalism and child welfare: the need to rediscover uncertainty and ambiguity. *British Journal of Social Work,* **28** (1), 5–27.

Parton, N., Thorpe, D. & Wattam, C. (1997) *Child Protection: Risk and the Moral Order.* Macmillan, London.

Pascall, G. (1986) *Social Policy: A Feminist Analysis.* Tavistock, London.

Pelling, H. (1984) *The Labour Government 1945–51.* Macmillan, London.

Philp, A.F. & Timms, N. (1962) *The Problem of the Problem Family.* Family Service Units, London.

Rose, N. (1989) *Governing the Soul: The Shaping of the Private Self.* Routledge, London.

Rose, N. & Miller, P. (1992) Political power beyond the State: problematics of government. *British Journal of Sociology,* **43** (2), 173–205.

Secretary of State for Social Services (1974) *Report of the inquiry into the care and supervision provided in relation to Maria Colwell.* HMSO, London.

Secretary of State for Social Services (1988) *Report of the inquiry into child abuse in Cleveland.* HMSO, London.

Sleeman, J.F. (1979) *Resources of the Welfare State: an Economic Introduction.* Longman, London.

Social Services Committee (1984) *Children in Care (HC 360).* HMSO, London.

Sullivan, M. (1992) *The Politics of Social Policy.* Harvester-Wheatsheaf, Hemel Hempstead.

Titmuss, R.M. (1958) *Essays on 'The Welfare State'.* Unwin, London.

Townsend, P. (1970) *The Fifth Social Service: A Critical Analysis of the Seebohm Proposals.* The Fabian Society, London.

Utting, D. (1995) *Family and Parenthood: Supporting Families, Preventing Breakdown.* Joseph Rowntree Foundation, York.

Walker, A. (1990) The strategy of inequality, poverty and income distribution in Britain 1979–89. *In the Social Effects of Free Market Policies* (ed. I. Taylor), pp. 29–48. Harvester-Wheatsheaf, Hemel Hempstead.

Walker, A. & Walker, C. (1997) *Britain Divided: The Growth of Social Exclusion in the 1980s and 1990s.* Child Poverty Action Group, London.

Webb, A. & Wistow, G. (1987) *Social Work, Social Care and Social Plannning: The Personal Social Services since Seebohm.* Longman, London.

Williams, F. (1989) *Social Policy: A Critical Introduction.* Polity Press, Cambridge.

Chapter 2

Child Welfare: whose responsibility?

Keith Bilton

Introduction – What do we mean by child welfare services?

The welfare services provided by the Children's and (from 1971) Social Services Departments of local authorities have made a relatively small contribution to the welfare, in the broad sense of well-being, of the majority of children, although for a minority their contribution has been critical. For most families, the universal services of health and education have been much more significant. Child benefit, introduced in 1978, is payable for all children, and before that family allowances were available for second and subsequent children. An increasing number of families have been wholly, or at least substantially, dependent on other social security benefits. Many welfare state services, therefore, contribute to the welfare or well-being of children. This book is, however, concerned with child welfare as a function of the personal social services, and the purpose of this chapter is to set personal social services for children in the context of other welfare state provision, and to consider how the interrelationships have affected child welfare services. The overall picture is one of policy changes in particular services made with little apparent concern for their effects on other services. Concern about inter-service relationships then tends to arise subsequently and reactively, and to be expressed either as exhortation or through the superimposition of various kinds of collaborative machinery and by the allocation of lead responsibility.

Collaborative machinery is then used, not to seek a consensus about proposed organisational and policy changes within agencies, but to mitigate their adverse consequences. The problems thus created for Area Child Protection Committees are discussed in Chapter 6.

By welfare state services I mean the publicly-funded or subsidised social services, broadly defined as income maintenance or social security, health, education, housing and the personal social services (Townsend, 1970). To include housing as a social or welfare state service has in recent years become contentious; the previous Conservative Government did not regard it as a welfare state service, despite the continuance of a social housing sector and of substantial public subsidy in the form of housing benefit and tax relief. Housing continues, however, to include a social housing sector and to receive substantial public subsidy in the form of housing benefit and mortgage tax relief. Until the second half of the 1970s, there was no doubt of housing's status as a social service, and its interrelationship with child welfare services has been important.

The use, copied from the USA, of the word 'welfare' to denote the social security system has in recent years encouraged a tendency to equate the welfare state, and reform of welfare, with social security alone, and has facilitated a perception of the welfare state as a system for transferring resources from the majority to an 'underclass' and as constituting not an aid but a threat to general social well-being. The recent Green Paper on social security reform (DSS, 1998) reasserts a broader view of the welfare state as including health, education and even, though less consistently, housing. Confusingly, it also continues to use 'welfare' as a synonym for social security.

Alongside these welfare state services, the juvenile or youth justice system has to be viewed as a special case. It consists of a network of publicly funded services, some of which form part of the child welfare services. Arguments for treating it as a welfare service became persuasive in the 1960s, but have since progressively lost ground in England and Wales, although in Scotland the establishment in 1968 of an alternative to the criminal justice system for children, based on the concept of social education, has institutionalised welfare values and, so far, ensured their survival.

To discuss the effects on child welfare services of changes in other fields of social administration is not of course to set these services and their clientele within the context of social change. Significant as the achievements of the welfare state have been, a social history of childhood in the last half century would show changes far more sweeping, and more significant in their effect on children's lives, than those which have resulted from administrative changes in public welfare provision.

The following sections in this chapter begin with an overview of the origins of modern child welfare services and move on to consider the implications for them of selected developments and changes in five related fields:

(1)   income maintenance and poverty
(2)   provision for homelessness
(3)   education services
(4)   early years services
(5)   criminal justice services.

The chapter concludes with some observations on present and future problems. It does not attempt to present a comprehensive review.

The reforms of the 1940s – how the Poor Law was laid to rest

Child care responsibilities were, before 1948, divided among a variety of agencies. Voluntary child care organisations provided predominantly residential care, with some foster homes. The public assistance committees of local authorities, administering the continuing Poor Law, looked after homeless children, often made homeless by separation from their destitute parents. The Children and Young Persons Act 1933 gave local education authorities responsibility for looking after children committed to their care by the juvenile courts, although it also allowed the courts to commit children to the care of other 'fit persons'. Other child welfare services were developed by local education authorities between 1906 and 1939 – school meals and school health services, necessitous clothing allowances, school attendance work and child guidance clinics – but these were retained within the education sector and did not pass to the new Children's Departments. Thus, even within child welfare services themselves, a division was made, which largely persists, between services provided as part of the emerging personal social services and those provided primarily to enable children to benefit from education.

The legislation of the 1940s has been presented as a radical departure from the pre-war approach, made politically possible by the wartime spirit of altruism and collectivism, and embodying the pursuit of an egalitarian society. Other commentators have stressed its developmental nature, building on earlier Acts and on municipal initiatives, and have presented the commitment to egalitarianism as a 1960s gloss on earlier objectives of equality of access and minimum standards (Glennerster,1991). Holman's account of the genesis of the Children Act 1948 (Holman,1996) challenges the popular view that its origins lay in the response to the death in 1945 of the foster child Dennis O'Neill. Holman shows how wartime experiences from the evacuation of children provided the impetus for the implementation of policies developed in pre-war times. It draws attention to the long gestation period which preceded the Act, and is thus consistent with Glennerster's account of mainstream welfare state developments. The tendency to attribute new Children Acts to recent events and to overlook their long gestation periods persists. The Children Act 1975 was not, save in one or two provisions which were at odds with its general philosophy of trusting the professionals, a response to the death of Maria Colwell. Nor was the Children Act 1989 a response to Cleveland, although the reaction to Cleveland may have contributed to an exaggeration of the extent to which the Act requires partnership with parents.

The Children Act 1948 was also part of an egalitarian project summarised in the opening words of the National Assistance Act of the same year, 'The existing poor law shall cease to have effect'. The aim was egalitarian in that it sought to abolish separate status and separate provision for destitute people. Thus, under the Children Act, children in care were to be able to use the same services as other children. Their best interests were to be furthered and opportunity provided for the proper development of their character and abilities. Declaratory legislation does not, however, demolish buildings, and its influence on attitudes is variable. For most welfare state services, with the exception of education, dealing with a legacy from the Poor Law was a practical necessity.

One of the basic strategies adopted was the separation of cash from care, a peculiarly British principle not found in American or Continental European systems. The local authority Public Assistance Committees had inherited both the Elizabethan cash-giving function of parish or outdoor relief, administered by the Relieving Officers, and the Victorian development of 'less eligible' accommodation for the destitute in workhouses. Outdoor relief, subsequently renamed public assistance, became a national function (national assistance) under the National Assistance Board, while local authorities retained responsibility for providing residential accommodation, including temporary accommodation for homeless families. There were three important consequences for child care services. First, the new Children's Departments did not acquire any responsibility for the prevention or the relief of homelessness, but had a duty to receive children into care if the local authority's response to homelessness did not enable parents to go on looking after them. Second, provision for homeless families continued in many areas to reflect Poor Law attitudes – fathers excluded from the accommodation, accommodation provided in a wing of a former Poor Law institution – administered by committees and departments whose main concerns were for elderly and disabled people and which had little incentive to move away from punitive attitudes towards a marginal and inconvenient group of service users. Third, social work, in child care as in other fields, developed within the care side of the cash–care divide, and did not inherit the combined responsibilities of the Relieving Officer. The National Assistance Board and its successors have looked to bureaucratic models and not to the exercise of professional judgement for the pursuit of justice and equity in the exercise of discretion, and have therefore seen no need to employ social workers for this purpose.

Within Children's Departments, efforts to bury the Poor Law were required by legislation which gave local authorities responsibility for each child's welfare rather than duties to provide types of service for categories of recipient. (Compare the duty in section 1 of the Children Act 1948 to receive a child into care if his parents are unable to care for him and his welfare requires it, with the duty in section 21 of the National Assistance Act 1948 to provide residential accommodation for persons in need of care and attention and, in so doing, merely to 'have regard to' their welfare.) Also, a training council for child care workers was set up before the new service was introduced, and, as Nigel Parton notes in Chapter 1, 'Child care officers were not drawn in any significant numbers either from Poor Law staff or the pre-war voluntary agencies'. The emphasis on fostering helped to reduce dependence on Poor Law and other institutional buildings for accommodating children, and in the 1950s a 'family group home' model for residential care gave added impetus to their replacement by buildings, usually on housing estates, designed as larger versions of ordinary family homes.

What primarily survived from the Poor Law was coercion and stigma. Child care officers in the 1960s were reluctant to accept the degree to which families' relationships with them were affected by the availability of coercive powers (Handler, 1968). They wanted to see their preventive family casework as a service which families welcomed positively, and, while this perception was no doubt accurate in part, they underestimated the extent to which fear that children would be taken away encouraged parents to cooperate. The emphasis currently placed in child protection work on making it plain to families exactly where they stand was not then so strong. It was, however, fairly usual to hear parents warn their children that, if they did not behave, the child care officer or NSPCC inspector would take them away. Katrin Fitzherbert studied the case histories of 150 'West Indian or half-West Indian' children in the care of the London County Council in 1964–65 (Fitzherbert, 1967). One of her conclusions aroused considerable controversy at the time:

'They [the parents of these children] do not have rooted inside them the same horror of seeing children institutionalised which restrains most English parents, who have all heard of Oliver Twist, from going to the Children's Department unnecessarily.' (p. 107)

Child care officers were at that time reluctant to recognise the extent to which they relied on stigma to achieve their preventive objectives. But times change. Colton and others (Colton *et al.*, 1997) found, not surprisingly, that residential and foster care are perceived as more stigmatising than services provided within the parental home, but also that there are various ways in which stigma can be reduced. They also found that service providers considered the social function of residential and foster care to be more stigmatic than did service users.

Child welfare, income maintenance and poverty

The impact of social security safety net provisions on child welfare services is seen most clearly in the area of family support. The Curtis Committee (Curtis, 1946) was clear that 'every effort should be made

to keep the child in its home ... provided that the home is or can be
made reasonably satisfactory', but it was not until 1964, with the
implementation of the Children and Young Persons Act 1963, that
Children's Departments received a statutory mandate for this preventive work. They also acquired a power in exceptional circumstances
to give assistance in cash. Primary responsibility for the relief of
immediate financial need, however, lay with the National Assistance
Board (NAB), and local authority assistance in cash was and has
remained a function exercised within narrow limits, generally exercised
only where other sources of financial help are unavailable.

In 1948, when national assistance was introduced, one million
people were dependent on it, and it was believed that dependence on
discretionary assistance would be contained at about this level by a
combination of full employment, national insurance benefits and
family allowances. By 1966, however, when the Supplementary Benefits Commission replaced the NAB, the figure was two million, and by
1979 it had doubled again to more than four million. The 1966 reform
was an attempt to manage the exercise of discretion within a rights-
based system. It created new complexities in the system but also new
opportunities for professionals who could master those complexities to
secure additional payments for claimants. Welfare rights work consequently become a specialist occupation, largely separate from social
work, although often advisory to it.

The replacement of supplementary benefit by income support in
1986 was intended to curb the cost, and in particular the administrative
cost, of discretion. Income support became a rule-governed means-
tested system, more an integral part of the national insurance system
than a safety net below it, and requiring in turn its own safety net in the
form of the Social Fund. The cost of discretion in the Social Fund was
controlled by giving it a limited budget, and by defining very narrowly
the circumstances in which assistance could be given by way of a grant,
the effect being that most applicants can receive help, if at all, only in
the form of a loan. Thus many families are further impoverished by
loan repayments, which may take up to 25% of their income support
entitlement, while others are denied loans because they are judged
unable to afford to repay them. Figures for Social Fund assistance are
shown as gross expenditure, without deducting income to the Fund
from loan repayments, thus presenting as an increasing volume of state
assistance a process of temporarily redistributing the resources of the
poorest. The Social Fund is therefore ineffective as a safety net, and
needs a safety net of its own, which the State does not provide.

There would have been some logic in giving responsibility for the
Social Fund to Social Services Departments, specialists in meeting social
need within budget limits through the exercise of discretion. The
responsibility would have been formidable, but it would have considerably strengthened their family support role under Part III of the

Children Act 1989. This would, however, have been seen as breaching the separation of cash and care. For child and family social work practice, the main effect of the introduction of the Social Fund has been that charities have replaced the social security system as the best hope of defending local authority assistance in cash against the unwanted role of safety net of last resort. It has never been easy for social workers in child welfare services to see themselves as being well-placed to tackle problems of poverty, but in the 1960s this was a much discussed issue. Although the Children Act 1989 has introduced new duties to provide support to families in need, child and family social work now appears more than ever disconnected from measures to tackle poverty.

Before concluding discussion of the effects of the separation of cash and care functions, it is interesting to note the emergence of a contrary trend in services for adults. Under the NHS and Community Care Act 1990, responsibility for funding adult residential care placements in the independent sector was transferred from Social Security to Social Services Departments and cash-limited. However, as payments by Social Services Departments were made to the providers of care and not to the service users, this particular service became on transfer a care rather than a cash function. The contemporaneous introduction of purchaser–provider separation then stimulated pressure for disabled service users to be given the option of becoming their own purchasers, that is, of receiving cash from the local authority with which to buy personal social services, a development which represents a more obvious blurring of the cash–care divide. Whereas financial assistance from child welfare services has been seen as a service in itself, and often as one which may reinforce dependency, community care direct payments are viewed as an alternative to services and as a way of promoting greater independence. There have also been suggestions that the Government might consider transferring to Social Services Departments responsibility for assessing the need for and paying disability living allowance and attendance allowance, perhaps with a view to imposing cash limits, but the Green Paper on social security reform appears to rule this out by stating an intention to retain them as universal and national benefits. One may conclude that the boundary between cash and care, and between national and local responsibilities, is now discussable, and that some adjustment is conceivable.

The effects of changes in the administration of income maintenance systems on family support services have been less significant than the growth of family poverty. Donnison (1998, p. 14) concludes that:

'inequality remained remarkably stable between 1949 and 1963. There was then a move towards greater equality which continued with fluctuations till about 1977. After that, inequality increased – most dramatically from 1985. That increase, bringing inequality to the highest levels recorded since the Second World War, may have been checked in the early 1990s, but it is too early to be sure of that.'

For the poorest tenth of the population, between 1979 and 1990–91, growing inequality was reflected not merely in their exclusion from rising living standards but in an actual decline in income of 14% in real terms after allowing for housing costs. The growth of poverty and inequality particularly affected families with children. In 1979, 10% of children lived in households which, after meeting housing costs, had an income of less than half the national average. By 1991–92, one third of children lived in these poorer households.

The growing inequality in family incomes has arisen from increasing inequalities in earned and private income, from the abandonment of the link between benefit levels and average earnings, and from the mal-distribution of paid employment – in this case the tendency of families to polarise into the work-rich, with more than one working adult, and the work-poor, with no one in work or at best intermittent casual earnings. Lister (1996) draws attention to the way in which the 'spouse's unemployment trap' contributes to this phenomenon. Where one partner is on benefit, the effect of the other partner's earnings on the benefit entitlement often means that he or she cannot afford to stay in work.

Polarisation into work-rich and work-poor households is commonly advanced as an explanation of the coexistence in the UK, when compared with other European countries, of relatively high levels of employment (70% of the working-age population) with a relatively high proportion of workless households (19% of households with a working-age member) (1994 figures). Willetts (1998), who quotes these figures, attributes them instead to high levels of family break-up resulting in large numbers of small households and therefore in a worsening ratio of workers to households. That work-rich, work-poor polarisation is a significant fact and a serious problem has, however, been amply demonstrated, for example by Gregg & Wadsworth (1995).

Local community development strategies offer another response with some positive potential, and one with which a family support service ought to have close links. A series of mishaps has hampered their development. In the late 1960s and early 1970s the Home Office was active in promoting community development projects (Social Work Service, 1972; Fuller & Stevenson, 1983), but it was in the middle of this period that responsibility for child care services was transferred from the Home Secretary to the Secretary of State for Social Services. The Seebohm Report (Seebohm, 1968) had advocated that Social Services Departments should:

'engage in the extremely difficult and complex task of encouraging and assisting the development of community identity [noting that]

social work with individuals alone is bound to be of limited effect in
an area where the community environment itself is a major impedi-
ment to healthy individual development.' (pp. 147–8)

The report therefore stressed the need for Departments to undertake
community development:

'a process whereby local groups are assisted to clarify and express
their needs and objectives and to take collective action to attempt to
meet them' (p. 151)

and to develop citizen participation:

'the maximum participation of individuals and groups in the community in the planning, organisation and provision of the social
services [which] should reduce the rigid distinction between the
givers and the takers of social services and the stigma which being a
client has often involved in the past.' (p. 151)

Social Services Departments, established between January 1971 and
April 1972, have made various attempts to engage in community
development and maintain a community social work approach. Despite
substantial growth in their budgets in the years 1971–75, most of them
found it extremely difficult in this early period to allocate resources to
this objective within area offices which were intended to encompass
both work with individuals and a community approach. Priority in
child and family fieldwork services had to be given to discharging case
accountability for children in care or in need of protection, a demand
reinforced in the case of child protection by the Maria Colwell Report
(Secretary of State, 1974) and reaffirmed by subsequent child death
inquiries. In 1976, budget cuts described by Brown (1995) as:

'far larger, not only than any before, but also than any later achieved
by Conservative governments despite their rhetoric about rolling
back the frontiers of the State,'

aggravated the difficulties. The Barclay Report (National Institute for
Social Work, 1982) attempted to redefine community social work in
such a way as to strengthen the case for its becoming a mainstream
activity of the personal social services, but this did not lead to a
widespread implementation of the committee's proposals. Indeed, two
minority appendices to the committee's report, one expressing a more
radical and the other a more conservative approach, attracted more
attention. A minority of local authorities organised their services on the
principles of the more radical neighbourhood-based community social
work advocated in the appendix by Brown, Hadley & White. Some
commentators, particularly on the work of Wakefield Social Services
Department, argued that this approach succeeded in supporting community strengths, was able to meet requirements of case accountability

for children in care and in need of protection, and reduced the numbers of children coming into care. In other authorities, however, worrying failures in child protection work and in the management of residential child care services led to organisational structures based on a neighbourhood approach being regarded as unsafe, and they have now been largely abandoned.

Homelessness and child welfare

In the 1960s, child and family social workers were still contending with a family homelessness service which retained clear signs of its Poor Law origins. The local authority's duty, discharged under the National Assistance Act 1948 through a Welfare or combined Health and Welfare Department, was restricted to the provision of 'temporary accommodation for persons who are in urgent need thereof'. Temporary accommodation provided no clear route into or right to permanent public sector housing. Except in the county boroughs and, from 1965, Greater London, housing services were the responsibility of one tier of local government: children's and welfare services of another. Access to public housing was governed by local rules which showed considerable variation. Many used points systems, but in some the allocation of each tenancy was determined by the Housing Committee. Temporary accommodation might be provided for as little as 28 days. Fathers were often excluded from it, and it was typically communal in nature, offering little privacy. The splitting up of families and the use of communal accommodation were roundly criticised in a government joint circular of 31 October 1966.

The prevention of homelessness was crucial to the success of the duty to prevent children's reception into care placed on Children's Departments by the Children and Young Persons Act 1963, but the departments had little power to achieve it. Not surprisingly, homelessness was a key policy issue for the Association of Child Care Officers, whose response was to declare reception of children into care on the grounds of homelessness to be contrary to its members' professional responsibilities. In the early 1960s, much homelessness was precipitated by the largely unregulated eviction practices of urban private landlords (Rachmanism) and rural caravan site owners.

Prevention of these abuses was a high priority for the Labour Government elected in 1964, which speedily introduced the temporary Protection From Eviction Act 1964, followed by the Rent Act 1965, which introduced 'fair rents' and gave sitting tenants some protection from eviction. These Acts significantly assisted the preventive work of Children's Departments, but government was unable to solve the underlying economic problem. Few private landlords could in fact run a profitable business by providing low-income families with reasonable housing and secure tenancy at a rent they could afford. Despite the introduction of rent allowances, the private rented sector continued to decline (from 52% of all household tenures in 1951 to 12% in 1981), and the eviction of families from public sector housing became the greater problem.

The creation of Social Services Departments brought together in one agency the responsibility for preventing the reception of children into care and responsibility for accommodating homeless families. Statutory duties towards homeless families and their relation to housing law and provision were, however, unchanged. The Local Government Act 1972, implemented in 1973, continued in the 'shire' (non-Metropolitan) counties of England, and throughout Wales the pattern of placing housing and personal social services responsibilities with different tiers of local government. Social Services Departments' performance in engaging constructively with the problem of homelessness was patchy. Some Social Services area offices developed with their housing counterparts good early warning systems which enabled both agencies to work together to prevent or respond effectively to evictions. Others avoided involvement until actual eviction precipitated a crisis, and then hoped that the family would find its own solution or disappear. Gradually, more order was imposed on this chaotic situation, partly through the curious system of rent guarantees, whereby Social Services Departments used their General Rate Fund budgets to insure the Housing Revenue Account against tenants' failure to clear rent arrears, thus staving off eviction. Nevertheless, the conflicting interests of Housing and Social Services Departments remained a serious problem and were at times played out in tense negotiations between Chairs of Housing and Social Services Committees.

The Seebohm Report (Seebohm, 1968, p. 127) recommended:

'that housing departments should, as a few already do, assume responsibility for providing accommodation for homeless families [and that] as homeless families require permanent accommodation ... a further and necessary responsibility should be placed upon housing departments to give whatever help may be necessary to achieve this.'

In 1977 this recommendation was implemented in the Housing (Homeless Persons) Act, which enacted a Private Member's Bill introduced by Stephen Ross, Liberal MP for the Isle of Wight, and gave housing authorities a duty to house people who had become homeless unintentionally and were 'vulnerable'. Having dependent children constituted vulnerability. This normalising and welcome development can be seen as marking the end of the Poor Law approach to homelessness, and therefore as a particularly significant achievement by a back-bench MP.

Unfortunately, pressure of demand led to increasing delays in housing homeless families, and they were, in increasing numbers, consigned to highly unsuitable yet comparatively expensive 'bed-and-breakfast' hotels, often away from their home area – a highly inappropriate use of private sector resources. Thus, although reception into care was avoided and families were not split up, their welfare was severely prejudiced, not least by loss of contact with previous schools, GPs and health visitors. The situation has since been improved through measures to bring empty housing into use, first by local authorities leasing privately-owned properties and subsequently by housing associations either leasing them or acting as managing agents. This has provided temporary housing of much better quality, although problems for families arising from being moved out of their previous home areas remain, and complicate the provision of family support services where they are available.

The Housing Act 1996, which was defended in part by references to the need to prevent young women from using pregnancy and homelessness as a way of jumping the housing queue, has removed the duty to provide homeless families with permanent housing, and thus abandons the central requirement of the 1977 Act. Its practical effects have been less significant than might have been expected. Housing authorities are responsible for the cost of providing temporary accommodation, which generally exceeds that of permanent housing. While the 1996 Act requires that homeless families be housed only through the housing waiting list, housing authorities have discretion as to the priority they give within waiting list points systems to homelessness and to residence in temporary accommodation.

Education and child welfare

The Education Act 1944 established a tripartite system of secondary education in grammar, technical and secondary modern schools. The technical sector was never developed, and secondary modern schools were never able to achieve anything approaching parity of status and esteem with the grammar schools. The result was a system which failed to develop the potential of about four-fifths of its pupils (Hattersley, 1997), and in which the educational expectations of the majority of children were low. This may perhaps have obscured the particular problem of the low educational attainment of children in care. That this problem existed was not surprising. Social and economic deprivation is associated with coming into care (Bebbington & Miles, 1989) and also with educational failure (Heath *et al.*, 1994). Child care officers tended to take the view that children in care, emotionally damaged by separation and loss, could not be expected to make much educational progress until their more fundamental needs had been met. This may have been a reasonable working hypothesis, but there was little impetus to test it by trying to disprove it; nor did the child care service provide or generally have access to a special education service designed to fit in with these needs.

Heath *et al.* (1994) cite studies published in 1976, 1987, 1988 and 1989, showing that children in care perform educationally below national norms for their age groups, and Fletcher-Campbell (1998) similarly dates awareness of this issue from the late 1980s. From the point of view of the child care practitioner, however, what seems to have arrived in the late 1980s is not so much a new awareness that children in care (or looked after) were not doing well at school, as the idea that something might, and if possible should, be done about it. Fletcher-Campbell argues that looked-after children do not need special educational privileges, but do need special support, related to the abnormal structure of their lives, 'so that they may gain access to those curriculum experiences engaged in by their peers'. She suggests that this special support:

> 'may have to be "additionally special" in order to compensate for the damage accorded to the young people through their having been within the care system.' (p. 5)

Clearly, special measures are needed in relation to such basic necessities as ensuring that looked-after children have a place in an appropriate school, and in managing the problems which arise when children move frequently. The Department for Education and Employment Regulations which place responsibility for a child's education with the authority in whose area he or she is fostered, rather than with the care authority, need to be changed. Responsibility for education should remain with the care authority, irrespective of where the child is placed. Children's and Social Services Departments have not performed well in carrying the parental role in relation to schools – attending parents' evenings, participating in parent–teacher associations, encouraging and helping with homework and all the other ways in which concerned parents involve themselves with their children's education. These roles should be built into the practice of residential work, foster care and fieldwork where it is impracticable to help parents to carry them. The Looking After Children forms and records introduced by the Department of Health in 1995 direct attention to seven dimensions of children's development, of which education is one, and they are intended to make educational needs more central to Social Services Departments' work with looked-after children. There is a danger, however, that these forms and records will be seen by field and residential workers as an additional administration imposition, and that their potential value will not be realised.

The approach recommended by Fletcher-Campbell may not, however, be sufficient on its own. The longitudinal study by Heath *et al.* of the educational progress of children in long-stay foster homes, compared with that of children from similar backgrounds receiving family support services, found that even six or seven years in the same substitute family (and irrespective of whether custodianship or adoption orders were made in the course of the placement) did not reduce educational disadvantage attributable to the children's early histories before entry to care. Greater than average educational inputs led to a degree of catching up, but there was also some evidence that earlier intervention of this kind was more effective than remedial work in middle childhood (approximately 8–14 years). While the study in no way contradicts findings about the educational damage associated with insecure and disruptive in-care experiences, it does strongly suggest that for most looked-after children these experiences will aggravate earlier educational disadvantage, which would have been best addressed before the children came into care. There is a two-way relationship between educational failure and being a looked-after child, and cooperation between Education and Social Services Departments needs to be based on a recognition of this. The education contribution to family support work is as crucial as the education of looked-after children.

Early years services and child welfare

The Children Act 1948 is not the only significant child welfare measure whose fiftieth anniversary falls in 1998. The Nurseries and Childminders Regulation Act of the same year affirmed the need for regulation of day care services for all young children. This was initially a responsibility of local authority community health services. It became a personal social services function in 1971. In April 1998 responsibility for the strategic development of early years services passed to Education Departments. The move reflects a desire to expand nursery education and to prioritise the educational component of other day care provision. Certainly departmental boundaries have created problems in the past, not least the exclusion from nursery education of disadvantaged three- and four-year olds in Social Services day nurseries. There have been too few integrated local authority nursery centres. Concerns have been expressed, however, that the education service may favour parents' rather than children's interests, in line with the bias in education legislation towards parents' rather than children's rights and responsibilities.

A wider concern is that Government's approach to support for parents and to childcare provision is too much influenced by the Home Office view of parenting as a crime prevention strategy and by the objective of bringing lone parents into the labour market. More traditional attitudes would have sensed some conflict between these two objectives. Neither of them suggests an approach rooted in a clear family policy. The new Childcare Tax Credit will substantially advantage working parents to the relative detriment of those who choose full-time parenting. Even if more workers are in fact needed in a country which already has the highest employment participation rate in Europe, no argument has been advanced as to why this should be achieved by recruiting lone mothers earlier in their children's lives rather than by retaining more employees in their fifties, whose family responsibilities are likely to demand less of their time. It is difficult to resist the inference that younger women are judged more likely to be willing to accept insecure low-paid work. Anxieties also arise about the type of childcare provision likely to be stimulated by the availability of the tax credit. Buckingham (1998) reports growing interest from relatively large commercial firms in providing nurseries with more than 100 places offering education-based curricula for children from the age of six months.

Criminal justice and child welfare

The Children and Young Persons Act 1969 gave Children's/Social Services Departments lead responsibility for providing services to young offenders – through residential services expanded by the integration of approved schools and remand homes with children's homes into the 'community homes' system, and through supervision in the community, to be strengthened by the development of 'intermediate treatment' (i.e. a service of intermediate intensity between fieldwork supervision and residential care). Several factors then undermined the discharge of this lead responsibility. The low success rate of approved schools (in terms of reconviction rates two years after discharge) was not affected by their redesignation as Community Homes with Education or CH(E)s. The use of residential care for offenders conflicted with local authorities' pessimism about residential care generally, with their struggle to deal with offending by children placed there for other reasons, and their wish to use it only as a last resort for children with nowhere else to live. (For a brief discussion of the history of the relationship between residential child care and the criminal justice system, see Bilton (1995).)

The committal to care of young offenders was also attacked by liberal youth justice theorists as a disproportionately harsh sentence masquerading as a welfare disposal. But if residential care for offenders was to be discouraged, then intermediate treatment would have to be convincing as not only an effective but also an adequately tough disposal; the local authorities' response to offending would otherwise appear too soft.

Unfortunately, the Government gave priority in the implementation of the Act to the community homes system over intermediate treatment, which therefore developed late and slowly. Nevertheless, a number of schemes were developed, both by local authorities and by voluntary organisations, which demonstrated the positive contribution that child welfare services could make. Intermediate treatment was subsequently fatally undermined by an economically convenient approach to diversion from the criminal justice system which, instead of seeking active engagement with young offenders, opted for minimal intervention justified by the statistical probability that they would grow out of their offending. In these circumstances, there was little chance of success in the difficult task of persuading the courts, Government and public opinion of the compatibility of welfare with justice and punishment, of the need to combine reparative and restorative justice with the provision of worthwhile and adequately attractive alternatives to offending.

Both in the courts and within Social Services Departments, the youth justice system has been progressively re-separated from the child welfare system. The Crime and Disorder Bill will extend the youth justice system, through child safety and parenting orders, into non-criminal areas of behavioural and social problems for which the Children Act 1989 enacted child welfare provisions. For children in trouble, this may mean an increase in the randomness of their allocation between child welfare and youth justice systems.

A similar dominance of justice over welfare considerations, attributable to the demands of the criminal justice system, can be seen in post-Cleveland developments in child protection work. While Thoburn (1998) rightly notes that the Cleveland Report (Butler-Sloss, 1988) 'catalogued the harm done to children removed precipitately from homes when child sexual abuse had been alleged', other commentators (e.g. Wattam, 1992) have drawn attention to the effects of the report's emphasis on the need to secure evidence which meets judicial requirements as a key task of child protection investigations (or enquiries). These include treating the child as a potential witness rather than as a child in need, the domination of investigations by 'Memorandum of Good Practice' interviews (Home Office, 1992) and the subjection of children in court proceedings to 'systems abuse of a very harmful kind' (Utting, 1997). These effects are discussed in more detail in Bilton (1993).

Some present and future problems

Many of the problems in relationships between child welfare and other welfare state services arise from gatekeeping, rationing and other restrictive, and sometimes deterrent, policies and practices designed to limit access to selective and last-resort services. They are to be found in the administration of income- and disability-related social security benefits, the Social Fund, homelessness services, and in child welfare services themselves. While they often arise from the need to contain expenditure, some of them also constitute responses to the fundamental policy problem of how the State should respond to the needs of citizens who have not met its general expectations as to what they themselves should do to meet their responsibilities. The Children Act 1989 reflects a belief that the great majority of parents want to meet their responsibilities and can and should be helped to do so.

The Green Paper on social security reform (DSS, 1998), although containing many positive proposals, envisages a social security system based on the observance of a social contract both by the State and by claimants. It avoids the issue of how to meet the needs of claimants (and of their children) who do not keep their side of the bargain. By rejecting the idea of the welfare state as 'a safety net for the destitute', it avoids confronting the awkward fact that no contractually-based system can function humanely without one. It makes no mention of the Social Fund. The Green Paper also declares an aim 'to rebuild the welfare state around work', and alleges that 'the vast majority of single parents want to work', a statement supported by evidence only if the words 'at some stage' are added to it. While the Green Paper does not propose to make it obligatory for lone parents to work, it appears to pave the way for further discrimination against those who do not, under the guise of offering them what they want. Proposals for social security reform therefore contain the seeds of future conflicts of policy and philosophy between income maintenance and child welfare services.

Other problems in coordinating the child welfare contributions of different agencies have arisen from the Government's pursuit since the late 1980s of reorganisations of the internal structures and processes of health, education and personal social services authorities without apparent regard for effects on their ability to work together (Jones & Bilton, 1994). Sanders *et al.* (1997) found in a study of involvement in Area Child Protection Committees that:

> 'a significant factor accounting for variations in the levels of involvement is the fragmentation which has taken place as a result of government "reforms", most notably in education and health.' (p. 87)

The response to these problems has been a renewed emphasis on collaborative planning and on coordination through the exercise of lead responsibility. Essential as these activities are, it is disappointing that the challenge they face is that of compensating for organisational mismatches and conflicting policies.

Underlying many current problems is a failure to develop a coherent family policy to underpin all welfare state contributions to child welfare. The social security Green Paper makes some contribution to its formulation. The increase in child benefit, the national minimum wage, the implementation of the Working Time and Parental Leave Directives, and the more gradual reduction of Working Families' Tax Credit as earnings increase, are all moves in the right direction; however, there is some way to go, and the emerging shape of the policy is distorted by the refusal to contemplate giving parents who look after their own children the same level of assistance as those who employ other carers.

Conclusion

From this selective and impressionistic review, it is difficult, even dangerous, to draw conclusions. However, of the issues discussed, the following points stand out.

First, children and families in need have not been well-served by a social security system which has struggled with the difficult task of both observing rules and exercising discretion. The fundamental problems, however, have arisen, particularly since 1977, not so much from the system itself as from the context of increasing family poverty within which it operates. Families applying to the Social Fund have suffered from the tendency, in a social, economic and political system which lacks a strong commitment to equality, to treat those in the greatest need as the least eligible. The history of homelessness services also illustrates this tendency, although improvements since 1977 may not be lost, despite the 1996 Housing Act. Both the operation of the Social Fund and the application of homelessness legislation suffer from decision-making procedures which largely exclude the application of social work knowledge and skill from the exercise of discretion, too often confining it to a special-pleading role.

Second, children looked after by local authorities have been damaged by the failure of the child welfare service to replicate the parental contribution to their education. This failure may have some of its roots in the view that, when addressing serious problems in children's emotional development, concern about educational progress can be postponed. These children are also gravely disadvantaged, however, from the inability of the education service to redress the adverse effects of social disadvantage. As with the social security system, problems arising from the social and economic context are significant, but the interrelationship between system and social context is here more complex. Given the importance of early remedial intervention, the current emphasis on the educational component of early years services is welcome, but there is a risk that the fostering of young children's healthy emotional development through the experience of secure relationships will receive insufficient attention.

Third, in the youth justice system, the essential compatibility of justice and welfare objectives is obvious: it is in the interests of young offenders that their offending should cease. Too many opportunities to demonstrate how this compatibility may be translated into practice have been missed. For child victims of crime, a criminal justice system which aggravates the harm they have suffered is clearly a travesty of justice, but the problems which give rise to this unjust treatment seem more intractable.

Underlying these issues lies a more fundamental matter – the lack of a family policy which, despite the tensions and conflicts inherent in such a contested area, would have sufficient coherence to ensure a drive to improve the lot of children in need. The experience of the last 50 years shows that, even when services specifically intended for 'deprived' children are targeted for improvement, efforts are seriously hindered when other key elements in children's welfare systems are deficient or are in conflict with the goals of such services.

References

Bebbington, A. & Miles, J. (1989) The background of children who enter local authority care. *British Journal of Social Work* **19** (5), 349–68.

Bilton, K. (1993) *Child Protection Practice and the Memorandum of Good Practice on Video Recorded Interviews with Children*. British Association of Social Workers, Birmingham.

Bilton, K. (1995) *Specialising in residential child care: a discussion paper*. Department of Health for the Support Force for Children's Residential Care, London.

Brown, J. (1995) *The British Welfare State: A Critical History*. Blackwell, Oxford.

Buckingham, L. (1998) Nanny state is failing to learn its nursery lessons. *The Guardian*, 11 April.

Butler-Sloss, E. (1988) *Report of the Inquiry into Child Abuse in Cleveland*. HMSO, London.

Colton, M., Drakeford, M., Roberts, S., Scholte, E., Casas, F. & Williams, M. (1997) Social workers, parents and stigma. *Child & Family Social Work* **2**, 247–57.

Curtis, M. (1946) *Report of the Care of Children Committee*. Cmnd 6922, HMSO, London.

Department of Social Security (1998) *New ambitions for our country: A New Contract for Welfare*. Cmnd 3805, HMSO, London.

Donnison, D. (1998) *Policies for a Just Society*. Macmillan, London.

Fitzherbert, K. (1967) *West Indian Children in London*. Occasional Papers on Social Administration, G. Bell & Sons Ltd, London.

Fletcher-Campbell, F. (1998) Progress or procrastination: the education of young people who are looked after. *Children & Society* **12**, 3–11.

Fuller, R. & Stevenson, O. (1983) *Policies, Programmes and Disadvantage*. SSRC & DHSS, Heinemann, London.

Glennerster, H. (1991) Social policy since the Second World War. In *The State of Welfare: The Welfare State in Britain since 1974* (ed. J. Hills). Clarendon, Oxford.

Gregg, P. & Wadsworth, J. (1995) *More Work, Fewer Households?* National Institute for Economic and Social Research, London.

Handler, J. (1968) *Coercion in the caseworker relationship: a comparative overview.* Paper presented at the National Institute for Social Work Training, London.

Hattersley, R. (1997) *Fifty Years On: A Prejudiced History of Britain Since the War.* Little, Brown and Company, London.

Heath, A., Colton, M. & Aldgate, J. (1994) Failure to escape: a longitudinal study of foster children's educational attainment. *British Journal of Social Work* **24**, 241–60.

Holman, R. (1996) Fifty years ago: the Curtis and Clyde Reports. *Children & Society* **10**, 197–209.

Home Office (in conjunction with Department of Health) (1992) *Memorandum of Good Practice on Video Recorded Interviews with Child Witnesses for Criminal Proceedings.* HMSO, London.

Jones, A. & Bilton, K. (1994) *The Future Shape of Children's Services.* National Children's Bureau, London.

Lister, R. (1996) Blurring the vision. *The Guardian*, 3 July.

National Institute for Social Work (1982) *Social Workers: Their Role and Tasks.* Bedford Square Press, National Council for Voluntary Organisations, London.

Sanders, R., Jackson, S. & Thomas, N. (1997) Degrees of involvement: the interaction of focus and commitment in area child protection committees. *British Journal of Social Work* **27**, 871–92.

Secretary of State for Social Services (1974) *Report of the Committee of Inquiry into the Care and Supervision Provided in Relation to Maria Colwell.* HMSO, London.

Seebohm Committee (1968) *Report of the Committee on Local Authority and Allied Personal Social Services.* Cmnd 3703, HMSO, London.

Social Work Service Development Group (1972) *Community Development Project and the Social Work Service.* DHSS, London.

Thoburn, J. (1998) The swings and roundabouts of fifty years of family placement. *Family Support Network Newsletter* No. 12, 10–12. University of East Anglia, Norwich.

Townsend, P. (1970) *The Fifth Social Service: A Critical Analysis of the Seebohm Proposals.* The Fabian Society, London.

Utting, W. (1997) *People Like Us: The Report Of The Review Of The Safeguards For Children Living Away From Home.* The Stationery Office, London.

Wattam, C. (1992) *Making a Case in Child Protection.* Longman, Harlow.

Willetts, D. (1998) Let me explain. *The Guardian*, 8 April.

Chapter 3

Children Still in Need, Indeed: prevention across five decades

Pauline Hardiker

Introduction

Two approaches to prevention are explored in this chapter. First, a framework is outlined which serves as a way of thinking about social policy issues in child welfare. This framework (or grid) (see Figure 3.1) has been used in Great Britain in relation to children's services planning. Second, prevention is used as a further heuristic device to locate the concerns of child welfare professionals during the welfare state era. This pragmatic approach may serve to make the enormous and ambitious project implied in the chapter's title perhaps a little more manageable. As Freeman (1992) suggests, there is always an element of rhetoric and reality in discussions of prevention:

> 'nowhere is there agreement about quite what prevention is, while everywhere there is agreement that it is a good thing.'

> (Freeman, 1992: p. 47)

On the other hand, many policies and practices are pursued on the basis of preventive goals. As Parker (1990: p. 98) argues, '...the principle of prevention ... had been invoked from the earliest days of organised child care.' Nevertheless, prevention meant different things in different contexts and eras.

The social policy contexts of prevention in child welfare

Figure 3.1 outlines a framework (Hardiker *et al.*, 1991a, b; 1996) which locates preventive concepts in their social policy contexts. This identifies contrasting views about the role of the State in child welfare and the levels of intervention prioritised by services. The framework was originally formulated in a feasibility study of policies and practices in preventive child care for the Department of Health in the late 1980s (Hardiker *et al.*, 1991a). This latest version has been revised through

THE ENABLING AUTHORITY

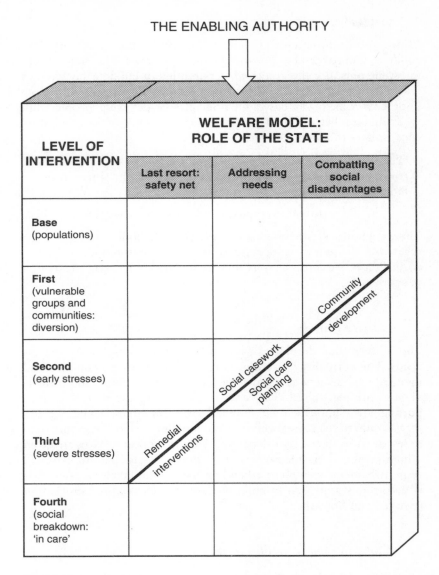

Fig 3.1

dissemination and developmental activities in the child welfare community.

The role of the State (horizontal axis)

The role of the State is one means of locating the value systems which legitimate welfare interventions. Three models of welfare are summarised:

1. Last resort.

In this approach, parents are held to be responsible for rearing their children, and parental rights and duties are stressed. The State should intervene only as a last resort when parenting or children's behaviour reach 'damaging' levels. This approach was readily recognisable in the Poor Law which was based on principles of deterring people from applying for relief and from pauperism. The principle of 'less eligibility' encapsulates this value precisely:

> 'The situation of the relief recipient on the whole shall not be made really or apparently so eligible (i.e. desirable) as the situation of the independent labourer of the lowest class.'

> > (Royal Commission on the Poor Laws, 1834: p. 228)

The workhouse was held out as a threat to able-bodied applicants for relief with the aim of reducing destitution, pauperism and, of course, costs. Preventive concepts were then understood in terms of preventing pauperism.

2. Addressing needs

The welfare state developed as a major social institution to address needs. The normality of stresses in rearing children in a complex and multicultural society is acknowledged. Life transitions and vulnerabilities are recognised. The State is given a significant role in supporting and supplementing families' own resources. Child welfare services aim to reintegrate children and families into society rather than to rescue children and punish parents. Family support services are given a high profile alongside professional approaches to welfare. Parental responsibilities are emphasised and partnership principles espoused. It is within this approach to child welfare that ideas about prevention emerged and flourished.

3. Combatting social disadvantages

This approach sees social problems, including those experienced by children and families, as rooted in social inequalities, which welfare agencies combat. The State is thus given a proactive role in child welfare. The Children Act 1989 Guidance and Regulations illustrate some of these principles (DOH, 1991): giving parents more power *vis-à-vis* the law, addressing children's rights, taking into account the views of local communities and user groups, anti-discrimination. Community development and educational priority area projects in the 1970s and safe city plus anti-poverty strategies in the 1990s are other examples. Prevention has a rather different meaning within this approach and focuses on 'primary prevention for populations', i.e. draining the swamp rather than rescuing drowning people.

Levels of intervention (vertical axis)

Preventive concepts were originally developed in medicine, locating primary, secondary and tertiary levels (prevent disease arising in the first place; provide help once problems have arisen; avoid the worst consequences of treatment). In social welfare, it is more appropriate to identify levels of intervention in terms of stages in problem development and targets for intervention.

1. Base level

This level identifies overall populations for whom universalist services are mobilised. The ideology of the post-war welfare state in Britain was based on a vision that such services would provide primary prevention bulwarks against the five giants: want, ignorance, disease, squalor and idleness (Beveridge, 1942; Glennerster, 1995; Stevenson, 1995). The welfare state was designed to sustain and support the patriarchal nuclear family, though its effectiveness in this was precarious (Tunstill, 1997). Moreover, it is now recognised that base level services actually generate 'needs' for significant social groups. Changes in political economy have produced increased fragmentation of services for children and young people through NHS and education reforms, plus housing and social security policies (Sutton, 1997). Rises in school exclusion and youth homelessness relate to free market developments which create new agendas for the politics of prevention.

2. First level

Services at this level target vulnerable groups and communities. Interventions aim to divert these groups from Social Services Departments and to enable vulnerable children and families to use universalist and community-based resources wherever possible. Advice, guidance and signposting services in health centres, libraries, churches, temples, schools, leisure and community centres may serve these purposes.

3. Second level

This level targets early stresses such as those experienced by families in temporary crisis or early difficulties; it includes 'children in need', including disabled children. Approaches include short-term or task-centred methods and placements. The aim is to restore personal and social functioning so that direct interventions by Social Services Departments are no longer needed. Children and parents may be enabled to use family centres, day care, accommodation and befriending networks.

4. Third level

This level targets serious stresses including the risk of significant harm, family breakdown or compulsory entry into the care system. Problems may be well-established and crises may be serious: homicide, sexual abuse, cruelty, grievous bodily harm, wilful neglect. The aim of interventions is to mitigate these difficulties, to restore family functioning and links between parents and children and to facilitate 'good-enough' parenting. Children and families may be enabled to use a range of therapeutic and community facilities.

5. Fourth level

This level addresses a diverse range of issues and problems from social breakdown, placements outside of the home to children abused within the care system. The aims of intervention may be damage limitation, therapy or permanency planning. Skilled interventions of a high order, including interprofessional and interagency co-ordination, are indicated.

Profiles of prevention (the diagonal)

It is important to relate levels of intervention to models of welfare because these locate the preferred targets of intervention:

- In a model of combatting social disadvantages, the preferred approach will be at the first level, using community development methods.
- In a model of addressing needs, the preferred response will be at the second level, using social casework and social care planning approaches.
- In a last resort model, interventions may not take place until the third level is reached, when remedial methods will be called for.

These profiles indicate tendencies and are not necessarily mutually exclusive. Hardiker and Barker's research on significant harm and disability, for example, shows the importance of task-centred and developmental work at third and fourth levels of intervention (Hardiker & Barker, 1994; Hardiker *et al.*, 1995; Seden *et al.*, 1996).

The enabling authority (the third dimension)

There has always been a mixed economy of social care in child welfare services, including the statutory and the independent sectors plus informal carers.

1. Pre-1948 Children Act

The major voluntary organisations were significant providers of child welfare services. Rescue and salvation rather than prevention were dominant approaches to welfare. Parker (1990) describes this as the age of separation.

2. Post-1948 Children Act

The major voluntaries continued to be important providers of child welfare services during this period. Packman (1968) discusses the complex links between the new statutory and the established voluntary child care services.

> '... the relationship between the variations in numbers of children in voluntary society care and the variations in numbers in local authority care is complex ... The fact that there is no consistency in the relationship between the proportion in local authority care and in voluntary society hands does not, however, invalidate the assumption that the two child care systems are closely related and that the activities of one can and do influence the activities of the others.'
>
> (Packman, 1968: pp. 115–16]

Packman concludes that numbers are less related to assessed need or level of activity of the local authority Children's Department than to historical accident, patchy coverage of the country, and the skills and personalities of individual workers.

3. Preventive activity

After 1948 voluntary child care organisations moved away from a predominantly separatist provision of child welfare services. Barnardos is a good example of this trend, refocusing its services to work with families in communities, and basing its values on challenging social disadvantages. Projects span several levels of intervention, including professional and developmental initiatives in residential units and family centres (Stones, 1994).

Overview

It has been suggested that developments in preventive concepts largely belong to the Welfare State era, during which wide-ranging needs were interpreted and addressed. One development relates to need interpretations. With the growth of social science and professional knowledge, a wider range of psychosocial needs in children, families, groups and communities was recognised. Some of these became translated into legitimate targets for governance. The other development relates to need-satisfactions. The relative balance between families, the State and the market in satisfying child care needs shifted across the five post-war decades.

The grid (Figure 3.1) is useful in locating child welfare issues but its specific relevance to prevention still needs to be clarified. There is an assumptive base in the framework outlined. As Parker (1980) argues, within a needs-based model of welfare, prevention is a relevant aim at every level of intervention. A professional approach to child welfare aims, wherever possible, to prevent the need for a more intrusive intervention, in line with the dominant values of social work. What is or is not a more intrusive intervention is, of course, a very complex equation (Hardiker, 1992). One Children's Services Strategy Group (Children and Young People Services Plan, 1998) is operationalising these ideas, defining prevention as:

- stopping worse things happening later
- action earlier to prevent more intrusive interventions at a later date
- restoring or enabling people to move on to a better level of functioning
- avoiding the necessity of emergency measures.

This strategy group is using the grid to map and cost its constituent children's services. This suggests that the grid is a useful framework for mapping, planning and evaluating services (Hardiker *et al.*, 1996).

Spheres in which child welfare is operated

As we have seen, prevention can mean rather different things depending on the social policy contexts in which it is promulgated. In the nineteenth century prevention largely meant deterrence, rescue and salvation. As Parker (1990) shows, prevention also meant preventing children returning to 'cruel and neglectful' parents; there were many structural and ideological impediments to restoring children to their own parents during 'the age of separation'. This tide altered course somewhat following the Children Act 1948.

An exploration of preventive aims over the last 50 years helps to locate the spheres in which child care social work chose to operate. Some of the changing circumstances of children and families were interpreted as psychosocial needs. Some laws, policies and practices were interpreted as targets for intervention. Consequently, preventive child care social work came to be associated with addressing the following spheres: institutionalism, family breakdown, deviant careers, drifting in care, family support for children in need. These preventive aims often need to be 'read into' the policies and practices reviewed. For example, Tunstill (1997) observes that the Children Act 1948 did not include the word 'prevention' as such.

The prevention of institutionalism

The Curtis Report (1946) contains vivid descriptions of institution-alism in residential settings:

> 'For the most part the children are housed in large gaunt looking buildings with dark stairways and corridors, high windows, and unadapted baths and lavatories ... the traditional chocolate and buff paint remained, with bare boards and draughts, and a continual smell of mass cooking, soft soap and disinfectant.'

> (The Curtis Report, 1946: para 141)

> '... the defects were not of harshness, but rather of dirt and dreari-ness, drabness and over-regimentation ... children were being brought up by unimaginative methods, without the opportunity for developing their full capabilities and with very little brightness or interest in their surroundings ...
> [There] was a lack of personal interest in and affection for the chil-dren which we found shocking. The child in these Homes was not recognised as an individual with his own rights and possessions, his own life to live and his own contribution to offer ...
> ... he was without feeling that there was anyone to whom he could turn who was vitally interested in his welfare or who cared for him as a person.'

> (The Curtis Report, 1946: para 418)

These regimes were said to affect the children's behaviour in a pathological clamouring for attention and petting; slowness, back-wardness and lack of response; habits of destructiveness and want of concentration. It was also noted that it was unusual for children to have any regular contact with relatives by visits.

The major explanations for these problems were seen to be in administrative structures, the selection and training of staff and, of course, the value base of the service. It was these that the Children Act 1948 aimed to address. The gestation of the new system, though, was fought out during World War II at central government level between the major departments, the Ministry of Reconstruction and the Cabinet (Parker, 1983). Plans were set in train for selecting and training a new generation of boarding-out officers even before the legislation was passed. The new value base of the services was enshrined in the Chil-dren Act:

- to further the child's best interests, rather than to relieve and set him to work
- to afford opportunities for the proper development of the child's character and abilities
- to make use of facilities for children in the care of their own parents.

Adoption, emigration and the creation of smaller residential units also underpinned these reforms, which were clearly located in different models of welfare at fourth levels of intervention. Nevertheless, throughout the 1940s and to some extent before, child welfare concerns addressed the boundaries between children in their own homes and children 'in care'.

The Curtis Report describes this boundary very clearly:

'We have not regarded ourselves as called upon to deal with children who though suffering from neglect, malnutrition or other evils, are still in their own homes under their parents' care. During the period leading up to a child's removal from his home, he may indeed be said to be deprived of a "normal" home life.

The consideration of the welfare of children deprived of home life has inevitably raised in our minds ... the question whether this deprivation might not have been prevented.'

(Curtis Report, 1946: p. 6)

The Report identified some dilemmas. Some children were returned to homes in which they had been neglected because it was thought better for them than the conditions under which they would have to be cared for in the workhouse (The Curtis Report, 1946: para. 40). Furthermore, the extreme seriousness of taking away a child from an indifferent home was noted; every effort should be made to keep the child in its own home (The Curtis Report, 1946: para. 447).

The idea of positive discrimination for children in care was phrased in terms of compensation for the deprivation of a 'normal home life'. A substitute home should offer something much better. The Curtis Report argued that this need for compensation was not recognised in any existing legislation, something which was rectified in the Children Act 1948.

This same issue of relative deprivation and social justice (Runciman, 1966) was rehearsed in the Review of Child Care Law 1985 in relation to a simple welfare or best interests test (DHSS, 1985a).

'Taken to its logical conclusion a simple 'best interests' test would permit the state to intervene whenever it could show that the alternative arrangements proposed would serve the child's welfare better than those proposed by their parents. But "the child is not the child of the state"....'.

(DHSS, 1985a: p. 6)

The following vignette illustrates some ways in which the reversal of the principle of less eligibility subsequently impacted upon children in care in the community and children not seen to be deprived of a normal home life.

'Mr and Mrs A and their five children lived in a four-bedroomed, semi-detached council house in the 1950s. Mr A was a semi-skilled manual worker and Mrs A worked in a local cotton mill. There was a close extended family. The two older A children undertook many household tasks, including cooking, cleaning and looking after the younger children.

There was a "family group home" next door. Mr and Mrs B looked after five children (two sets of siblings) who were "in care". Mr B went out to work while Mrs B stayed at home to look after the house and children. A cleaning lady came daily, provisions were delivered to the home, and the house was very well-furbished. The A and B children played together.

The A children sometimes pondered about the contrasting conditions and circumstances in these two homes, and would often conclude, "but we are a family!"'

Post-war developments in the theory and practice of group care may be used as one measure of evaluation in respect of preventing institutionalism and using substitute care settings as both methods and targets of intervention. Contemporary projects identifying key indicators for evaluating services for looked-after children also illustrate the contrast between the Curtis heritage and the Children Act 1989 (Ward, 1997). Nevertheless, Stevenson (1997) sadly observed that,

'... the failure ... to address satisfactorily the provision of "good enough" residential care is one of the tragedies of post-war child welfare services in the United Kingdom.'

(Stevenson, 1997: p. 197)

We might also add that the Curtis solution of boarding-out has not been a universal success (Berridge & Cleaver, 1987).

The prevention of family breakdown

Deprivation, neglect, delinquency and problem family were typical words used in child care books in the early days of Children's Departments (Donnison, 1954; Wilson, 1962; Philp, 1963). To some extent, these social problems were limitations in the welfare state's aim to support the patriarchal nuclear family. A fine new generation of feminist social policy analysts also explored ways in which social workers were engaged in the State organisation of domestic life and social reproduction (for example, Wilson, 1977). The 'problem of the problem family' illustrates that these Welfare State controls did not always succeed in shoring up some families. The same can be said about 'lone parent families' today.

Child care social workers defined family breakdown in terms of children being admitted to (and possibly 'lost in') care. They did not mean family breakdown through divorce, for example, which increased significantly after World War II (Holterman, 1995; Owusu-Bempah, 1995; Utting, 1995; Owusu-Bempah & Howitt, 1997). It is in this context that the prevention of reception into care through working with families in communities became spheres of child care policy and practice. This was the seed-bed for developments in social casework in Children's Departments (Timms, 1962; Heywood, 1978). The focus was upon children deprived of a 'normal' home life with their parents and children at risk of admission to care (third levels).

This type of prevention is sometimes identified with the Children and Young Persons Act 1963; however, the policies and practices developed from the earliest days of Children's Departments through, for example, the appointment of family caseworkers to focus on this target group (Donnison, 1975; Packman, 1981; Thoburn, 1993). The literature illustrates the growing impact of social work upon the careers of children in care, from admission, to being in care, through to discharge (Jehu, 1963; Stevenson, 1963; Central Council for Education and Training in Social Work, 1978; Aldgate, 1980).

Preventive work, especially through the provision of cash and material aid, faced in two directions. One boundary related to income support (Stevenson, 1973), the other to conformity in exchange for welfare (Handler, 1973). Throughout its history, social work has never moved very far from the dynamics of the 'gift' relationship, implying sacrifice, prestige and obligation (Stedman Jones, 1971; Titmuss, 1971). On any definition or ideology, though, preventive work was undertaken with families at the most basic levels of need. Heywood & Allen (1971) concluded that the new legislation achieved some success in averting short-term crises rather than maintaining better care in the long-term for children in their own homes. There were also consequences for the child care service as it began to supervise far more children in their own homes, increasingly working at the interface with other government departments and public utilities (Packman, 1981).

The prevention of deviant careers

Delinquency has been an important preoccupation in child welfare. From the nineteenth century there were concerns that delinquency, neglect and deprivation arose from similar social circumstances; social policies were also developed to provide services for delinquents outside of the penal system. The aim was to prevent delinquency and its amplification into deviant careers (Boss, 1967; Bottoms, 1974; Parsloe, 1976; Platt, 1977; Packman, 1981; Eekelaar *et al.*, 1982). The high watermark for these ideologies was reached in the 1960s (Packman, 1981).

One way to encapsulate this sphere of prevention is the 'treatment model of delinquency' (May, 1971; Hardiker, 1977):

- Delinquency can be explained in terms of the motivational and behavioural systems of delinquents and not of the law and its administration.
- Delinquents are constrained in their behaviour which limits their responsibility.
- Delinquency is a presenting symptom of underlying problems and a sign of the need for intervention.

The treatment model contrasts with the infraction model, which explains delinquency largely in terms of chance and police activities because delinquents behave conventionally most of the time. Consequently, the family rather than the legal system became an important target for social work intervention in relation to preventing delinquency (second and third levels).

Although earlier child welfare legislation addressed the needs of delinquents, the Children and Young Person's Act 1969 may be taken as a zenith. For example, Harris (1991) analyses the issues in relation to the Care Order (Criminal), which was born in 1971 as section 7(7) and met its demise in the Children Act 1989. The Order began with a set of benign therapeutic aspirations, and survived a period of confusion in relation to diversion, punishment and welfare. Harris found that this order was used in disparate ways, and was not simply an intermediate step between supervision and custody; it was used for:

- minor offenders who could have been dealt with by less intensive treatment strategies, such as supervision plus;
- minor offenders whose social needs meant they were properly in care but who could have been committed using the civil jurisdiction on non-offence grounds (s. 1(2)(a)–(e)); and
- offenders whose repeated delinquency and poor response to non-residential alternatives posed a serious policy problem.

The Order was replaced by Supervision Order with conditions.

Hardiker's research on probation officers' ideologies (Hardiker, 1977) found that treatment models were not pervasive in relation to juvenile offenders. These ideologies were mediated by tariff and need considerations plus agency and court policies. Nevertheless, treatment ideologies were sometimes used in relation to adolescents. For example, David, a 13-year-old boy, was charged with theft as a trespasser and had no previous convictions. The probation officer thought that his offence behaviour was partly associated with problems in his family, arguing as follows:

'I think it is a marital problem, *not* related to cultural difficulties; his family came from Fiji in the hope of improving their circumstances and perhaps found it more of a struggle than they expected and in that sense frustrations have not helped the marital relationship. Father has tended to seek a bit of escape in drink at times. Mother has had to go out to work and has begun to try and achieve a certain amount of independence from the husband, which doesn't fit in with his expectations. I think this has some direct bearing on the boy's behaviour because the family situation is one in which conflict is quite apparent; it doesn't help him feel secure in his family and again he has this problem of finding out his own identity. The parents have unrealistic ambitions for their children. Therefore, he committed this offence along with his mates for reasons of status and group membership.'

(Hardiker, 1977: pp. 140–41)

A Supervision Order was recommended, 'to provide support and guidance to David, giving the opportunity to offer assistance in examining and resolving family conflicts'. This is quite a sophisticated version of a 'treatment model', identifying family conflicts, adolescence and group status dynamics. An 'overcultural' approach was avoided. Diversionary principles would have led to a different approach and outcome, had the case been processed 20 years later (Owusu-Bempah, 1994). A treatment ideology was more pervasive then in Social Services Departments, until diversionary ideas began to impact upon policies and practices (Thorpe *et al.*, 1980; Harris & Webb, 1987). Diversion was one response to concerns that 'treatment' approaches amplified rather than prevented deviance!

Preventing deviant careers was also relevant to parents in child welfare. There is a long history of decriminalising aspects of parenting; for example, infanticide and non-wilful neglect. The Doshi case (Hardiker & Curnock, 1984) illustrates ways in which social work processes facilitated a down-tariffing welfare approach in relation to a mother charged with assault, actual bodily harm and ill-treatment. Such an approach might, though, amplify deviance in other family situations.

The prevention of drift in care

Throughout the history of child care, even during the 'age of separation', there were concerns about the importance of returning children to their parents or other carers. Rehabilitation was enshrined as a duty in the Children Act 1948 (fourth level). The debate about children 'drifting in care' was stimulated in the 1970s by Rowe & Lambert's (1973) study of 'children who wait'. The importance of planning for children was also reinforced by new coalitions of interest such as the National Children's Bureau (Pugh, 1993) and the Permanency Planning Movement (Maluccio *et al.*, 1986). Some commentators suggest that these developments reflected the growing influence of child protection and 'State as parent' value perspectives (Harding, 1997).

The Children Act 1975 is one sphere in which to locate the issue of the prevention of drift though, as Rowe (1985) comments, this Act focused largely on adoption and sought to address the following problems: the labyrinth of adoption societies; the lack of legal emphasis on the child's rights or the welfare principle; social workers' misuse of adoption in attempts to sort out family relationships; confused attitudes about adoption versus rehabilitation, in the absence of permanency planning strategies. Rowe suggested that:

'... facing up to the chilling possibility of permanent separation galvanises social workers into action ... referral to an adoption unit not infrequently turns into successful rehabilitation.'

(Rowe, 1985: p. 27)

Attempts to prevent 'drift' included new controls on parental powers to remove their children received into care. There were many vested interests making different claims in respect of the new legislation, e.g. critics of 'tug of love' scenarios together with the poverty lobby which pressured for more 'preventive' and community services (Equality for Children, 1983; Holman, 1988; Rowe, 1989). 'Permanency planning versus prevention' was a familiar motto during this era.

Hardiker & Barker (1986, 1988) illustrate ways in which social workers experienced the impact of these changes upon their practices. One child was taken into care with a view to eventual rehabilitation. The practitioner commented:

'I felt previously that the policy was towards keeping up parental contact for as long as possible, but my new senior is very concerned that we could end up drifting into a situation rather than planning; the child might suddenly be found to be having destructive visits from parents and becoming very upset and disturbed. So we are now looking at terminating parental contact... I feel the mother is now doing what is expected of her and no more, and is going to force us to make the decision for her. I think it will probably end up as relinquishment.'

(Hardiker & Barker, 1986: p. 39)

The skills required in facilitating and maintaining links between parents and children in care subsequently became the focus of vigorous debate and research (DHSS, 1985b; Millham *et al.*, 1986; DoH, 1991).

The next example illustrates the sphere of prevention-versus-permanency planning as it was defined in the 1980s. Sylvie was brought up in an African–Caribbean family. She ran away from home when she was 15 and was received into care when her parents refused to have her back. She became pregnant and went to live in a purpose-built housing complex. Before and after the birth of her baby, Gemma, Sylvie adamantly requested adoption and made no preparations for Gemma's care. Following a visit from her maternal grandmother, Sylvie requested time to make up her mind and asked for Gemma to be received into care.

The social worker and hostel staff supported Sylvie in her wish to build an independent life for herself and, meanwhile, to reach her own decision about Gemma's future. During two-and-a-half-years, the following resources were mobilised: income support; facilities at the hostel, where Gemma could stay full-time or part-time, with staff backup; payment of fees and fares for Sylvie to train as a community volunteer; negotiation with the Housing Department in relation to accommodation and rent guarantee; provision of nursery and part-time care facilities.

Sylvie did well in care, maintaining a job and moving into her own accommodation. She was encouraged to visit Gemma, to take her home for weekends and to plan for her future care. There were long periods when there was no contact between Gemma and Sylvie, who began to avoid contact but was unwilling to consent to any long-term plans for Gemma. There was intensive social work input in respect of support, planning and resources. Eventually, the social worker recommended that Gemma should be 'freed for adoption', and concluded:

> '... all necessary resources were made available to facilitate Gemma's rehabilitation to her mother. It was a very painful piece of work. Any social worker would feel absolutely ridden with guilt about taking a big step like freeing for adoption. It has not been easy, but I am very satisfied with the outcome. I feel in my heart of hearts that I did everything to the best of my ability to try to rehabilitate the child with her mother and then to facilitate the relinquishment and adoption processes.'
>
> (Hardiker & Barker, 1988: p. 114)

These examples illustrate some ways in which social workers straddle kinship, welfare, and legal systems as they negotiate different interpretations of parents' and children's needs. They also illustrate ways in which families *and* social workers are caught between conflicting structural imperatives in respect of culture and social change. Adoption within the extended family or community is an integral part of the fabric of African–Caribbean society, but Sylvie was partly dislocated in time and space from such imperatives.

Family support services for children in need

The Children Act 1989 (Schedule 2 Part 1) refers to preventing: the need to bring proceedings for care/supervision orders or criminal prosecutions; placement in care; criminal offences. Prevention may be equated with diversion here (Masson, 1992). 'Family support services for children in need' has replaced the term 'prevention'. The duty is framed more positively as support rather than diminishing the need to receive children into care but it is owed to a restricted group of children. Hardiker, *et al.* (1991b) observed that:

> 'the language of "needs" ... sits oddly in our new residualist era, and it remains to be seen how it will be operationalised ... This new ideology of residualism ... will continue to provide a challenge for good practices in child care.'

> Hardiker, 1991b: pp. 356–7)

The language of needs was used in children's and community care legislation in the 1990s, which referred to needs-led assessments, targeting and eligibility criteria (Hardiker & Barker, 1994, 1996; Aldgate & Tunstill, 1995; Hardiker & Everitt, 1996). These influences have produced some exciting developments in children's services planning (Sutton, 1995; Cohen & Hagen, 1997; Sinclair *et al.*, 1997). As Fraser (1989) argues, evaluators should be able to choose between 'better' and 'worse' need interpretations. This is one challenge ahead (Association of Directors of Social Services & NCH Action for Children, 1995).

The 'refocusing debate' aims to collapse the bifurcation between protection-versus-prevention, especially in relation to child abuse. Seden *et al.* (1996) found, however, that family support packages were mobilised in every case in a study of significant harm. Protection and prevention are relevant aims at every level of intervention, and the refocusing debate points to the importance of addressing earlier levels of intervention in both respects (DoH, 1995).

Conclusion

No assumptions are made in this chapter about evolutionary progress, functional imperatives or the role of 'great' people and events in forming public opinion or social policy (Goldthorpe, 1962; Cretney, 1997, 1998). The domain of prevention illustrates continuities and discontinuities, facilitators and inhibitors, consensus, compromise and conflicts in social policy processes (Parker, 1986, 1990; Smith, 1996). Different and increasingly complex coalitions of interest have also shaped the ways in which prevention and need have been used as political instruments in policy processes and justifications for practice.

Social workers know 'in their bones' that there are limits to prevention in the spheres of interventions with people-in-situations. That is why, while the earth remaineth in societal form, there will be children in need.

Acknowledgement

I wish to acknowledge the help, support and wise advice from my friends and colleagues at the University of Leicester School of Social

Work, especially Professor Jane Aldgate, Mary Marker, Dr K. Owusu-Bempah, Lucy Panasiuk and Professor Noel Timms.

References

Aldgate, J. (1980) Identification of factors influencing children's length of stay in care. In *New Developments in Foster Care and Adoption* (ed. J. Triseliotis). Routledge and Kegan Paul, London.

Aldgate, J. & Tunstill, J. (1995) *Making Sense of Section 17*. HMSO, London.

Association of Directors of Social Services & NCH Action for Children (1995) *Children Still in Need*. Northallerton and London.

Berridge, D. & Cleaver, H. (1987) *Foster Home Breakdown*. Blackwell Science, Oxford.

Beveridge Report (1942) *Social Insurance and Allied Services*. Cmd 6404. HMSO, London.

Boss, P. (1967) *Social Policy and the Young Delinquent*. Routledge and Kegan Paul, London.

Bottoms, A. E. (1974) On the decriminalisation of English juvenile courts. In *Crime, Criminology and Public Policy* (ed. R. Hood), pp. 319–45. Heinemann, London.

Central Council for Education and Training in Social Work (1978) *Good Enough Parenting*. Central Council for Education and Training in Social Work, London.

Children and Young People Services Plan 1998–2001: The Final Report of the Prevention and Family Support Network (1998) *Social Exclusion in Milton Keynes: Towards a Multi-agency Family Support Strategy*. Milton Keynes Council.

Cohen, B. & Hagen, U. (1997) Children's Services: Shaping up for the Millennium. Supporting Children and families in the UK and Scandinavia. HMSO, Children in Scotland, Edinburgh.

Cretney, S. (1997) The Children Act 1948: Lessons for Today. *Child and Family Law Quarterly Seminar*, Oxford, 1 July.

Cretney, S. (1998) The Children Act 1948: The state as parent. *Law Quarterly Review* July, 419–59.

Curtis Report, The (1946) *Report of the Care of Children Committee*. Cmd. 6922. HMSO, London.

Department of Health (1991) *The Children Act 1989 Guidance and Regulations. Volume 2: Family Support, Day Care and Educational Provision for Young Children*. HMSO, London.

Department of Health (1995) *Messages from Research*. HMSO, London.

Department of Health and Social Security (1985a) *Review of Child Care Law: Report to Ministers of an Interdepartmental Working Party*. HMSO, London.

Department of Health and Social Security (1985b) *Social Work Decisions in Child Care: Recent Research Findings and their Implications*. HMSO, London.

Donnison, D. V. (1954) *The Neglected Child and the Social Services*. Manchester University Press, Manchester.

Donnison, D. V. (1975) *Social Policy and Administration Revisited*, Rev. edn. George Allen and Unwin, London.

Eekelaar, J. M., Dingwall, R. & Murray, T. (1982) Victims or threats? Children in care proceedings. *Journal of Social Welfare Law* 67, 68–82.

Equality for Children (1983) *Keeping Kids Out of Care.* Review of the evidence given to the House of Commons Social Services Select Committee on Children in Care 1982–83.

Fraser, M. (1989) Talking about needs: interpretive contests as political conflicts in welfare state societies. *Ethics* 99, 291–313.

Freeman, R. (1992) The idea of prevention: a critical review. In *Private Risks and Public Dangers* (eds S. Scott, S. Platt & H. Thomas). Explorations in Sociology, 43, British Sociological Association.

Glennerster, H. (1995) *British Social Policy Since 1945.* Blackwell Science, Oxford.

Goldthorpe, J. H. (1962) The development of social policy in England, 1800–1914. *Transactions of the Fifth World Congress of Sociology* 4, 41–56.

Handler, J. (1973) *The Coercive Social Worker.* Rand McNally, Chicago.

Hardiker, P. (1977) Social work ideologies in the Probation Service. *British Journal of Social Work* 7 (2), 131–54.

Hardiker, P. (1992) The Children Act 1989: Family support services for children with disabilities. In *Family Support and the Children Act* (ed. J. Gibbons). HMSO, London.

Hardiker, P. & Barker, M. (1986) *A Window on Child Care Practices in the 1980s.* Research Report, University of Leicester School of Social Work.

Hardiker, P. & Barker, M. (1988) A window on child care, poverty and social work. In *Public Issues, Private Pain: Poverty, Social Work and Social Policy* (eds S. Becker & S. Macpherson). Social Services Insight Books, London.

Hardiker, P. & Barker, M. (1994) *The 1989 Children Act: Social Work Processes, Social Policy Contexts and 'Significant Harm'.* Research Report, Leicester University School of Social Work.

Hardiker, P. & Barker, M. (1996) *The NHS and Community Care Act 1990: Needs-Led Assessments and Packages of Care.* Research Report, University of Leicester School of Social Work.

Hardiker, P. & Curnock, K. (1984) Social work assessment processes in work with ethnic minorities – the Doshi family. *British Journal of Social Work* 14 (1), 23–47.

Hardiker, P. & Everitt, A. (1996) *Evaluating for Good Practice.* Macmillan, Basingstoke.

Hardiker, P., Exton, K. & Barker, M. (1991a) *Policies and Practices in Preventive Child Care.* Avebury, Aldershot.

Hardiker, P., Exton, K. & Barker, M. (1991b) The social policy contexts of prevention in child care. *British Journal of Social Work* 1991, 21 (4), 341–59.

Hardiker, P., Exton, K. & Barker, M. (1996) The prevention of child abuse: a framework for analysing services. In *Childhood Matters: Report of the National Commission of Inquiry into the Prevention of Child Abuse,* Vol. 2. HMSO, London.

Hardiker, P., Seden, J. & Barker, M. (1995) Children first: protection and prevention in services to disabled children. *Child Care in Practice: Northern Ireland Journal of Multi-Disciplinary Child Care Practice* 2 (1), 1–17, Part I; and 2 (2), 1–9, Part II.

Harding, L. (1997) *Perspectives in Child Care Policy*, 2nd edn. Longman, London.

Harris, R. (1991) The life and death of the Care Order (Criminal). *British Journal of Social Work* 21 (1), 1–17.

Harris, R. & Webb, D. (1987) *Welfare, Power and Juvenile Justice*. Tavistock, London.

Heywood, J. S. (1978) *Children in Care*, 3rd edn. Routledge and Kegan Paul, London.

Heywood, J. S. & Allen, B. K. (1971) *Financial Help in Social Work*. Manchester University Press, Manchester.

Holman, B. (1988) *Putting Families First*. Macmillan, Basingstoke.

Holterman, S. (1995) *All Our Futures*. Barnardos, Barkingside.

Jehu, D. (1963) *Casework – Before Admission to Care*. Association of Child Care Officers.

Maluccio, A. N., Fein, E. & Olmstead, K. A. (1986) *Permanency Planning for Children*. Tavistock, London.

Masson, J. (1992) Managing risk under the Children Act 1989: diversion in child care. *Child Abuse Review* 1, 103–22.

May, D. (1971) Delinquency control and the treatment model. *British Journal of Criminology* 11 (4), 359–70.

Millham, S., Bullock, R., Hosie, K. & Haak, M. (1986) *Lost in Care*. Gower, Aldershot.

Owusu-Bempah, J (1994) Self-identity and social work. *British Journal of Social Work* 24 (2), 123–36.

Owusu-Bempah, J. (1995) Information about the absent parent as a factor in the well-being of children of single-parent families. *International Social Work* 38, 253–75.

Owusu-Bempah, J. & Howitt, D. (1997) Socio-genealogical connectedness, attachment theory, and child care practice. *Child and Family Social Work* 2 (4), 199–207.

Packman, J. (1968) *Child Care: Needs and Numbers*. George Allen & Unwin, London.

Packman, J. (1981) *The Child's Generation*, 2nd edn. Blackwell and Robertson, Oxford.

Parker, R. A. (1980) *Caring for Separated Children*. National Children's Bureau, London.

Parker, R. A. (1983) The gestation of reform: the Children Act 1948, In *Approaches to Welfare* (eds P. Bean & S. Macpherson). Routledge and Kegan Paul, London.

Parker, R. A. (1986) Child care: the roots of a dilemma. *Political Quarterly* 57 (3), July–September, 305–14.

Parker, R. A. (1990) *Away From Home: A History of Barnardos*. Barnardos, Barkingside.

Parsloe, P. (1976) Social work and the justice model. *British Journal of Social Work* 6 (1), 71–89.

Philp, A. F. (1963) *Family Failure*. Faber & Faber, London.

Platt, A. M. (1977) *The Child Savers: The Invention of Delinquency*, 2nd edn. University of Chicago Press, Chicago.

Pugh, G. (1993) *30 Years of Change for Children*. National Children's Bureau, London.

Rowe, J. (1985) Children Act 1975: Piecemeal distortion. *Community Care* 21, November, 25–27.

Rowe, J. (1989) Caring concern. *The Guardian*, 2 June, p. 30.

Rowe, J. & Lambert, L. (1973) *Children Who Wait*. Association of British Adoption Agencies, London.

Royal Commission on the Poor Laws (1834). Report. Fellowes, London.

Runciman, W. G. (1966) *Relative Deprivation and Social Justice*. Routledge and Kegan Paul, London.

Seden, J., Hardiker, P. & Barker, M. (1996) Child protection revisited: balancing state intervention and family autonomy through social work processes. *Child and Family Social Work* 1 (1), 57–66.

Sinclair, R., Hearn, B. & Pugh, G. (1997) *Preventive Work with Families: The Role of Mainstream Services*. National Children's Bureau, London.

Smith, R. S. (1996) *Values and Practice in Child Care*. PhD thesis, University of Leicester.

Stedman Jones, G. (1971) *Outcast London*. Clarendon, Oxford.

Stevenson, O. (1963) Reception into care – its meaning for all concerned. *Case Conference*, 10 (4), September.

Stevenson, O. (1973) *Claimant or Client*. George Allen & Unwin, London.

Stevenson, O. (1995) Reviewing post-war welfare. In *Targeting Those Most in Need: Winners and Losers* (ed. I. Allen). Policy Studies Institute, London.

Stevenson, O. (1997) Review of M. Hill & J. Aldgate, Child Welfare Services; Jessica Kingsley, London. *Child and Family Social Work* 2 (3), 194.

Stones, C. (1994). *Focus on Families*. Macmillan, Basingstoke.

Sutton, P. (1995) *Crossing the Boundaries*. National Children's Bureau, London.

Sutton, P. (1997) All in the same boat – rowing in the same direction? Influences on collaboration over children's services. In *Children's Services: Shaping Up for the Millennium* (eds B. Cohen & U. Hagen). HMSO, Edinburgh.

Thoburn, J. (1993) Prevention and reunification – an historical perspective. In *Prevention and Reunification in Child Care* (eds B. Marsh & J. Triseliotis). Batsford, London.

Thorpe, D. H., Smith, D., Green, C. J. & Paley, J. H. (1980) *Out of Care*. George Allen & Unwin, London.

Timms, N. (1962) *Casework in the Child Care Service*. Butterworths, London.

Titmuss, R. M. (1971) *The Gift Relationship*. Allen & Unwin, London.

Tunstill, J. (1997) Implementing the family support clauses of the 1989 Children Act: legislative, professional and organisational obstacles. In *Child Protection and Family Support: Tensions, Contradictions and Possibilities* (ed. N. Parton). Routledge, London.

Utting, D. (1995) *Family and Parenthood*. Joseph Rowntree Foundation, York.

Ward, H. (1997) *Identifying Key Indicators for Monitoring Services and Assessing Outcome*. Dartington Social Research Unit and School of Social Work, University of Leicester.

Wilson, E. (1977) *Women and the Welfare State*. Tavistock, London.

Wilson, H. (1962) *Delinquency and Child Neglect*. George Allen & Unwin, London.

Chapter 4

Children's Rights

Lorraine Harding

Introduction

This chapter will first consider different meanings of a term which has been in common use in recent decades – 'children's rights'. Essentially, what will be explored is the distinction between the protectionist and liberationist understandings of the concept of children's rights. On the one hand, a protectionist understanding is concerned about child welfare but fundamentally sees adults as the guardians or protectors of children, while children are construed as dependent and in need of special treatment; one variant of this is the 'caretaker thesis' (Archard, 1993). On the other hand, the liberationist understanding stresses the need to empower children themselves, seeing them as competent and not dissimilar to adults, and seeking to free them from arbitrary age-based restrictions. A recent example of liberationist thinking is the work of Franklin (1986, 1995). It will be argued that such views give rise to some difficulties in the debate about children. Dangers arise from an inappropriate 'adultisation' of children. Nevertheless, the liberationist case does have some positive aspects.

As an illustration of recent trends reflecting 'children's rights' thinking, the chapter will also consider briefly the liberationist elements in the UN Convention on the Rights of the Child.

The chapter will conclude by highlighting some key points in current debates.

Protectionist and liberationist understandings of children's rights

A protectionist understanding of the concept of children's rights is the approach that, while concerned about children's 'rights' to a number of things such as welfare, care, health, education, and adequate standard of living, sees adults (and adult-controlled systems) as the guardians or protectors of children; that is, children are construed as unable fully to defend and exercise their rights for themselves, although obviously with increasing ability, and decreasing need for adult protection, as they age.

In this view, then, it would not be appropriate, or helpful to children, to give them the power or autonomy or rights which adults character-istically have. Children's 'rights' are *different* from those of adults, and include, as well as provision of certain services and types of care, the need for a measure of control in the cause of effective socialisation. Thus while children may still be argued to have 'rights' in this context, for example the right not to be abused, adults are firmly in control as far as decisions affecting children are concerned. Children are protected from adult abuse, for example, by the actions of other, more benevolent adults, and by various adult-controlled systems for detecting and acting on abuse.

This approach, which might also be termed a welfarist under-standing of children's rights, can be seen as the more 'traditional' one, if the twentieth century and the latter part of the nineteenth century is considered. There is, for example, in Britain a history of child law and policy which embodies this general orientation. It was manifested in the appearance of 'industrial schools' in the mid-nineteenth century; in the instituting, and then the extension to older age groups, of compulsory schooling from the 1870s and 1880s; in Acts protecting against cruelty and neglect, beginning with the Prevention of Cruelty to, and Protec-tion of Children Act 1889; in provisions for child and maternal health in the early years of this century; and in a host of statutes and policies relating to children and their well-being in the post-Second World War era (of which the Children Act 1948 is one famous milestone, and the Children Act 1989 another).

One variant of the protectionist approach is what Archard (1993: p. 51) calls the 'caretaker thesis'. This is based on the claim that children should *not* be seen as self-determining agents; this thesis:

'offers an account of why children should not be free to make autonomous decisions, and of how their caretakers should be guided in making decisions for them.'

(Archard, 1993: p. 51)

It denies to children the rights of self-determination, doing so from within a general philosophy that *does* accord self-determination a central, valued place. But children are excluded from this general emphasis, as are certain adults, because they cannot make the choices that they would make if rational and autonomous. Children merit adults paternalistically making choices for them because of children's stage of cognitive and emotional development; and adults choose for them as children would choose if they were adults – if they were competent to choose. A particular consideration with children is the question of the child's future interests: the choice should be made with regard to the interests of the adult person that the child will in time become. This is relevant to the notion of 'future-oriented consent' which is discussed further below. Another way of looking at the adult caretaker in this context is in terms of a trustee for the child's present and future interests: 'The purpose of the trust is to safeguard the future adult's interests, which the child is itself unable to do' (Archard, 1993: p. 53). Archard goes on to identify problems with the caretaker approach, such as the difficulty of considering children as a group, the assumption that age is a valid criterion for discrimination, and the question of how caretaking should be conducted, including 'future-oriented consent'. The inadequacies of caretaking, paternalistic or protective approaches to children now lead us into the alternative, liberationist view.

By contrast with the protectionist approach, the liberationist understanding of children's rights stresses the need to empower children, seeing the protectionist standpoint as basically flawed in this respect. Indeed it is thought that the protective approach does not actually protect children because it still leaves them subject to adult power. Adult power is construed as oppressive, with children's greatest need being for more power and autonomy of their own in order to withstand this destructive force. Furthermore, children should not be subject to restrictions only on the grounds of their age (these limits being essentially arbitrary and discriminatory), and should have most, if not at all, of the rights which adults usually have – to work full-time for wages, to vote, to live where they choose, to go to school or not as they wish, and perhaps (although expressed with some hesitation) to experiment with sex and drugs. This type of more extreme writing on children appeared in the 1970s as an extension of black and women's liberation movements, and names associated with it include John Holt in *Escape from Childhood* (1975). Holt's title indicates his underlying orientation: modern childhood is basically perceived as a prison, from which children need liberating. Something of this vein of discussion has been carried forward by Franklin in two edited collections (1986 and 1995) (see below).

In the modern era the liberationist construction of 'children's rights' constitutes a relatively recent development (although it might also be argued that it bears some resemblance to the mediaeval construction of childhood – see Franklin (1986) and below), with manifestation as indicated in the 1970s (Foster & Freed, 1972; Farson, 1974; Holt, 1975) and further expression in the 1980s and 1990s, both in writings (for example, Franklin, 1986, 1995; Newell, 1989, 1991, 1993; Rosenbaum & Newell, 1991; Children's Rights Development Unit, 1994), and in action (for example in changing practices on child punishment, children as witnesses in court, and children's consents; in the setting up of various child-oriented organisations such as Childline and the Children's Rights Development Unit; and in the changing position of children in public and private family law).

There are some obvious basic points of difference between the protectionist and the liberationist views. Fundamentally, the concept of childhood is different, in that the protectionists see primarily the vulnerability of children, along with their need for direction and control. The liberationists on the other hand think that the competence of children is underestimated – that they can do more than they are given credit for, and are not necessarily less rational and mature than adults. They are conscious of injustices to children in an adult-controlled world, seeing increased power for children as the means to end such injustice. An analogy is drawn between the 'oppression' of children by adults, and other oppressions, such as of black people by white people, of women by men, of disabled people by non-disabled people, and so on. Discrimination against children is seen as being equally unfair as discrimination against these groups. The basic position is that children are essentially no different from adults and should be treated (virtually) the same – a long way from the protectionist view.

The liberationists may also look to the history of childhood, in particular the work of Aries (1962), to argue that childhood is essentially a modern construction, and that the mediaeval world had no concept of children as different or special, or at least not once they had reached the age of six or seven, and it incorporated them into, rather than excluded them from, adult society. This understanding of earlier times is contested (see, for example, Pollock, 1983), but the view that the experience and understanding of childhood, and the response to it, are culturally determined and vary with time and place, is a point well made. The liberationists' challenge to modern concepts of childhood may or may not have a sound historical base, in terms of the notion of childhood as a separate and distinct stage of life being a recent invention; but they usefully ask fundamental questions: why do modern industrial societies segregate children into special environments, why are children deprived of some fundamental rights of citizenship, why is it an offence for them to do certain things which are not an offence if done by adults, and so on.

The protectionist and liberationist viewpoints also have different views of the family and the State. The protectionists tend to see a family structure with some parental authority as generally an appropriate context for children, while in this view the State also has a beneficial protective role. Liberationist writers (see Holt, 1975) give little credence to either family or State as beneficial for children. Both are seen as adult-controlled and therefore oppressive. Holt comments: 'The family was not invented, nor has it evolved, to make children happy or to provide a secure emotional and psychological background to grow up in' (1975 p. 38); and: 'Most children who lose their families remain wards of the State – i.e. they are prisoners' (1975: p. 23).

Despite these obvious, and sometimes stark differences, there are also points of convergence between the two points of view: both have a genuine concern for children's welfare, although they construe how it might be achieved differently. Both would presumably agree that standards of living, health, recreation, and education (where children choose to take it up) should be high. (For differences and similarities, see Fox Harding, 1997: pp. 158–170.)

In debates in the 1980s and 1990s liberationist arguments, or at least a moderate version of them, have tended to have a higher profile, and a number of changes in the treatment of children have also occurred, as indicated, which move, broadly speaking, in the direction which liberationists would prefer. Recent writing in this genre will be explored further by means of an examination of the writing of Franklin (1995) in an introductory chapter to his edited collection *The Handbook of Children's Rights*. Some difficulties and dangers of the liberationist approach will then be examined.

The work of Franklin

In an earlier collection edited by Franklin and published in 1986, *The Rights of Children,* to which he also contributed, he challenged modern and common sense conceptions of childhood, and the criterion of rationality in distinguishing between children and adults. A more up-to-date and topical example of his work will be examined here. Franklin began his 1995 chapter, entitled: 'The case for children's rights: a progress report', by recalling a 'cynical and disparaging' reaction to his previous publication, which now seemed 'barely credible' (sic) (p. 3) at the time of this later writing. The debate had moved on in the intervening decade, he claimed, and children's rights 'seemed to come of age' (p. 3). After a review of policy developments and their roots – and an admission that in the 1990s there was also an ideological and policy reaction *against* children's rights – Franklin refers to other writings on children's rights from the 1970s to the 1990s, and goes on to introduce his book. He contextualises the book's contributions by examining the phrase 'children's rights' and assessing various strands in the debate. His main argument is as follows.

Childhood and its world are essentially a social construct and are not universal. Childhood has often been mythologised as a 'golden age' despite its obvious hardships and difficulties. Franklin criticises inconsistent and shifting age boundaries, and the categorisation of everyone under 18 as 'non-adult'. There appears to be an inconsistency in Franklin's own argument here, in that he seems simultaneously to complain that 'the age boundary between childhood and adulthood is established at different ages in different spheres of activity', and that 'the definition of everyone under 18 as a child' obscures diversity and recognised development over the age range with, usually 'different needs, rights and responsibilities being judged appropriate for the different age groups' (p. 8). It is not clear how age boundaries could simultaneously be consistent, and variable for different stages.

Franklin further contrasts the mythologised understanding of childhood with modern realities. Childhood in his view is essentially a condition characterised by powerlessness, and expresses more about power than chronology. Moving on to the definition of rights, Franklin finds this less problematic – theoretical discussion and the UN Convention had mapped out much of the rights terrain. Distinctions are made, however, between legal and moral rights, and between welfare and liberty rights, the latter corresponding broadly to the distinction made here between protectionist and liberationist understandings of children's rights. Welfare and liberty rights are said to carry different prerequisites (Archard, 1993).

In a section entitled 'Children's rights: the debate' (1995: p. 10), Franklin highlights the denial to children of rights which adults take for granted, and challenges the rationalisation for this. One strand in the paternalist argument concerns rationality, and the other the wisdom which follows experience. Franklin takes issue with both: for him, children have a competence for rational choice and do make informed choices; they 'display remarkably sophisticated skills in decision-making and evaluating outcomes' (p. 11). (However, no supporting evidence or reference is offered.) Children need experience of decision-making in order to become experienced, while adults also make ill-judged decisions. Franklin seeks to minimise any differences between children and (often inadequate) adults, and opposes 'double standards' for adults and children (p. 11). Also, who should decide competence? (This question may in fact be taken as an argument for standardised age limits rather than individualised judgements of competence – see below.)

Strangely, Franklin does not see children's exclusion as a temporary state, because children cannot grow prematurely to the age of majority, and because children *as a group* are permanently excluded. Three further arguments are considered by him and dismissed: that children are less self-sufficient than adults; that children's rights undermine adult rights and are essentially a demand for protection; and that paternalism is justified by the concept of 'future-oriented consent' – which returns us to the 'caretaker thesis' examined by Archard (1993). The protectionist and caretaker argument is that children, when adult, will acknowledge the validity of decisions which constrained them when they were younger. Franklin is sceptical. In particular, 'the consent of the child at some future date may simply be a product of the very process of intervention' (Franklin, 1995: p. 13). 'Brainwashing' may occur; in other words the adult intervention becomes self-justifying. Franklin then goes on to examine Hart's (1992) eight-level 'ladder' of children's participation.

In general, Franklin stands firmly in the liberationist camp as a defender of the equal, or near equal, status of children relative to adults. He is essentially arguing for the similarity of children to adults, and therefore their empowerment and self-determination rather than their protection; he is arguing against paternalism and the notion of adults as caretakers or trustees. In the next section some problems with this type of approach will be addressed.

Difficulties and dangers in a liberationist approach

Attention will now be given to some difficulties in the liberationist strand of argument of which Franklin's work is an example. The first objection is that the legal status of minority, and the age restrictions which are associated with it, while not entirely logical or an accurate reflection of children's actual capacities in every case, are in fact advantageous for children in some ways. That is, the status of minority may be seen as a benefit for children rather than an oppression, and it may be argued that the differentiated position of children in society is not so much an example of oppression or unjustified discrimination, as a means of protecting them and facilitating their development. The child liberationists have misread the nature of the differential treatment of children, misperceiving difference as oppression. Sometimes the treatment of children is *better* than the treatment of adults, for example under the criminal law in some respects and in the labour market. Sometimes services are provided for children which are not provided for adults, such as universal free education and various protective services. On the other hand, adult status carries burdens and liabilities. Differential treatment of children is thus not analogous to discrimination against women or black people, it may be said.

One specific feature of minority status is the existence of age limits below which certain activities are prohibited. These are criticised by liberationist writers because they are arbitrary, create a different legal situation at a specific moment in time, and do not relate to the differential maturity of children of similar chronological ages – the argument that we cannot generalise about individuals of any particular physical age. Age limits are also inconsistent between themselves (young people acquire different rights at different ages) and have shifted over time (for example the age of majority itself was reduced from 21 to 18 in 1969) (Franklin, 1995).

However, the alternative, apart from *no* age limits, would seem to be individualised decisions relating to how mature the young person seems to be and therefore what they are allowed to do – decisions which may be biased and subjective, or indeed not neutral to considerations of class, ethnicity or gender. Also, who is to make such decisions? It is interesting that Hafen & Hafen (1995: p. 20) comment that: 'The experience of American courts ... reveals that in practice customised findings of maturity are not very workable'. Generalised age limits arguably protect children from damaging experiences including exploitation in the labour market, and sexual abuse by adults partly because disputes do not have to be entered into regarding 'consent' to sexual activity, as is the case with adult rape and sexual harassment cases. They protect from situations where children are not equipped to make judgements about consequences (as may be the case with consensual sex and drugs), and from activities which they may be technically competent to carry out but which require psychological maturity for safe handling (such as driving).

In the field of education, compulsion below a certain age arguably protects the child's need to learn at a stage of life when learning ability is at its most receptive, but when children may not be well able to judge the importance of education for themselves. Generally, then, the argument goes, age limits are protective against activities which may damage children (and indeed others).

Another related strand of criticism is that generally the liberationist argument tends to overlook the evidence of child development, and the reality of growth and change with chronological age. Although Franklin, for example, at times acknowledges different stages through which childhood moves, much of his argument speaks globally of children and is couched in terms which do not distinguish younger from older children, while, as already noted, he seeks to diminish what might be thought the self-evident differences between children and adults in terms of rationality and competence.

The essential area of disagreement between protectionists and liberationists seems to be to do with how far development, and progress through a number of developmental stages are biologically based, and how far socially constructed and shaped. It might be argued that this dichotomisation is sterile, and that what is crucial is understanding the balance between the two sets of factors – the interaction between what is inherent and what occurs in the social environment in which the child is placed. Overemphasis on the biological leads to the conclusion that children will always develop in the same way, whatever the circumstances of their upbringing, while the opposite pole of the argument is that children are so totally moulded by experience that if they are treated as adults they will behave as adults. What requires acknowledgement in this debate is that while the ability to learn is inherent, what is actually learnt is widely, although not infinitely, variable; yet while childhood and individual children *are* variable, there are some constraints arising from biological developmental stage. Child liberationists arguably overstate the importance of experience and underemphasise that of developmental stage. This is a flawed understanding of childhood.

A third difficulty with the liberationist argument concerns the interrelationship between rights and duties, which it tends to overlook.

There is a problem with an approach which tends to see children (or indeed any group) mostly or only as bearers of rights. While it may be helpful to stress children's rights in a society which traditionally paid attention mainly to their duties, it may be questioned if the neglect of duties can itself be carried too far.

Much might be said on why these concepts are linked in principle and practice, but in brief the argument is that if rights are to be made a reality, this may require action – or inaction – from others. Sometimes rights merely require being allowed to do something without let or hindrance. Sometimes others may have to actively provide or do something such as find resources, contribute labour, take part in some civic activity, or give up something themselves. If rights-bearing is to be widespread in a society, then the duty to respect rights, and to help make others' rights a reality, must also be widespread. True, it is arguable that the bearing of rights by a group does not necessarily incur corresponding duties by that same group (so, for example, the right to receive education does not imply the same person's duty to be involved in providing it). Nevertheless if children are to have adult rights, it might be claimed that they should also have some adult duties and liabilities, with some penalties incurred if they breach these duties and liabilities, including action under the civil and criminal law.

Liberationist writers may be ambivalent on this point (see, for example, Holt, 1975). In fact, there is a strong argument that children should never be burdened with the full range of adult duties and liabilities under the law. As Flekkoy (1991: p. 224) says: 'it would be maltreatment to burden them with fully equal responsibilities'. But if not, are they then entitled to full adult rights?

A fourth point is that dangers arise in practice from an inappropriate 'adultisation' of children, which can be connected conceptually with the related notion of the 'disappearance of childhood' (Postman, 1983 cited in Hendrick, 1997). There are dangers in the removal of age-related restrictions and measures. As suggested earlier, these may in fact be a necessary protection to children. There are also dangers in the removal of specific social controls over children applied by teachers, parents and other adults. Difficulties arise in solving the control or discipline problem represented by children through, as might be suggested by liberationists as an alternative, applying the penalties which adults normally face. It might be regarded as harsh and utterly inappropriate, for example, to subject a small child who has physically attacked another to the same processes awaiting an adult who commits an assault. It *is* appropriate that there should be a minimum age for any criminal responsibility (currently ten in Britain – relatively low in international terms). As noted above, when children above this age *are* processed by the criminal law, their treatment is currently often more lenient than that facing adults (for example, their privacy is protected in a special court, their home circumstances are more fully taken into account, they are not below a certain age placed in adult prisons). Moving to adult-type responses would often be harder on children. There is a need for child-specific mechanisms.

Nevertheless, in recent years governments have sought harsher treatment under the criminal justice system of young offenders; for example, through tough secure 'training centres' for persistently offending 12–14-year-olds; proposals for curfews; and proposals for stricter supervision, by the probation service, for 10–14-year-olds; and for making youth courts more public (for example, the Crime and Disorder Bill 1997). In 1997 'adultisation' in the negative sense was exemplified by the Conservative Government's proposed ending of the ancient *doli incapax* rule (later confirmed by the Labour Government), which had ensured that in the case of 10–14-year-olds charged with offences, their knowledge of right and wrong was not assumed by the court but had to be positively demonstrated. The ending of this rule is a move towards treating children more like adults which is also more likely to lead to their criminal conviction.

Reducing the age of criminal responsibility to *below* ten, the current level, was apparently considered by the Conservative Government at one stage (Cervi, 1997). 'Treating children like adults' is not always consistent with their 'liberation' in any sense. Indeed a hostile backlash against children and young people, overlooking their special needs and vulnerabilities, may be detected in political and public opinion, existing in time, interestingly, alongside a movement against physical punishment of children. The hostility is seen, for example, in the public and media response to the young killers in the James Bulger case, 1992 (see, for example, Franklin, 1995; Franklin & Petley, 1996; King, 1997). Such harsh 'adultisation' is not what liberationist writers intend, but it is an agenda which could be inferred from some of their arguments.

Fifth, there may be concern that an emphasis on rights in the liberationist sense legitimates adult neglect of children. Hafen & Hafen (1995: p. 19) comment: 'the idea that children should have more freedom has been growing in recent years, perhaps reflecting a lessening of adult responsibility for children'. They suggest that when adults disengage themselves from child-rearing in the name of children's autonomy, their purpose, even if not fully conscious, may be to increase their own autonomy by freeing themselves from the burden of care. So, in practice, children's autonomy may equal less adult responsibility, more adult indifference (although liberationist writers may cherish the hope that adults will continue conscientiously with their *responsibilities* while forfeiting their *powers*). One related concern which I have aired elsewhere (Fox Harding, 1996) is that ideas of children's autonomy may be, as it were, hijacked by governments who wish to reduce various services and benefits for children under the cloak of arguing for stronger 'parental responsibility'. If such responsibility is not monitored and enforced, then it may not provide adequate protection for children and young people, who may be left in a vacuum where *no one* has responsibility, and they are inappropriately left to take responsibility for themselves. The ulitmate expression of this is 'street children' – the responsibility of neither parents, nor the State, nor anyone else. The concept of children's autonomy may potentially be misused to defend such a situation. Indeed, street children do have a kind of autonomy.

It is admitted that the liberationist case does have some positive aspects. In some ways it is a useful corrective to more traditional approaches to childhood and children's needs and welfare. There is an uneven power balance between children and adults, to which the liberationist argument usefully draws attention. Traditional and authoritarian views of children and their place emphasised children's duties and obedience in relation to adults rather than their rights (for example, Hendrick, 1997). Even those more 'progressive' views which emphasise adult responsibilities towards children do not necessarily endow the latter with rights. So it may well be salutary to emphasise children's rights to correct a historical imbalance – although with the risk that the 'duties' of children now become as invisible as their 'rights' once were. The liberationist approach also forces a re-examination of any particular – present or past – concept of childhood, and a recognition that concepts are relative, that childhood is at least to some degree socially and culturally defined. In addition, it usefully draws our attention to weaknesses in claims of future-oriented consent in arguments about deciding for children – to the dangers of the type of indoctrinating, authoritarian or oppressive socialisation process which edits out any present or future criticism of itself, so that adults may be unable to see that they *were* indeed damaged by certain childhood experiences, or that they suffered, not only as children but *as adults*, because certain decisions were made over their heads or certain types of upbringing were applied. Archard (1993) deals effectively with this point, defining a 'self-justifying paternalism' which:

> 'brings about its own subsequent vindicatory consent . . . It is obvious that a child's upbringing could produce an adult who approved of how it had been brought up, and that this need not involve anything like the objectionable means of brainwashing. Nevertheless why should we approve of an upbringing just because it can produce retrospective approval of itself?'

> (Archard, 1993: p. 54)

Thus the notion of future-oriented consent, a major plank of paternalism, can mislead or be misused.

Finally, Archard, who himself adopts something of a moderate or compromise position (1993: p. 65), acknowledges two particularly sound arguments of the liberationist case. One is to do with the ideology of childhood commonly held in western societies: 'an ideological presumption of "childishness" on the part of children is a characteristic feature of the modern conception of childhood' (1993: p. 68); the second is that the presumption that children are incompetent is something of a self-fulfilling prophecy – because of it, children are denied opportunities to learn competence.

It is argued then, that while the child liberationist standpoint has some merits, it also carries some difficulties in principle and dangers in practice. This chapter will conclude by considering a recent development which shows the influence of the liberationist case, albeit in an attenuated form.

The UN Convention on the Rights of the Child

The UN Convention (an international legal instrument passed in 1989, ratified by the UK in 1991) comprises both protectionist and liberationist components in the sense in which these terms have been used here. What may be seen as more conventional or traditional articles include those relating to general welfare (Article 3), standard of living (Article 27), social security (Article 26), health care (Article 24), education (Article 28), child labour (Article 32), and rights requiring protective measures (such as Articles 19 and 43/5 on the responsibility to protect children from abuse and neglect, and sexual abuse). Of greater interest here, however, are those elements which have a liberationist cast – notably Article 12, but also articles concerned with, for example, freedom of expression, assembly and privacy.

Article 12, probably the most well-known and innovative, provides that children be given the right to express their views in matters affecting them (although this is subject to their age and maturity), and that in administrative and judicial proceedings affecting them, they shall be provided with the opportunity to be heard. This may be directly, or through a representative, or through an appropriate body. The precise wording of the article is that governments:

> 'shall assure to the child who is capable of forming his or her own views the right to express those views freely in all matters affecting the child, the views of the child being given due weight in accordance with the age and maturity of the child.'

> (CRDU, 1994: p. 316)

Children have a right to a say and are to be taken seriously when important decisions about them are being made (although their view would not necessarily be decisive). The separateness of the child is recognised. Liberationists must surely give their blessing to this article, although they may feel that it does not go far enough, or that there may

be problems of interpretation. The article concedes children's competence in some areas, but without according them an across-the-board
right to have their wishes respected. (It may be noted that a similar
principle is embodied in the Children Act 1989, section 1(3).)

Other articles tend in a similar direction, stresssing the civil liberties
of the child. Article 13 acknowledges the child's right to freedom of
expression including the freeedom to receive information; this could
have major implications for parent–child relationships. Article 14
provides for the child's freedom of religion, and Article 15 for freedom
of association and peaceful assembly. There are debates as to how
realistic and important the latter right might be for children, whereas
with regard to religion, there are of course difficulties in establishing
what a young child's religion might be, as distinct from that of his or
her parents. Article 16 refers largely to the child's right to privacy, and
states that no child shall be subjected to arbitrary or unlawful attacks
on his honour and reputation. Article 17 concerns access to information aimed at the promotion of the child's well-being and health. These
articles may be seen as extending to children's basic civil rights which
adults have long fought for and, to a degree, had established.

This discussion of the Convention has necessarily been brief, but the
influence of liberationist thinking should be apparent. It should be
noted, however, that these articles are not uncontentious, for example,
in the Swiss parliament huge concerns were raised about the potential
violation of the family and parents' rights of autonomy and control
over their children, with the State and the UN seen as threatening
presences in this regard (unpublished communication). Certainly the
liberationist articles embody a notion of the child as a distinct set of
interests. This could entail conflict with the parents' interests, or at least
wishes. In principle, for example, children could receive information
which parents think they should not have, adopt a different religion
from their parents, attend gatherings which parents feel are unsuitable
for them, and have a right to keep secrets from parents.

There are doubts as to how far nation states do in fact implement the
Convention with respect to these articles (or indeed the Convention as a
whole). The Convention does not become part of the law of nation
states who sign it and cannot be enforced in their courts, although it
may be seen as an influential ideal triggering debates and recon-
sideration of national laws (van Bueren, 1996). In Britain, it may be
argued, the Children Act 1989 and the Family Law Act 1996 go some
way to meeting Article 12 as far as court and local authority decisions
are concerned. The Scottish Children Act also requires the child's
wishes to be taken into account in decisions made within the family.
However, how are general rights to freedom of expression, association,
privacy and access to information being made a reality for children?
How great is the gap between international expression of intent and
national practice?

Conclusion

This chapter has examined the distinction between the protectionist and liberationist understandings of children's rights, focusing on the work of Franklin (1995) and some problematic, as well as some positive aspects of the liberationist approach. Current debates seem to revolve around the claims and competence of children and their similarity to adults, the meaning of a rights-based discourse in relation to children, and whether differential treatment is equivalent to unjust discrimination. The coming to prominence of rights-based discourses in relation to children should be noted, with the attenuation of some child–adult distinctions (a trend which is not necessarily in children's interests). Alongside all this, older protectionist discourses continue, and in addition there is a degree of hostile or negative 'adultisation' of children. International pressure for children's rights exists, and the Convention on the Rights of the Child provides an interesting balance between liberationist and protectionist thinking, which may be criticised equally for going too far and for not going far enough in a child liberationist direction.

References

Archard, D. (1993) *Children: Rights and Childhood*. Routledge, London.
Aries, P. (1962) *Centuries of Childhood*. Penguin, Harmondsworth.
Children's Rights Development Unit (1994) *UK Agenda for Children*. CRDU, London.
Cervi, B. (1997) Two peas in a pod. *Community Care* 27 February–5 March 1997, 8.
Farson, D. (1974) *Birthrights*. Penguin, New York.
Flekkoy, M. (1991) *A Voice for Children: Speaking Out as their Ombudsman*. Jessica Kingsley and UNICEF, London.
Fox Harding, L. (1996) Recent developments in 'children's rights': liberation for whom? *Child and Family Social Work* 1 (3), 141–50.
Fox Harding, L. (1997) *Perspectives in Child Care Policy*. Longman, Harlow.
Franklin, B. (1986) *The Rights of Children*. Blackwell Science, Oxford.
Franklin, B. (1995) *The Handbook of Children's Rights: Comparative Policy and Practice*. Routledge, London.
Franklin, B. & Petley (1996) Killing the age of innocence: newspaper reporting of the death of James Bulger. In *Thatcher's Children? Politics, Childhood and Society in the 1980s and 1990s* (eds J. Pilcher & S. Wagg). Falmer, London.
Foster, H.H. & Freed, D.J. (1972) A bill of rights for children. *Family Law Quarterly* VI (4), 343.
Hafen, B. & Hafen, J. (1995) Abandoning children to their rights. *First Things* August/September, 18–24.
Hart, R. (1992) Children's participation: from tokenism to citizenship. In *Innocent Essays No. IV*. UNICEF, London.

Hendrick, H. (1997) *Children, Childhood and English Society 1880–1990.* Cambridge University Press, Cambridge.

Holt, J. (1975) *Escape from Childhood: The Needs and Rights of Children.* Penguin, Harmondsworth.

King, M. (1997) *A Better World for Children: Explorations in Morality and Authority.* Routledge, London.

Newell, P. (1989) *Children are People Too: the Case Against Corporal Punishment.* Bedford Square Press, London.

Newell, P. (1991) *The UN Convention and Children's Rights in the UK.* National Children's Bureau, London.

Newell, P. (1993) *One Scandal Too Many ... The Case for Comprehensive Protection for Children in All Settings.* Calouste Gulbenkian Foundation, London.

Pollock, L. (1983) *Forgotten Children: Parent–child Relations from 1500–1900.* Cambridge University Press, Cambridge.

Rosenbaum, M. & Newell, P. (1991) *Taking Children Seriously: A Proposal for a Children's Rights Commissioner.* Calouste Gulbenkian Foundation, London.

van Bueren, G. (1996) The 'Quiet' Revolution. In *Children in Charge: The Child's Right to Protection* (ed. M. John). Jessica Kingsley, London.

Part II

Policy and Practice in the Delivery of Care

Chapter 5

Social Work with Children and Families

Olive Stevenson

Introduction

This chapter traces and reflects upon the development of social work in child welfare, from the creation of Children's Departments in 1948 to the present day. It is an attempt to locate our present preoccupations and dilemmas within their historical context. I am keenly aware that the account suggests a loss of confidence and of impetus in the 50 years we are considering. In so doing, it does less than justice to many individuals who have contributed significantly and who, in important ways, have challenged the trends. In particular, a group of social workers in the field of fostering and adoption have pursued developments in knowledge and skills, sometimes with little support. Chapter 7 of this book by June Thoburn expands on this subject. The period under review was by any standards, exciting, challenging and problematic, as other chapters in this book illustrate well. Of central importance in the policy and practice of child welfare was the emerging profession of social work, and its troubled history is inextricably entangled with children's issues, especially those relating to child protection.

The impetus for change

The early post-war days saw the beginnings of specialised training based in universities for child care officers (as they were then known), encouraged and funded by the Home Office. These courses were a direct consequence of the powerful drive to improve services for deprived children A number of factors had converged and in so doing reinforced each other to produce a considerable degree of social, political and professional enthusiasm for radical change in the care offered to children who could not live at home or whose home circumstances were unsatisfactory. Although the implications of the Children Act 1948 have been described as purely administrative – the

creation of Children's Departments – the context in which it was passed
and the principles which it enshrined give it an importance not always
recognised by those who readily appreciate the significance of the
Children Act 1989.

The context was, of course, of post-war years in which the experiences of evacuated children and those who looked after them were
still fresh. In the official history of the war, Richard Titmuss wrote
brilliantly of the effects of the social dislocation on children and
families (Titmuss 1976). Many people who would otherwise have
remained unaware of children's suffering saw it for themselves in the
behaviour of children separated from their parents and learnt for the
first time at first hand the poverty and hardship of the conditions in
which some urban children lived. The need which some of those children had for expert help was recognised by some of those such as
Clare Winnicott (formerly Britten) who later taught social work students at the London School of Economics. At the same time, the
work of John Bowlby and his associates, (Bowlby, 1951) coming
from a different direction, brought the links between deprivation and
disturbed behaviour increasingly to the fore. Although his earlier
research was disputed (Rutter, 1972), the contribution which Bowlby
made to theories of bonding and attachment and its influence on a
rising generation of social workers cannot be overestimated. The
films of James and Joyce Robertson (Robertson, 1952), which
showed the behaviour of young children separated from their parents, made a huge impact on professionals working with young children. (It should not be forgotten that today's hospital policies which
enable parents to stay with their children were much influenced by
those films.)

The context, then, was a growing awareness of the damage which
can be done to children's confidence, psychological and intellectual,
and physical well-being, by the disruption of family ties and by insensitive care away from home. This powerful sense of unease was symbolised by the now famous letter written by Lady Allen of Hurtwood to
The Times (Allen, 1944), confirmed by the Curtis Committee's 1947
report on the disorganised state of residential and foster care, and
fuelled by the tragic story of Dennis O'Neill who was maltreated and
who died in a foster home. (Home Office, 1945). Everyone who
undertook training in child care at that time, knew of these events and
of current concerns.

Behind such immediate anxieties, however, there lay also powerful
optimism, as Packman (1981) has shown. Post-war society, although
weary, was also committed to a 'welfare state', in which fraternity
(though, less, sorority) and egalitarianism were valued and epitomised
in a wave of legislation of which the Children Act 1948 was but a small
part. These values were a central theme of the Act. As Heywood (1959,
1978) pointed out:

'Finally, in a clause, perhaps unmatched for its humanity in all our legislation, the Act defines the general duty of the local authority towards the child in care... Where a child is in care of the local authority, it shall be the duty of that authority to exercise their powers and duties so as to follow his best interests and to afford him opportunity for the proper development of his character and abilities... The vision of the purpose of the legislation is based on the social, psychological, material and spiritual needs of the child as a citizen.'

(Heywood, 1978 : p.158)

The phrase 'the child as a citizen' is a powerful reminder that this Act required the local authority, *in loco parentis*, to act as a good parent would. This ideal was in striking contrast to an earlier era, embodied in the nineteenth-century novels of Dickens but alive and well in the pre-war years of the twentieth century (Hitchman, 1956) which accepted without questions lower standards for children in public (or indeed voluntary) care.

To the social worker of today, these optimistic intentions to provide a good life for children in care evoke painful and sorrowful feelings. The impression of residential care in this period is one of betrayal of trust; the evidence is inescapable, although as Bullock in Chapter 8 shows, it is only a partial picture. The difficulties of finding and keeping foster homes for severely disturbed and disruptive children are everywhere to be seen. Furthermore, as Stein in Chapter 9 describes, local authorities have been inadequate as 'good parents' in their support to young people leaving care. The point here is to stress the initial mood of optimism and the principled intentions of the first entrants to the new career of Child Care Officer, It was, however, to be 'more difficult than we thought' (Stevenson, 1998).

The number of qualified 'Child Care Officers' entering the new Children's Departments was initially very small and the quality of service and care offered in many local authorities dubious or simply bad. As Packman (1981) recounts, certain authorities, as their reputations grew, drew qualified staff like magnets but, in the early years, the demand for trained staff far exceeded the supply.

The Curtis Committee (1946) expected that the chief officers (children's officers) would be women. They should be:

'highly qualified academically, not under 30, with experience of work with children and with "marked administrative capacity". Her essential qualifications, however, would be on the personal side. She should be genial and friendly and able to set both children and adults at their ease. She should have a strong interest in the welfare of children and enough faith and enthusiasm to be ready to try methods new and old of compensating by care and

affection those who have had a bad start in life. She should avoid
institutional correctness.'

(Curtis Committee, 1946: p. 148)

This 'job specification' proved attractive to a group of women, some in
senior civil service posts, who were successful, with some men, in
offering dynamic leadership at a time when women's occupational
positions were much less established. Whilst it is easy to smile at the
emphasis on personal qualities and the underlying assumption that this
was somehow 'women's work' akin to child-rearing, it is still heart-
warming to see the value base made explicit, the stress on creativity and
innovation and, not least, an appreciation of the administrative complexity of the work. These children's officers also had the backing of
exceptionally committed senior civil servants, including specialists,
mostly women, in the Home Office and there was close communication
between them and those who were developing training.

This was also a time when the emergent profession of social work
was beginning to stake a claim. With hindsight, one can see that trends
and developments in that sphere had both positive and negative effects
on the nature and quality of social work in the child welfare field. At the
beginning of the period under review, various branches of social work
had separate occupational identities, mirrored in professional associations and separate training.

Between 1950 and 1970, it was apparent that there would be major
advantages in bringing these groups together into one generic profession, based on common training and linked by one professional
association. The influence of the USA at that time was powerful and
'the giants' of social work education (Charlotte Towle, Florence Hollis,
Harriet Bartlet, for example) played a significant part in the way social
work education in the UK developed. This was particularly evident at
the London School of Economics which was one of the first to offer a
'generic' course to replace, amongst others, the child care course.

The intellectual arguments for 'a common base of social work' were
powerful. By a curious quirk of history, however, the implications of
this debate for the British scene came out differently from those in the
USA. Whereas in the USA, the debate centred upon the methodology of
social work, the similarities and differences, for example, between case
work and community work, the issue of fields or settings in Britain (for
example, probation or medical social work) seemed much more significant to social workers. The 'generic' arguments were focused on the
common and distinctive characteristics of work in settings and with
particular types of client, rather than upon method.

It appeared to me then, as it does today, that social work could and
should share a common base in terms of values, knowledge and skills.
Furthermore, there were obvious political and social advantages in a
unified profession. Many of us worked enthusiastically to that end,

despite the doubts and warnings of those whose commitment to the development of child care practice was single-minded. But, as we shall see throughout this chapter, a number of factors conspired to weaken the energy and purposefulness of the child care enterprise. In those early days, there were four interlinking problems.

First, it soon became apparent that the number of qualified child care officers were quite insufficient and the handful of pioneer courses could not meet the need. Coincidentally, however, and quite understandably, the needs of other branches of social work for improved levels of training became clear, not least because there was a perceived danger of 'elitism' within the local authorities in which child care officers might be the only qualified workers in main stream departments. (At this time, medical and psychiatric social workers were largely employed outside local authorities.) In particular, there was concern about the quality of service offered to elderly people and other vulnerable adults. What more sensible, then, than to develop generic training that could embrace all fields of work?

Second, however, in simple terms of size and logistics, this was a major exercise which involved very rapid expansion in the field of higher education. Between 1950 and 1970, social work courses mushroomed.

Third, this was a time when British social sciences, again following the USA, also grew significantly. Many of those recruited to Social Services Departments were involved in the teaching of social work students. They brought new dimensions, especially in sociology, to social work education which were valuable but controversial and which added to the growing volume of curriculum demands. Throughout this period, the knowledge explosion in the social sciences was revealed as a rich mine for social workers but also a constant source of anxiety concerning balance, eclecticism and conflict to those who planned the curriculum.

Fourth, this period saw the beginning of the still continuing debate about the appropriate length of training for social workers. One, two, three or four years (or even 18 months) undergraduate, post-graduate, non-graduate? All these were debated and contested, linked to ulti-mately unproductive attempts to define levels of training, according to tasks performed. In short, it was a muddle.

The effect of these four interacting factors, not surprisingly, was to disperse the concentration on child welfare which had been envisaged and initiated by the early educators, in which, incidentally, field work placements had played a crucial part. There were also the beginnings of a loss of confidence in the value and feasibility of the enterprise itself. Social work came under fire from the left: the nest-feathering of the professions; social workers' allegedly dubious claims to professional status; the Marxist critique of social work as part of the state apparatus of control, epitomised by the title of Handler's work *The Coercive*

Children's Officer (1968); all this and much more reinforced the insecurities and uncertainties of social workers and their teachers.

Too little teaching about too much, the highly variable quality of
some teaching, and a small proportion of students who fell below the
ability required to assimilate complex ideas for practice, contributed to
a professional climate which became increasingly anti-intellectual and
which at times attempted to fill the theoretical void with rhetoric.

This led to very particular difficulties in the field of child welfare. It
became the received wisdom of the time that psychoanalytic theory had
dominated the approach and activity in the early days of child welfare
as a specialism. The present author (Stevenson, 1963), somewhat naive
and certainly foolhardy, took on Barbara Wootten who, in a famous
polemic (Wootton, 1959), accused social workers of paying too much
attention to the unconscious minds of clients and not enough to their
material needs. I sought to show how useful such psychoanalytic theory
could be in understanding children's behaviour, which was a fair and
justifiable position to take.

However, in doing so, I appeared to collude with a view that social
workers were 'sort of' psychoanalysts. The reality was quite different
as every practising child care officer knew. The work was about long
cold car journeys (no heaters allowed in county cars), about trying to
bring warmth and stability to children's lives, about magnificent fat
foster mothers and about getting second-hand cookers. It was essentially busy rather than reflective work. It was, however, set in a context of attempting to understand often bizarre and disturbed
behaviour with the only body of theory which had been made available to us at that time. In the light of my recent work on neglectful
parents (Stevenson, 1998), Wootten now seems as naive as I was.
The difficulties of such families could not then, and cannot now, be
explained solely in terms of poverty. It is not an exaggeration to see
in the 1960s the beginning of a decline in the search for *meaning*
which dogs us today, when 'comprehensive assessments' may be
devoid of theoretical substance.

Social workers were introduced to other theories as well as psycho-
analysis. Behavioural psychology had an enthusiastic, though small,
following and there were flurries of interest in specialist applications,
such as family therapy, which derived only in part from psychodynamic
theory. The question, however, which has to be addressed is why the
general body of social workers remained so obstinately 'atheoretical' in
their approach to the work. A combination of factors outlined above
stifled the development of crucial elements in professional judgements
at precisely the time when the need for greater confidence and precision
in the management of child abuse was becoming apparent. The 1960s
saw the beginning of a decline; not only were there 'too many' ways of
understanding on offer to the intending social worker, they were often
inadequately applied to the day-to-day work and sometimes taught

from a position of hostility, masquerading as rational criticism, to the very business of social work.

Reorganisation: gains and losses

This, then, was the position as we entered the 1970s, which was to prove a momentous decade for British child welfare services. The first, highly significant event was, of course, the creation in 1970 of Social Services Departments, into which Children's Departments and other departments offering personal social services to adults were merged. As with the development of generic training, this was widely welcomed by welfare professionals and academics at that time, although there were the same reservations and anxieties voiced about the loss of specialisation. It seemed to many, including myself, a logical progression towards a better service to families: the famous phrase 'one door to knock upon' in the Seebohm Report (Seebohm Report, 1968) came to symbolise a sincere attempt to offer a service which would not compartmentalise families by bureaucratic divisions. 'Horror' stories of families subjected to numerous visits by officials with different roles were commonplace and used in support of the new arrangements. Today's readers may find it instructive to reflect on those debates in the late 1960s and on the intractable difficulties there have been in realising the generic ideal.

The motives for change to unified departments were, of course, mixed. The creation of much larger organisations gave power, status and resources to the personal social services in local government. There were genuine advantages in this for clients who needed service as well as the more dubious opportunities for organisational aggrandisement. Central Government also established that Directors of Social Services should be qualified social workers, a principle gradually eroded over the succeeding years. That specification in the early years was important because it marked the end of a regime of powerful Medical Officers of Health within the local authorities, some of whom may have expected to assume the leading role in the new departments. It was an important symbol (or so we thought) that, in the progress towards professionalisation, social work 'had arrived' even if the competence of some of those appointed proved disappointing. However, 1970 also saw the beginning of a marked gender shift in the ranks of senior management which has only been redressed in the past few years. With the end of specialist child welfare, the Curtis Committee's 'ideal women' were no longer much in evidence and, indeed, it seemed that the management and political skills required for large organisations were very different from those associated with the former children's officers. Some, of course, managed the transition successfully. But the work had changed. A number of experienced and well-qualified women social workers found the upper echelons of management an unattractive prospect and walked away. It is likely that this exodus played a part in creating a managerial climate less sympathetic to concensual and reflective practice which we shall later see has had detrimental effects in child welfare practice.

It seems clear now that the professional and organisational forces leading towards unification were overwhelming, especially when the creation of a single British Association of Social Workers from a number of separate associations is recalled. Furthermore, it seemed to fit the spirit of the age, just as the present day 'post-modernism' era favours fragmentation. So far as child welfare was concerned, the advantages of a holistic service to adults and children were beyond argument. As we look at the barriers which have grown up within Social Service Departments, we see that the problems and needs of mentally ill, drug-dependent and learning-disabled adults are often not connected properly with plans to protect their abused children. Why have Social Service Departments not fulfilled their early promise – to offer social work a sensible and safe structure within which to foster professional skills and deliver holistic services?

As is usually the case, it was in the combination of factors rather than single factors that serious difficulties arose. I have earlier suggested that social workers in child welfare were increasingly uncertain professionally by 1970. The professional and organisational implications of the 1970 Act were huge. It is one thing to proclaim a holistic ideal, quite another to evolve the sophisticated structures and professional identifications to give reality to the ideal. There was little recognition of the needs and anxieties of staff who became (in theory) 'generic' overnight. Many were not qualified. Many had experience in only one branch of social work and some had little inclination to change. Retraining and opportunities for professional development were minimal. Arguments raged as to whether we should be thinking about generic departments, generic teams or generic social workers. The uncertainties and difficulties of the mid-1970s were well captured by the research team (which I, with Parsloe, directed) which conducted a very large study of social service teams across the country. The findings were widely recognised as a fair (though worrying) picture of the longer-term effects of reorganisation, once the dust had settled (Parsloe & Stevenson, 1978).

In general, our research suggested that there was not widespread rejection of the idea of genericism; rather, our respondents were beset by doubts and anxieties about the best ways of organising work, and of enhancing their competencies, and of managing the varying pace and extent of client demand. We concluded:

'The portrait of social services departments ... is generally one of commitment and hard work, of concern and sympathy for clients and of valiant efforts by many individuals to cope with the pressures and strains....We fear however that the best endeavours of many individuals are to an extent undermined by several factors. First, there is an overriding lack of clarity about objectives and roles, about the proper functions of the personal social services and of social work in particular. Secondly, there is, quite bluntly (with some honourable exceptions) a lack of imagination and creativity which would lead to attempts to refine objectives and roles through experiment and to provide organisational structures to facilitate innovation... Thirdly, and not surprisingly, restraints and cut-backs have come at a most unfortunate time for the development of a type of agency new to the United Kingdom – a comprehensive statutory department for the provision of personal social services ... we have a very long road to travel before we can claim to be providing a service in which the deep compassion of many individual workers is contained within, and fostered by, sensitive and efficient organisational structures.'

(Parsloe & Stevenson, 1978: p. 328)

In the light of the above, it is perhaps understandable that the structures within which services were to be delivered occupied so much of the professional and academic debate in the 1980s. Internal reorganisations as well as major local government reform in 1974 dominated the discourse. There were, of course, practical, difficult questions about the best ways of cutting the cake but behind those lay ideological, perhaps even philosophical, issues which reflected the conflict within social work and between those academics who became involved. To today's social workers, the intensity of the debate about 'patch' social work and the enthusiasm with which some espoused it must seem strange and remote. It was based on a 'communitarian' and 'participatory' view of local culture, in which social workers would be fully involved in the life of small populations (between 5000 and 10 000) and would mobilise the energy of local people. The idea had many attractions and was vigorously advocated by some (Hadley & McGrath, 1980, Currie & Parrott, unpublished monograph). What it singularly failed to achieve was the integration of that model with essential specialisations and with the protective functions of child welfare.

Preoccupation with structure was illustrated by my own work at that time. In 1980, in *Specialisation in Social Service Teams* (Stevenson, 1981) I attempted to confront and resolve some of the dilemmas inherent in the generic ideal. I argued that there were three fundamental questions to be addressed. First, there was the need for professional expertise, where it was to be located and how fostered. This became more and more apparent as the research and knowledge of the social and behavioural sciences expanded. Second, there were complex issues concerning the formal and informal organisation of work. The vague notion of 'teams', at times reified to the point when it became almost holy, needed conceptual clarification in relation to the objectives of the work. Third, important matters of 'boundaries and connections' with other agencies who served the same clientele in different ways, were increasingly important. The creation of Social Service Departments did not resolve problems of communication and cooperation as had sometimes (unrealistically) been suggested. Inside and outside the local authority were agencies or other professionals critical to the well-being of children and families and others needing service (see Chapter 7). Experiments began with interdisciplinary teams, for example in the field of adult mental health.

The dominance of child abuse: a bureaucratic response

It was in relation to child abuse that the yearnings for cosy social work alongside local communities were finally stifled. The wave of anxiety about child abuse which swept the country and the professions from the mid-1970s ensured that two themes would be uppermost in the succeeding years. First, the importance of interprofessional coopera-tion, of establishing 'connections' in this sphere, became a priority. Second, the increasing emphasis on the legal responsibility to protect children made informal, voluntary relationships with the community seem increasingly unrealistic, even irrelevant. We have paid for this; social workers are not seen as community friends.

The impact on social work of the Maria Colwell Inquiry (DHSS, 1974), and of the spate of inquiries which followed it, have been much described and discussed and will not be reiterated here. In the context of this chapter, two points should be emphasised. First, it has been my aim to demonstrate the cumulative impact on the development of the profession of a number of distinct but interrelated phenomena, cul-minating in the post-Colwell 'moral panic'. Second, these factors – theoretical insecurity, structures in which professional work was not always appropriately managed or organised, resources which were perceived to be diminishing in the face of increased demand, and widespread public and political criticism of alleged failures – created an anxious climate in which the organisational response was almost pre-dictable. Systems of accountability and control are enforced when anxiety is high.

Now, as we are urged to 'refocus' on children in need and when the importance of professional judgements is on everyone's lips, it seems important to evaluate what may come to be called 'the era of pro-cedures' in the 20 years after the Colwell inquiry.

As the Birchall & Hallett (1995) and Hallett (1995) research makes clear, much has been achieved through the development of written procedures and few, if any, workers would want to do without them. They reflect the complexity of the processes involved in keeping children safe and the diversity of the situations in which protection is required. Although they are often referred to as 'step-by-step' guides, they also contain important base line definitions and, as they are revised, the fast-changing nature of the problems to be confronted can be identified. Thus, definitions of abuse and their indicators are important ways of influencing practitioners. 'Neglect', for example, is usually described as including failure to seek appropriate medical help or to keep necessary appointments. (Although educational and intellectual neglect is less often identified as significant.) Again, for example, most if not all include references to organised abuse and many now address the problems of children who abuse children.

These documents, revised seriously and systematically, provide at a moment in time, a view of what child protection means as well as a manual for action. Furthermore, they suggest an orderly way of proceeding in situations which are of their nature disturbing, complex, and sometimes urgent. It is noticeable that this emphasis on order and control is often used effectively at important stages of the process, such as case conferences. There is no doubt that the skills of chairing case conferences are highly developed in some areas and there now exists a core of highly experienced, purposeful and clear-headed social workers who bear no relation to the woolly warm stereotype of bygone days. Indeed, this is but one example of the greater precision in the exercise of legal and professional responsibility, generally, which has become apparent. Something important has been gained through the pain and misery of the child abuse 'scandals' and this, linked to the interagency achievements discussed in Chapter 6, should be acknowledged and valued in assessing children's social work in the past 20 years.

However, although there have been significant gains in terms of clarity and precision in risk assessment in cases (such as physical injury) which lend themselves to quasi-forensic investigation, the culture has had severe limitations for effective child protection and professional development.

Child abuse has increasingly been understood as an expression of complex interpersonal dynamics and to manifest itself in many different distortions of family (and other) relationships. Thus, an approach which is centred upon the investigation of 'incidents' or 'events' is seen as inadequate for purposes of assessment and consequently for planning and intervention. Nowhere is this seen more clearly than in the fields of neglect and emotional abuse. The numbers of children registered in these categories have risen sharply in recent years. Whilst this might reflect a real increase, it is more plausible to suggest that agencies and professionals are becoming increasingly aware of, and concerned about, such cases, perhaps as anxiety about other types of case is better contained through current practice. The characteristics of cases of chronic neglect, as every child protection worker knows all too well, are mess, disorder, inadequate parenting and 'long-running sagas', often over years.

Even in those cases of emotional abuse which are not also neglectful, the problems are typically long-standing, reflecting intractable relationship problems and may involve particularly difficult evaluations of the cultural dimensions of child-rearing. In both types of case, overall assessment of the impact on child development and of 'significant harm' is essential, which may take place over a considerable period of time. The issues have been explored in my recent work on neglect (Stevenson 1998) and further considered in small-scale action research (Glennie et al., 1998). It is quite clear that the needs of these families run counter to the brisk, short-term models of child protection practice which the policy and culture of the 1980s and 1990s has encouraged. That fact has radical implications, which cannot be here explored fully, for the way child welfare work is organised. It affords a latter-day illustration of the difficulty which we have had over the years in devising structures and systems which are sensitive to, and appropriate for, the range of problems and needs with which social work must deal. It also moves us on in our discussion of the problems and needs of the profession itself.

Discussions of procedures and of structures of managerial accountability are embedded within the concept of bureaucracy. The creation of Social Service Departments marked a critical moment for social work, not only because it brought field social workers together but also because these departments had a much larger workforce of social care workers, including 'home helps' and residential workers. Thus, size and occupational diversity, as well as the traditional model of local government, presented the managers of the new departments with a major challenge. On the one hand, social work was seen as pivotal to the departments; on the other, they were only a tiny (and sometimes troublesome) proportion of the staff. It is possible to analyse the years between 1970 and the present day in terms of deep conflict between bureaucratic and professional ideals and models. In 1970, fresh from a period as social work advisor to the (then) Supplementary Benefits Commission, I perceived an inherent tension between social work and income maintenance services as arising in part from the need for a balance between models of justice (Stevenson, 1970). Using the concepts of 'proportional and creative justice' (Tillick, 1960) – that is, on the one hand, fairness in terms of equity, on the other, fairness in terms of meeting special and unique needs – I argued that both were essential and were bound to exist in tension with each other, within families, justice systems and other social institutions.

Reflecting on these principles today in the context of Social Service Departments, it seems that the tension has not been held constructively. Rather, models of proportional justice have become dominant with all their associated paraphernalia such as proliferation of forms and 'paperwork'. As anxiety has mounted (especially in the child protection sphere), as rationing of resources (with consequent 'prioritisation') has become sharper, as the influence of managerialism from the world of industry penetrated local government, so the opportunities for creative justice, for flexible, creative responses within local government to unique individuals in difficulty, have diminished. Voluntary organisations, including large child care agencies with honourable traditions, have filled some of that gap and some have sought to develop partnerships with Social Service Departments, seeing the wider importance of such innovations. But these are a mere drop in the ocean.

Between 1990 and 1993, an Economic and Social Research Council (ESRC) funded study of the attitudes and decisions of field social workers (and those of their seniors) in cases of neglect and sexual abuse was undertaken in three local authorities. A large number of social workers were interviewed (Stevenson, 1996; Allsopp & Stevenson, 1995). Two methods were employed: group interviews using a vignette of an appropriate case; and individual interviews in which social workers brought their own cases to discuss. It was instructive to see how closely social workers *in groups* kept to task, in discussing the vignette in terms of the law and of their agency policy. In contrast, they talked at length, freely and often with much emotion about their difficult cases when seen individually. In the action research conducted recently in the Nottingham area (Glennie *et al.*, 1998), participants were encouraged to be reflective about their (exceedingly) difficult cases of neglect. One of the major findings was of the enjoyment and professional benefit they derived from this opportunity.

In short, social workers in local government have been professionally starved. Some of this has been a kind of occupational anorexia, derived from anxiety about elitism or any claim to special expertise. There is no denying the anti-intellectual bias which has existed even amongst very able students and practitioners. However, as pressure mounted and overload increased, the power of bureaucracy was seen by many to oppress rather than to support and to inhibit rather than to liberate. A better balance between the necessary two elements in the delivery of personal social services would be a hugely significant step forward, of benefit to users and workers alike. Indicators of such an improvement could lie, for example, in arrangements for supervision/consultation which encouraged creative thought about ways forward for difficult families, about the use of existing resources (such as pre-school provision) in flexible ways, and about the better development of informal community resources for family support.

The forces which drove social workers down this cul-de-sac were not counterbalanced by coherent and academic activity which might have provided them with alternative frames of references, based on the now substantial body of research and knowledge available concerning child development and family dynamics. An unacceptable situation has arisen, in which social workers are uncertain about the distinctive contribution which they have to make to the assessment and understanding of complex child protection cases, especially when courts are involved. The hunt for 'experts' is expensive and very time-consuming (and hence damaging to children) and sometimes of limited value. Social workers speak of coordinating and integrating views of others and this is of course necessary and valuable. However, there must be more to the social worker's contribution than that.

What, then, constitutes the social worker's contribution? There would seem to be four elements. First, it should not be necessary to turn to 'experts' to give evidence to the courts, if the research and knowledge relevant to understanding are well-founded, relatively uncontentious and easy to access. Why is it that guardians *ad litem* with the same qualifications as social workers can be accorded respect when giving such evidence? The problem is partly one of image but it also raises questions concerning the professional support (for example, ready access to research literature) available to local authority workers, the development of post-qualifying studies, and other related matters. Whilst there are welcome initiatives to facilitate individual study, the local authority remains an inhospitable environment for professional development.

Second, at basic qualifying level, knowledge and theory of human growth and development, essential for all social workers, needs radical curriculum review. Without it, child welfare practice lacks a sound base. A topical (and hopeful) example is the renewed interest in child observation as a part of learning about child development. This element in training, which was widely used in the early days, dropped out of the curriculum when we were bombarded by 'genericism', but is now being reconsidered and is well-illustrated by a recent Central Council for Education Training & Social Work (CCETSW) publication (Bridge & Miles, 1997) on child observation.

Third, the theory needed for professional renewal in social work has many facets. Social workers' expertise in no small measure lies in the capacity to see and weigh up interacting factors in the lives of those they seek to help. This is why analyses of the problems and dilemmas of families within a framework of social ecology are often greeted with relief and even enthusiasm by social workers. For example, in my recent work on neglect (Stevenson, 1998), the model was used to trace the influence of different factors on neglectful parents because it enabled me to appraise the significance of different spheres and dimensions of their lives on their difficulties. Everything becomes relevant: poverty, housing estates, extended families, individual characteristics and history, and so on. In this sense, rather than simply gathering up what others say, the social work assessment may be genuinely integrative and holistic. It will probably also involve the exploration of some dimensions rarely considered by 'experts' whose domains are often individualistic, or at best interfamilial.

Such a wide view may in fact lead to more creative interventions. The family group conference initiative is an example of this (Marsh & Crow, 1997). There are dangers (common in social work) of transient idealised enthusiasm and this could be one example. However, it also illustrates the capacity, and indeed hunger, for practice innovations based on a different perspective of the child's world. Thus, social workers, in adopting this way of looking at the situation, can contribute distinctively whilst acknowledging the need which the family or child may have for a narrower but more detailed expertise, for example in substance abuse and its effects in child-rearing.

The fourth important element in the social worker's professional domain is the development of professional skills, derived from the interplay between values and knowledge on the one hand and experience on the other. It is disappointing that the early promise of such work was not consolidated and further expanded in the child protection field, although there are heartening examples in the field of fostering and adoption, illustrated by Thoburn in Chapter 7. Whatever the reasons – pressure, insecurities, academic pretentiousness – it has proved difficult over the years to find and publish, in journals of standing, acceptable articles which describe and theorise practice. Yet such reflections are indicative of professional energy and are of considerable importance to the future of social work in child welfare.

However, behind work for change, whether within existing structures or through new patterns of service which may emerge, there remain fundamental questions in social work concerning education and training, basic and post-qualifying, and the academic input which it needs to develop lively and coherent arguments about the theoretical basis for the work.

This is not to deny or diminish the importance of academic research and reflection by social work educators which has found its voice again in recent years and is well-illustrated by Payne on social work theory (1998) who has found it necessary to make extensive changes to his first edition in 1991. Payne surveys a wide range of theories available to social workers, including those which directly bear on practice. The problem, however, remains the same as in the 1960s and 1970s: how to enable social workers to select, apply and integrate theory so that they address their work in child welfare more purposefully.

The oppression of social workers

It is my contention that the tensions and limitations of the organisational culture earlier described have left social workers peculiarly vulnerable to unhealthy and damaging pressure from two directions. The first of these concerns what can be described as bureaucratic dogmatism. To chart the progress of ideas and theories from their source, as they flow into the streams of politics and government shows public opinion and professional behaviour as complex and at times disheartening. Those who cast their theories upon the water can rarely foresee how they will appear downstream. This is particularly striking in matters concerning child welfare when feelings run high. The 'career' of John Bowlby's ideas is probably the best example (a sociological case study is called for) but, as Thoburn describes so graphically in Chapter 7, policies surrounding 'permanency placement' are equally disturbing.

Vitally important issues for child welfare, to avoid 'drift' in care, to have regard for the significance of bonding and attachment in young children, have led in some situations to rigidities which run against the spirit of good practice. For example, one cannot plan for a child's future around arbitrary time limits after which a permanent home must be found. As a guide, time limits are valuable; as a rule, they are foolish and conflict with the realities of parental involvement with their children. However, the problem is that 'a guide', if it is to be followed, needs a climate of professional support which has been shown to be lacking in Social Service Departments. Rules are therefore perceived to be necessary and the application of bureaucratic modes of enforcement follow.

Discussion of the second direction from which oppression has come is fraught with possibilities for misunderstanding. It concerns the effect on the profession of pressure by particular groups who, rightly, believed that vital aspects of their well-being had been ignored, or accorded low priority, by society including social workers. Issues concerning race are of particular significance in the child welfare field. There is no dispute about, and ample evidence of, the insensitive and neglectful treatment of children from different ethnic backgrounds and mixed heritage in the period here under review. Furthermore, the realisation that certain ethnic groups, or children of mixed heritage, were over-represented in care, belatedly provoked a wider debate about the social and family circumstances which lay behind this.

Inevitably, such considerations led to a recognition of the racism which was endemic in British society and an acceptance that racism is manifested in many subtle and hidden ways as well as in gross forms. Social workers were no different from other people in this respect, although arguably they were less prone to defensive rationalisations and more ready to accept social responsibility than some. For those who worked in child welfare, these issues were not simply theoretical. They were of immense importance in shaping policy and practice, for example in the placement of children. Here we see the interaction of the two pressures. Guilty and anxious social workers and their managers became caught up in the bureaucratic dogmatism to which earlier reference was made. The results were rigidities about transracial placements which could result, for example, in bad practice in which the needs of a particular child at a particular moment were ignored. As Thoburn (Chapter 7) shows, there is now evidence to support overall the importance of racial origins in planning, caring for and placing children. However, the central dilemma for child welfare workers, in this area as in so many others, is that the circumstances and needs of children are infinitely varied and unique, so that generalised policies are never a substitute for individualistic judgements and decisions.

It is not surprising, but none the less regrettable, that some of the trends identified within Social Service Departments were mirrored, from 1970, in the career of CCETSW, which is soon to be merged in the new General Council of Social Care. The rise and fall of that powerful and potentially valuable organisation, from which social work educators became progressively alienated, is a story in itself. For our purpose here, the correspondence between the bureaucratically dominated culture in CCETSW and that in local government is striking. In particular, the implementation of 'anti-oppressive' educational policies was in itself oppressive. Even more serious, CCETSW did not encourage serious attempts to tackle complex, controversial, and highly sensitive matters within a framework of informed academic debate, appropriate to the institutions of higher education within which courses were sited. There was a whiff of McCarthyism in the air. Reactions to the climate which was created on courses rather than to the vitally important substantive issues being considered were sometimes unconstructive. There were, however, significant contributions to the debate from some social work academics (Ahmed *et al.*, 1986; Dalrymple & Burke, 1995).

During these years, and in contrast to the sterile outcome of earlier Marxist influences on social work practice, feminist theorists began to make a significant contribution to social work practice. In addition to the overarching concept of patriarchy and the effect which this had on the view of the family, most particularly the place of mothers within it (Farmer & Owen, 1995), there was a subtler challenge to the management of ethos and style of Social Service Departments. This was neatly and humorously summed up by a group of students, who, in performing a role-play of women workers having an interview with 'management', insisted on sitting on the floor whilst men in suits sat uncomfortably at the desk.

It is difficult as yet to appraise the overall impact of the feminist movement on social work practice. It seems clear that it has profoundly changed the way social workers, both women and men, see the position of women in society and there have been valuable applications of this theory to child care (O'Hagan & Dillenburger, 1995). It remains to be seen whether that has laid firm enough foundations for the further development of skills for day-to-day practice with child welfare service users, although it has much potential. Its impact on organisational behaviour is unclear. The presence, again, of many more women in senior management may or may not affect the ethos and management style of Social Service Departments.

The bureaucratisation of CCETSW is epitomised (hopefully temporarily) in the proliferation of 'competencies' in the formal assessment of students, which splintered achievement into dozens of tasks. As the tasks mounted in complexity and subtlety, the process became more and more onerous and less and less convincing for the ultimate judgement of professional ability. This is not to suggest that greater precision in assessment of students was unnecessary; rather, it is to illustrate the extraordinarily pervasive nature of what has become an unbalanced search for certainty and safety through procedures, in practice and in training.

Fighting back

Some of the issues which I have discussed specifically in relation to child welfare have wider ramifications. In the years following the introduction of new community care legislation, and in the context of an emphasis on administrative case management activity, questions were raised as to whether social work as a profession with a distinctive role and function had a future; the detachment of probation from its social work associations was also damaging both to social work and to the probation service, and many, including myself, would argue strongly for a return to the contribution of social work to this field.

It is interesting, however, that the attack on the value of social work in child welfare was more muted. Indeed, despite harsh public and political criticism of child welfare social workers during the years of the Thatcher administration, it seemed as if no one could think of an alternative to this much maligned group. Perhaps this arose in part from a growing awareness of the extraordinary difficulty of the work and from more readiness to acknowledge the importance of children's well-being, and the complexities of safeguarding this, compared with that of other groups, such as old people. The understandings of politicians and the civil servants who worked for them was born not only of scandals and tragedies but also from sustained programmes of research, lacking in other fields, funded by the (then) Department of Health and Social Security and later the Department of Health.

Over 20 years, important studies have thrown light on the workings of the child welfare system. These programmes culminated in the publication in 1995 of the series *Studies in Child Protection* (HMSO, 1995), eight volumes which documented many aspects of the current situation. Furthermore, the Government became aware over the years of the importance of dissemination of research to managers and practitioners; the first major raft of research was summarised and widely used (DoH, 1991). The key themes of the most recent programme were promulgated in *Messages from Research* (DoH, 1995) and systematic dissemination work is continuing, supported by the Department of Health across many local authorities.

Clearly therefore, the importance of research utilisation has been seized, albeit in a rather centralised and perhaps somewhat authoritarian way. There is little sense that Central Government is committed to the professional development of its child welfare workforce beyond the assimilation of messages from the research which it has funded. Yet there is a vast amount of other work waiting to be tapped: for example, work on neglected children in the USA by academics such as Crittenden (see for example Crittenden, 1992) is eagerly used by British practitioners when it happens to come their way.

Furthermore, although the field has been enriched by some of the excellent studies in the most recent programme, they are, by and large, of the 'outsider looking in' variety, using conventional quantitative methods with modest qualitative supplements. There is, in fact, a dearth of the type of investigation which the preceding analysis has shown to be urgently needed. A great deal is known about the organisational context of practice and about what, in particular, social workers (and others) do in response to child protection problems. Much less is known about the thoughts and feelings involved in making judgements, dilemmas in decision-making and the effects on them of the organisational context. Most important of all, research in direct practice interventions is essential if professional expertise and skills are to be developed. There can be a benign, circular process in such activity by which theory underpins practice but is changed, modified or extended by practice. Moreover, such questioning activity, even when a particular intervention fails, lifts the level of practice in the process of what may be described as a spirit of 'cooperative inquiry'. The development of such research activity challenges a version of 'handed-down truth' which has accorded too well with the bureaucratic and hierarchical styles of management, earlier discussed.

It is easier to analyse trends with the passage of years. What will be the story of the next few years, let alone another 50? Whatever opportunities have been lost and wrong turnings taken, there are grounds for some optimism. Amazingly, throughout the buffeting of the past 25 years, child welfare has continued to attract highly educated, able and energetic people into its ranks. There are substantial numbers of such people who are now high experienced and competent. They need to be professionally liberated. Furthermore, although there is cynicism and even despair about the exhortation to refocus the work, to get a better balance between need and protection, there is also an underlying acceptance of the value of that approach. Some of these doubts arise from deep concern and anger about present shortages of resources, but they also illustrate the danger of seeking to *impose* policy changes in areas as complex as these and the need to work with the grain of the social workers. The refocusing initiative offers an opportunity to develop reflective practice and in so doing to uplift the spirits and the practice of social workers.

This challenge and local government reorganisation come at a bad time when stress and low morale are so evident. It requires dynamic leadership at different levels as well as some alleviation of destructive resource constraints. We can, however, build on some very sound foundations. There is extensive knowledge available both of children's developmental needs and of the work which must be done to nurture and protect them when their parents cannot fulfil the tasks alone. There is an excellent framework for interagency and interprofessional work. Most important, there is deep commitment in many social workers, and their colleagues, to the improvement of the lives of children and families.

References

Ahmed, S., Cheetham, J. & Small, J. (1986) *Social Work with Black Children and their Families*. Batsford, London.

Allen (Lady Allen of Hurtwood) (1944), *The Times*, 15 July.

Allsopp, M. & Stevenson, O. (1995) *Social workers' perception of risk in child protection: a discussion paper*. University of Nottingham.

Birchall, E. & Hallett, C. (1995) *Working Together in Child Protection*. HMSO, London.

Bowlby, J. (1951) *Child Care and the Growth of Love*. Penguin, London.

Bridge, G. & Miles, M. (1997) *On the Outside Looking in: Collected Essays on Young Child Observation in Social Work Training*. CCETSW, London.

Crittenden, B. (1992) Children's strategies for coping with diverse home environments: an interpretation using attachment theory. *Child Abuse and Neglect* 16, 329–43.

Curtis Committee (1946) *Report of the Care of Children Committees*. Cmnd 6922, HMSO, London.

Dalrymple, J. & Burke, B. (1995) *Anti-oppressive Practice. Social Care and the Law*. Open University Press, Bucks.

Department of Health (1991) *Patterns and Outcomes in Child Placement*. HMSO, London.

Department of Health (1995) *Child Protection: messages from research*. HMSO, London.

Department of Health and Social Security (1974) *Maria Colwell Inquiry: 1974, Report of the Committee of Inquiry into the care and supervision provided in relation to Maria Colwell*. HMSO, London.

Farmer, E. & Owen, M. (1995) *Child Protection Practice: private risks and public remedies*. HMSO, London.

Glennie, S., Cruden, B. & Thorn, J. (1988) *Neglected Children: maintaining hope, optimism and direction*. Notts County and City Area Child Protection Committees.

Hadley, R. & McGrath, M. (1980) Patch based social services. *Community Care*, 11 October, 16–18.

Hallett, C. (1995) *Interagency Coordination in Child Protection*. HMSO, London.

Handler, J. (1968) The coercive children's officer. *New Society*, October.

Heywood, J. (1959) *Children in Care*. Routledge Kegan Paul, London.

Heywood, J. (1978), *Children in Care*. Routledge Kegan Paul, London.

Hitchman, J. (1956) *King of the Barbareens*. Putnam, London.

Home Office (1945) *Report by Sir Walter Monckton on the circumstances which led to the boarding-out of Dennis and Terence O'Neill and the steps taken to supervise their welfare*. Cmnd 6636, HMSO, London.

Marsh, P. & Crow, G. (1997) *Family Group Conferences in Child Welfare*. Blackwell Science, Oxford.

O'Hagan, K. & Dillenburger, K. (1995) *The Abuse of Women within Child Care Work*.

Packman, J. (1981) *The Child's Generation*. Blackwell Science, Oxford.

Parsloe, P. & Stevenson, O. (1978) *Social Service Teams – the practitioners' view*. HMSO, London.

Payne, M. (1998) *Modern Social Work Theory*, 2nd edn. MacMillan, London.

Robertson, J. & Robertson, J. (1952) *A Two Year Old Goes to Hospital*. Concord Film Council, Ipswich.

Rutter, M. (1972) *Maternal Deprivation Reassessed*. Penguin, London.

Seebohm Report (1968) *The report of the Committee on local authority and allied personal social services*. Cmnd 3703, HMSO, London.

Stevenson, O. (1963) The understanding case worker. *New Society*, 1 August, 84–96.

Stevenson, O. (1970) *Claimant or Client? A Social Worker's View of the Supplementary Benefits Commission*. Routledge Kegan Paul, London.

Stevenson, O. (1981) *Specialisation in Social Service Teams*. Allen & Unwin, London.

Stevenson, O. (1996) *Social workers' perceptions of risk in child abuse*. ESRC Project Report. HMSO, London.

Stevenson, O. (1998) It was more difficult than we thought. Forthcoming in *Child and Family Social Work*.

Stevenson, O. (1998) *Neglected Children: Issues and Dilemmas*. Blackwell Science, Oxford.

Tillick, P. (1960) *Love, Power and Justice*. Galaxy Books, Oxford University Press, Oxford.

Titmuss, R. (1976) *The History of the Second World War*. HMSO, London.

Wootten, B. (1959) *Social Science and Social Pathology*. Routledge Kegan Paul, London.

Chapter 6

Children in Need and Abused: interprofessional and interagency responses

Olive Stevenson

Introduction

This chapter explores the development of policy and practice in inter-professional and interagency work with children and families in particular difficulties, especially in relation to abuse. As Birchall & Hallett (1995) and Hallett (1995a) explore in depth, there is considerable definitional awkwardness and ambiguity in the terms which are routinely used – in the precise meaning, for example, of 'coordination', 'collaboration' and 'cooperation'. The differing levels of organisational activity and the interaction between agency functions and professional roles within agencies add further complexities to the exploration of these issues and cannot be fully discussed here. In this chapter, the intention is to provide an analysis which traces the 'career' of this idea, i.e. that 'working together' is a desirable and important activity in child welfare. In so doing, it will become apparent, first, that we have moved towards a more sophisticated appreciation of what is needed to achieve that goal; second, that in so doing we have exposed some intractable problems and dilemmas; but third, that there have been substantial achievements over the years.

Working together: the development of an idea

In the years following the Children Act 1948, there was a growing realisation that the well-being of individual children was in some cases critically affected by the nature and quality of the communication and cooperation between agencies and the professionals who worked within them. This is now a well-rehearsed and well-worn assertion, bordering on the platitudinous. Yet looking back at this 50-year period, one can see emerging the recognition that the diverse systems and structures created to safeguard the health and well-being of children might fail to do so if they were not effectively co-ordinated.

In a sense, the Children Act 1948 was itself indicative of this understanding. The care of deprived children had before then been scattered between various different authorities and agencies with no clear lines of accountability. The location of new Children's Departments within each local authority and their accountability to the Home Office for regulation and guidance provided a focus for the coordination of policy and practice which, as the Curtis Committee (1946) showed so vividly, was much needed. Indeed, as Corby (1995) points out, even before this, the issue of interagency coordination in child care work was recognised. The report on the death of Dennis O'Neill (a foster child) (Home Office, 1945) found that two local authorities had not communicated effectively concerning this placement. The author of the report, Sir Walter Monckton, made the telling comment: 'What is required is that the administrative machinery should be improved and informed by a more anxious and responsible spirit' (Home Office, 1945: p. 18).

Furthermore, Children's Departments provided a springboard for work with children and families in the community, which became in the minds of child care social workers as important as the care of children in residential and foster homes. What began as a significant administrative change, designed to raise standards and to bring coherence to the organisation of children's care, led to a deeper appreciation of the difficulties created for families and for the authorities when community agencies were not working together effectively. (However, as Bilton points out in Chapter 2, certain key linkages, notably in the field of housing, were not adequately integrated into welfare services for children.)

Thus, it was not long after the passing of the Children Act 1948 that Central Government planted the first seeds of the idea that has come to assume very considerable significance in the British child welfare scene – that is, that agencies and professionals had a responsibility to share information about vulnerable families and children and (although this came later) to discuss together what needed to be done. It is interesting that the first official indication of this policy emphasis was in the context of work with 'problem families'. (This description was later dismissed as stigmatising; however, their characteristics bore an unsurprising resemblance to today's 'neglectful families'.) Clearly, then as now, many such families were in touch with a multiplicity of agencies and workers. In 1950, a Home Office circular (Home Office, 1950) recommended to Health, Education and Children's Departments that they set up 'coordinating committees' to review their work with such families. This was not yet dominated by concern about abuse but it moved the debate from general policies to particular families, from a broad recognition of the interdependence of policies to greater awareness of their impact on individual families and, crucially, of the ways in which the workers who mediate those policies affect the situation.

Yet it was to be another ten years or more before the growth of anxiety about child abuse (influenced by trends in the USA) initiated more systematic and frequent advice from Government and a more sophisticated discussion of the issues which arose from exhortations to 'collaborate' or 'cooperate'. It became apparent that rationality and goodwill alone were not sufficient. Considerations of agency function, of bureaucratic obstacles, of professional power, status, rivalry, insecurity and 'role blinkers', and much more besides, were to become necessary for the understanding of the processes involved.

It is perhaps, with hindsight, historically significant that I embarked on that search for understanding when sociological influences were making their impact on social work education. In 1963 *Coordination Reviewed* was published (Stevenson, 1963). The scene was set with a hypothetical example of such a committee on a July day in the town hall, in a small committee room decorated in beige and chocolate brown! Those present were: the children's officer (i.e. the chief as chair), the child care officer, the medical officer of health (who would then have been responsible for adult welfare services), the health visitor, the mental health officer (under the Ministry of Health), the probation officer, the officer of National Assistance Board Commission (the precursor of the Supplementary Benefits officer and of the contemporary Benefits Agency), and the housing manager.

The 'Long' family was described: the family was in difficulties with a seriously depressed mother, unemployed father and four children, two under five. The meeting had been called by the medical officer of health because of his and the health visitor's concern over the home conditions. There was no suggestion at that time that the children had been abused physically or should be removed. The focus of the article was an analysis of the underlying issues affecting the conference. These may be summarised as follows:

- Differing value systems between the participants. (For example, should Mr Long get a job? Is the family exploiting the benefits system? Should the family jump the housing queue?)
- Emotional identification with different members of the family by participants, according to worker's role (e.g. with depressed mother, needy children).
- Differences between participants in perception of nature and meaning of problems and therefore most effective forms of intervention (e.g. 'advice' or 'treatment').
- The role of senior managers in facilitating or preventing cooperative activity.

Thus, we can see that the essential nature of the interprofessional enterprise in those early years was not dissimilar to the present day in terms of the family problems presented and of the factors underlying the attempts to cooperate. However, it lacked the anxious focus upon risk and danger and it provided a forum in which those less concerned with individual welfare and more with equitable provision of resources (money and housing) could participate. In our contemporary language, the Long children and family were perceived (at least in my analysis) as much more 'in need' than 'in need of protection'. However, the principle that such forums for communication were needed for purposeful communication about individual families was accepted.

As Hallett (1995b) has pointed out, mounting concern about child abuse led to 'a stream of circulars of guidance from the late 1960s onwards, increasing in length and culminating in *Working Together under the Children Act 1989* (Home Office *et al.*, 1991); and added: 'interagency coordination lies at the heart of the system established in Britain for the management of cases in child abuse' (p. 2). The significance of the Maria Colwell inquiry in 1973 and the subsequent report (DHSS, 1974a) was part of a phase of growing activity, much influenced by medical practitioners in the USA and in the UK. Parton (1985) has traced these developments. He refers to 1963, as the year when British surgeons, Griffiths & Moynahan (1963), first published on the 'battered baby syndrome' in the *British Medical Journal*. Parton argues that the discovery of this 'syndrome' in the UK came from forensic pathologists and paediatricians and links this also with the work of the NSPCC. Thus a dialogue began between the medical profession and social workers, albeit in a specialised setting. The Maria Colwell inquiry consolidated child abuse as a topic of major social, political and professional concern. However, as Parton shows, in 1973, two days before the Colwell inquiry was announced, the Tunbridge Wells Study Group on Child Abuse, comprised of paediatricians, psychiatrists, social workers, health workers and police, held a major conference. Parton suggests that this group, together with the NSPCC and USA 'experts' influenced the (then) Secretary of State for Health and Social Security to set up the inquiry. He concludes: 'whilst the timing of Maria Colwell and Tunbridge Wells was coincidental, the combination was explosive' (Parton, 1985: p. 77).

Thus an analysis of this period demonstrates, first, that the notion of interprofessional activity in child abuse was established well ahead of the Colwell inquiry. Second, there were complex forces propelling work in that direction in which central government administration played a significant, but not the only, part. The direct interplay of politicians with the professionals, with doctors in a lead role, further confirmed interagency and interprofessional activity at different levels and in different ways.

The impact of the Maria Colwell Inquiry

So what light does the report into the death of Maria Colwell shed on these cooperative activities in the early 1970s and after its publication in 1974? It was inevitable that the media focused public attention more upon the tragic story of Maria herself than the subtler information which it conveyed about the state of interagency relationships.

The report's publication marked the beginning of a series of media onslaughts upon social workers, usually at field level. Whatever the justification for those criticised in particular cases, there was an understandable dismay amongst social workers that, despite the exhortations 'to work together', when disaster struck, it was the social workers who bore the main burden of criticism. This was certainly the case in the reaction to the Maria Colwell report. (A striking exception to this was the Cleveland Inquiry (Butler-Sloss, 1988) to which I shall refer later.) Yet the report's conclusions were striking in the emphasis they placed upon:

> 'failures in the system ... compounded of several factors of which the greatest and most obvious must be that of the lack of, or ineffectiveness of, communication and liaison. The overall impression created by Maria's sad history is that while individuals made mistakes, it was the system, using that word in the widest sense, that failed her.'

(DHSS, 1974a)

As the member of the inquiry who wrote a controversial minority report, it has not always been clear that I also wrote the fourth chapter, agreed by the members, on 'communications'. The choice of the term 'communications' is in itself interesting, indicating, as it does now, a somewhat naive emphasis on the passing of information as all-important. The chapter illustrates a phase of child protection work in which cooperative activity was relatively undeveloped, whether in assessment or intervention. Rereading my observations on 'communications' nearly 25 years later, two points stand out in the context of work today.

First, in relation to the Colwell report, many of the observations on interagency matters merely serve now to confirm the extent and nature of the progress which has been made in the last 25 years. The report as a whole (and indeed, my recollections of the 41 days of hearing) strongly suggests the sense of shock, of being unprepared, of outrage at being challenged which, in differing degree, the professionals showed. There was an overall naivity in their responses.

Although the inquiry contained many 'messages' for policy and practice, one of its most significant contributions was to push Central Government further and faster down the road it had already taken, towards the development, elaboration and refinement of cooperative structures and procedures with their attendant training implications. As Hallett (1995a: p. 3) comments, in the context of an important DHSS circular (Department of Health and Social Security, 1974b), 'uppermost in the Department's mind was undoubtedly the case of Maria Colwell'. This circular strongly recommended the creation of Area Review Committees (ARCs) at local level. (These were precursors of today's Area Child Protection Committees.) In some areas, these were already in place; as has been noted earlier, the beginnings of this coordinating activity went back to 1950 and had been followed up by government advice.

The 1974 circular was, however, much more explicit and detailed in what was suggested. It listed 11 functions for the ARCs 'about the diagnosis, care, prevention and local organisation necessary for the management of cases involving non-accidental injury to children' (p. 1). Included in these functions, the committees were to:

- advise on the formulation of local practice and procedures to be followed in detailed management of cases
- approve written instructions describing the duties *of all personnel* [author's italics] concerned with any aspect of these cases
- review the work of case conferences in the area
- provide education and training programmes to heighten awareness.'

Hallett (1995a) points out that this circular 'constituted an administrative mandate to cooperate' (p. 4) and was followed by other guidance, with major extension and consolidation in 1988 when the first *Working Together* was published (DHSS, 1988). This, with its subsequent 1991 revision (Home Office, 1991), has formed the basis for cooperative activity until the present time. As this chapter is being written, the Government has issued a consultative paper to form the basis for further revisions in the near future (DoH, 1998).

Thus it can be seen that from the early days of the period under review, there has been a growing commitment to, and interest in, coordinating activity in those aspects of child welfare which involved abuse. After 1974, this drive was fuelled by successive child abuse scandals and their attendant publicity. In addition to the very genuine professional distress that these tragedies caused, there was also mounting anxiety about professional accountability, about being 'found wanting'. It became clear that failure to liaise effectively with other professionals could be the grounds for censure and disciplinary action.

Second, and more specifically, the interaction (or lack of it) between the education systems and the Social Services Department emerged as fundamentally unsatisfactory in the report. This section in the report is by far the longest and includes discussion between education welfare officers and schools; between social workers, teachers and education welfare officers; and between staff in school, including medical and nursery staff. It demonstrates that the systems for recording and transmitting information about Maria were totally inadequate. It may be recalled that the junior school teacher (who was also trained as a nurse) was a crucial person in Maria's life. She observed Maria's determination and ravenous hunger, yet failed to get her anxiety heard. At this time, procedures, including case conferences, for the management of child abuse concerns were still embryonic and the word 'amateurish' describes, though understates, the impression given of the many different school staff who were seen at the inquiry and whose inadequate communications were subsequently criticised. The question for today's readers is whether any such extensive incompetence could occur now. The age of innocence is over; teachers are well aware of child abuse concerns, not least in relation to sexual abuse.

The participation of educational administrators and teachers in various aspects of child protection work at various levels and in different ways is in principle well-established and the appointment of designated teachers in child protection is important. However, it is salutary to remind ourselves of the findings of Birchall & Hallett (1995):

> 'There is evidently a large unresolved question about the place of the front line profession of teaching. They appear to be well-placed to identify and refer children to the specialist agencies but clearly are not well-integrated into the network. Remarkably few of them have received any training on the topic ... Teachers vary widely in their attitude to pastoral aspects of their job.'
>
> (Birchall & Hallet, 1995: p. 238)

There are grounds for concern that the overall situation now, some years after the research was conducted, may be worse rather than better, because the structural changes in the educational system and the political emphasis in raising school standards do not always sit comfortably with well coordinated systems which are sensitive to the risks and needs of individual vulnerable children. Of particular concern (and a worry for some teachers) are neglected children with poor educational attendance and low levels of achievement (Stevenson, 1998) whose needs, though pervasive, do not provoke immediate action as do physical or sexual assault. This is, of course, bound up with the nature of the expectations of teachers and school staff in the child protection process. The Colwell report concentrated on the responsibility of schools to note and to make known concerns about the well-being of pupils. The Birchall & Hallett study, 20 years later, also emphasises this dimension of cooperation. However, this leaves unaddressed another crucial question about the part which schools can play in the lives of those pupils who are inadequately nurtured, supported or controlled in their own families. Even to write those words sounds unrealistic in a climate of extreme resource constraints, linked to the general preoccupations with 'league tables' and standards, and to rising numbers of school exclusions.

We are overdue for a national debate on the part to be played by educational services in interagency child protection. We are seeing a steady increase in the numbers of children registered for neglect and emotional abuse, to the point when they are overtaking numbers of children physically or sexually abused. As research indicates (Stevenson, 1998), educational deficits in such children have long-lasting adverse effects on child development. If schools are not structured and resourced in ways which attempt to meet the needs of these children, we heap up trouble for the future as Stein (see Chapter 9) shows so clearly in relation to care-leavers 'in need'. In particular, children identified as 'needy' in the early years may be identified as 'villains' a few years later – small local criminals on the edges of (or excluded from) school, heading for the 'social exclusion' about which there is currently much political discussion.

However, there are wider issues in relation to the refocusing initiative and the present trend towards increasing educational responsibility for 'early years' services (see Bilton, Chapter 2). It has long been understood that the intellectual input to under-school-age children is crucial to subsequent educational attainment. Teachers have been rightly dissatisfied with a child protection system which involved 'heavy' investigations when, on occasion, these may not have been necessary. They have argued that this has acted as a deterrent to their involvement. However, the need for effective interagency cooperation for assessment and intervention for children in need, is often as great for less dramatic cases, especially for young children.

In short, the 25 years since the Colwell inquiry have seen a formalisation of educational involvement in child protection and strong commitment on the part of some individuals, administrators and teachers, to the improvement of cooperative work. But the weakening of local education authorities, the devolution of responsibility to individual schools, the competing demands on resources (for example, repairs to a leaking roof versus a teacher's presence at a training course), all create a set of formidable problems which it is urgent to address.

Underlying issues

As expectations of cooperative behaviour became established, the dimensions of the phenomenon of child abuse were widened to include, from the 1980s, sexual abuse. The powerful effects of this were to be illustrated in the second half of the 1980s by the Cleveland débâcle. In 1980, Christine Hallett and I had published on interagency cooperation without referring to sexual abuse (Hallett & Stevenson, 1980) By 1990, that would have been unthinkable. As the Cleveland report (Butler-Sloss, 1988) showed, those events challenged – some would say blew apart – the consensus which had begun to emerge about the basis for co-operative work. The spectacular rifts between police, paediatricians, police surgeons and social workers were only matched by the splits *within* some of those professions. For the first time, professionals other than social workers were under public and media scrutiny. Shared accountability became reality, not simply comfortable rhetoric. The effects have been long-lasting, notably amongst individual paediatricians whose responses vary between powerful, dedicated commitment to child protection work and extreme reluctance to become involved.

Leaving aside the debate at that time as to whether certain children had in fact been sexually abused and the medical disputes about physical symptoms, what this episode illustrated so powerfully was the uncertainty and ambivalence in society at large (including the professionals) about sexual abuse. What constituted sexual abuse, what was acceptable and unacceptable parental behaviour, what action to take if there were good grounds for suspicion but no actual proof – these issues were revealed as contested and raising passionate feelings in which the gender of the onlookers and the professionals played a significant part.

Yet the drama and intensity surrounding sexual abuse is only one powerful illustration of the deep and controversial issues which underlie much cooperative activity in child protection. Some of those concern the differences in value systems, in priorities for children's upbringing and in perceptions of acceptable adult behaviour to children; see, for example, Birchall & Hallett's (1995) work, and Hallett's (1995a) work which explores these matters using vignettes to elicit the ways in which professionals perceived standard child abuse situations. Both studies raise important questions concerning the similarities and differences between professionals in these perceptions.

Nonetheless, the overall findings of both studies that there was a high level of consensus between professionals is notable, especially in the light of the tensions following the Cleveland inquiry only a few years before. Birchall & Hallett (1995) conclude:

'The most striking impression is that the need to cooperate in child protection is widely recognised and valued. Most respondents with relevant experience assert that the coordinating system works fairly well and the majority report that others in the network are fairly easy to collaborate with.'

(Birchall & Hallett, 1995: p. 241)

The authors remind us, reassuringly, because otherwise their findings would be suspect, that this means that 'only a minority think everything and everyone works very smoothly together' (p. 241). Furthermore, they identify many deficits and limitations, some of which are discussed later in this chapter. Yet it remains important to stress the central findings of the studies.

Given the emotions and conflicts which bubble along just below the surface and the complexity of the work, how do we explain the comparative success of long-standing, government exhortations? There seem to be three major ingredients in the achievement.

Ingredients in the achievements

The first of these concerns the existence of *sufficient* consensus for cooperative action. Thus, for example, if there were not agreement that a child seriously and deliberately injured by a parent must be removed; if some were still operating on the basis that parents 'owned' a child and the State need not intervene, the basis for joint action would not exist. Value differences exist but in many respects there are shared systems of belief.

Within the second ingredient in the achievement there lie also weaknesses. Hallett (1995b: p. 325) reports that 'the study revealed that widespread routinised interagency coordination was central to child protection practice'. There were, of course, 'lapses', 'frictions' and 'difficulties' in the early stages of the process (up to the time of an initial child protection conference) but the process was essentially accepted as multidisciplinary, 'reflected in a routinised and relatively clear division of labour' (p. 325). Thus, we can see that an orderly system, sensibly bureaucratised, has been put in place. The process has become taken-for-granted, a relief for overburdened workers who can follow clear and probably well-rehearsed steps. There is nothing inherently wrong in such an approach: routine is economical of effort. The procedures which have been evolved in every part of the country serve this purpose. However, as I have discussed at length in the preceding chapter, it is increasingly recognised that an overemphasis on procedure may mask the need for critical professional judgements within the procedural process. It is possible (and I am tentative) that this emphasis serves to mask underlying differences and conflicts between professionals. How much this matters if there is urgent work to be done is unclear. It is epitomised in talk of 'thresholds' – that is, the points at which decisions must be taken to investigate, register, remove and so on.

In recent months, I have been involved in the creation of new Area Child Protection Committees, consequent on local government reorganisation. This has understandably been unwelcome to some of the agencies outside local government who resent the upheaval. One of their fears centres upon the possibility of differing 'thresholds' arising between the two Social Service Departments, in whose areas they would have to operate, despite agreement that there would be common procedures between the two. Nothing could illustrate better the dimension below 'routine' cooperation. The problem is that is coordination is 'mandated' and if sensible procedures are devised, professionals and agencies can jog along together reasonably comfortably until some dramatic events disturb the status quo. Then, because differences may have been disguised or deflected, and because the whole edifice of local cooperation, based upon consensus and not on authority, may have shaky foundations, there can be a mighty falling out. It is interesting to note that three such episodes, Cleveland (Butler-Sloss, 1988), Orkney (Secretary of State for Scotland, 1992), and 'the Broxtowe Case' of alleged ritualistic abuse in Nottingham, were all focused on sexual abuse on which there is less social consensus than (say) serious physical abuse.

A further weakness which the two research studies (Birchall & Hallett, 1995; Hallett, 1995a) discuss at some length is obliquely indicated in the earlier quotation on page 108. The success of the cooperative endeavour was much more apparent during the early process of assessment than in the execution and review of the protection plans. 'Working together' did not, by and large, extend to intervention. Birchall & Hallett (1995: p. 326) found that in almost 40% of the cases in their sample, 'there was no mention in the child protection plan of other agencies beside the social service departments.'

A third ingredient in the not inconsiderable achievements we are considering, lies in the development of interprofessional training by a small but committed core of mainly social workers, who have been interested in, and sensitive to, the complex issues which interprofessional work raises. Our book (Hallett & Stevenson, 1980) was one of the first to address underlying questions and was widely used by those initiating training for Area Review Committees (later Area Child Protection Committees (ACPCs)). In particular, the implications for those who chaired case conferences were readily grasped and resulted in many training courses for this group. Within the last two years, a new forum PIAT (Promoting Interagency Training) has received enthusiastic support nationally and the critical importance of training activity is well-recognised by most ACPCs (Glennie & Hendry, 1996). However, the scale and complexity of the training required may not always be recognised. First, there is the question of levels of training, from the most cursory 'awareness raising' to the most delicate interviewing of sexually abused children. Second, programmes of training *within* agencies and for particular groups of personnel have to be organised and coordinated. Third, interprofessional training has to be arranged to take account of different educational traditions between professionals, in a manner which promotes interaction and understanding between the different groups. Fourth, the numbers involved at basic levels of training are very large and the turnover high.

A recent study of Welsh Area Child Protection Committees (Sanders & Thomas, 1997) serves to confirm much of the foregoing discussion and adds a valuable dimension to the analysis by its focus on these particular committees' structures and their effects on cooperative activity. Sanders & Thomas make three broad concluding points. In acknowledging the 'many difficulties which lie in the way of achieving real collaboration' (p. 133), they point to the confusion between policy and procedures and suggest, to put it baldly, that busy people in senior roles with much else to do unrelated to child abuse, may take refuge in this comfort of routine rather than develop carefully articulated policies. This is a related but not identical point to my earlier concern that a focus on procedures may distract from the importance of judgements made by individual professionals.

Neither procedures nor policy formulations remove the need for judgements at the level of the individual. But well-argued policies which are owned by an interprofessional forum, such as ACPCs, certainly facilitate and channel judgements. A recent example in my experience is agreement between police, social workers and other agencies on the way child prostitution should be managed.

The second conclusion to which Sanders & Thomas come is a recognition of the amount that has been achieved. Their view that the 'determination which many unsung professionals have shown in the attempt to make the system work is truly impressive' (p. 133) is one which my own experience strongly reinforces. This is particularly striking when one considers the extent of the organisational and professional upheaval to which staff in so many agencies have been subjected for nearly two decades. Most of this change was apparently unrelated to child protection but in fact had major implications which had to be worked through. The creation of health care trusts and of the purchaser–provider splits are but two examples of many such instances of organisational turmoil. Most recently, local government reorganisation has placed heavy burdens upon ACPCs.

Finally, Sanders & Thomas join in the prevailing criticism of the 'limited view of child protection' which ACPCs embody, and cite the frustration expressed by some of their respondents:

'at being compelled to focus so much of their energy on one narrow aspect of service provision and at the compartmentalisation of child protection from other child welfare services.'

(Sanders & Thomas, 1997: p. 134)

This leads to discussion of present trends and emerging policies to which I shall turn at the end of the chapter. Before doing so, however, there remain some issues of general importance in the story of inter-agency relationships over the years.

Ongoing issues and dilemmas

Earlier in this chapter, reference was made to growing awareness during the period under review of the factors underlying agency func-tions and professional roles which had to be taken into account to achieve effective cooperation. In the United Kingdom, the dominance of the medical profession of welfare services was challenged by the rise of social work as a quasi-profession and, more specifically, by the creation, first, of Children's Departments in 1948 and then of Social Service Departments in 1970, neither of which were to be led by doc-tors. In child protection, this trend was confirmed by the fact that statutory accountability to the Courts was located in Social Services. In the 1988 guidance (DHSS, 1988) local authority Social Service Departments were confirmed as the lead agency. In the words of sub-sequent guidance (Home Office, 1991) they had:

> 'the primary responsibility ... in relation to child care and protection ... [but that] does not diminish the role of other agencies or the need for interagency cooperation in the planning and provision of services for a child or family.'

> (Home Office, 1991: p. 9, para. 3:5)

However, despite, or perhaps because of, the primacy accorded to Social Service Departments in this field of activity, the reality at local and field levels is much more confused and, on occasions, tense. At agency level, there is often ambivalence and resentment. Social Services may believe they are too often left to 'carry the can'; other agencies may believe that Social Services only pay lip-service to consensus and seek to impose their wishes on others. At an individual level, many tales are told of incompetence or bureaucratic rigidity amongst social workers or of comparable failings in their professionals including idiosyncratic authoritarian behaviour by a few. Given that some tensions of this kind are inescapable in human situations, it nonetheless illustrates the complexity and delicacy of work in which grave and life-threatening situations involve a network of people who are not professionally or organisationally accountable to each other. Perhaps we should marvel at how much goes well rather than focus upon what has gone badly.

Nonetheless, in addition to the major challenge discussed earlier, of constructing effective cooperative systems between schools and other agencies, there are other persisting problems; one concerns the role of general practitioners and the primary health care teams in child pro-tection and 'children in need'. From the earliest days in 1973 when the general practitioners presented legal arguments to the Maria Colwell inquiry why they should not be defined as 'an agency' within the terms of reference, to the present day, this is noted as an intractable difficulty. As with teachers, Birchall & Hallett (1995) found there to be a mis-match between the perception of the importance of general practi-tioners by other practitioners and disappointment about the fact that they were not adequately integrated into the protective network. The recent consultation document (DoH, 1998) seems to understate the problem, perhaps to avoid alienation.

It is, of course, the case that there are committed general practitioners who, in close liaison with practice-based health visitors, have striven to achieve good cooperation. However, this is essentially achieved by personal and individual effort and leaves others who are effectively still 'outside the mandate'. The impact of the future changes in primary health care structures and in health visitors' roles needs to be carefully monitored in terms of their impact on cooperative working. After so many years in which these difficulties have remained unresolved, there is a strong case for reviewing the current expectations and seeking alternative arrangements, for example, in relation to attendance at case conferences. Doctors, as teachers, can rightly claim that they are only involved in protective work occasionally: that does not alter the fact that, on occasions, their contributions are crucial to the life and well-being of the child. Furthermore, if refocusing is successful, more chil-dren in need will be identified as requiring particular health imputs. The cooperative structures in place must include these key personnel but their roles may need to be redefined.

A further area which required careful monitoring concerns the police. The years under review demonstrate, most strikingly, the pro-cess of inclusion of police in the cooperative structures. Hallett (1995b: p. 532) describes this as 'a profound transformation from the position existing in the 1970s.' The existence in nearly all police forces of specialised units to deal with either child abuse or abuse more generally has been a remarkable achievement and, at local level, there are often constructive and harmonious relationships with other agencies. It is in that context that some persisting difficulties should be understood.

First, it has to be acknowledged that some of the personnel in specialist units feel somewhat marginalised and isolated within the mainstream police where 'targets' and 'outputs' are so different from those of their specialist colleagues. Leaving aside the implications of that fact for the status of the work and the morale of individuals, it is also problematic if 'ordinary' police are insufficiently aware of the links between crime and abuse. As suggested earlier, this is of particular salience when the local juvenile offenders are from seriously neglectful homes. There is a danger of encapsulating this dimension of police work within a small section of the force.

Second, there is a need for careful examination of the present state of 'joint interviewing' between police and social workers, usually in cases of sexual abuse. There is an impression that sound, early cooperative efforts have had some unintended consequences, in creating a cadre of police who are more expert than social workers in the processes. Of itself, this would not necessarily matter, but the imbalance raises problems at the heart of police involvement.

This leads to the third and fundamental dilemma – the relationship between the civil and criminal justice systems in child abuse cases. Behind benign and sensible cooperation between individuals, there may be unresolved tensions about the role of the criminal justice system in child abuse. As is well-known in some other European countries, the legal framework lays much less stress on the investigation and prosecution of adult alleged perpetrators. Hallett (1995b: p. 532) points out that the central role of the police in British child protection services has been questioned by commentators in Europe, who see the judicial model as unhelpful (Lampo & Marneffe, 1993). For such observers, the move away in Britain from the medico-social model of earlier years is regrettable. Others believe strongly that judicial process in the criminal law is a formal signal that child abuse is socially condemned. Such a major theme cannot be elaborated here but its significance to interagency work may assume greater importance if the refocusing initiative is effective at local level. Fears are already being expressed by some police that they will not be consulted and involved so routinely where children are hovering on the edge between 'in need' and 'protection'. To some in the protective network, that may be welcome and, indeed, a foreseeable and desirable outcome of the policy change. The point at issue here is that it may create or exacerbate tension in the work.

One of the most demanding aspects of interprofessional relationships arises from the emphasis on 'partnership with parents' which developed in the latter part of the period under review. The term itself does not appear in the Children Act 1989 although, as Petrie and James (1995) point out:

> 'the words ... leapt into the vocabulary of those working with children and their families as though as it was a new activity that stood alone without reference to the framework in which it was placed.'
>
> (Petrie & James, 1995: p. 313)

The phrase does, however, recur in guidance following the legislation.

The implications of this ideal for interprofessional work have been little explored; to do so adequately would involve an empirical examination of the attitudes of various and diverse groups of professionals, shaped by their education and their conception of role, to relationships with parents. However, there is nothing inherently unacceptable to other professionals in the notion of 'partnership with parents'. Indeed, it accords well with the ethos of many professionals, especially in health, some of whom have been dismayed by increasingly forensic, socio-legal trends which had in part replaced the socio-medical approach of earlier years. Such trends were perceived as leading to a 'blaming' culture, which, in conjunction with the significance of the criminal justice system in British management of child protection, was not conducive to cooperative work with parents. Thus, although the 'partnership with parents motif' was led by legislation and guidance emanating from the social services branches of the Department of Health, it was not in principle contentious amongst other professionals.

Acceptance in principle, does not, of course, imply easy application in practice. The sociological critique of the professions, perhaps especially in the field of health, has demonstrated how difficult it is to use expertise in ways which are genuinely participative and how subtle and strong are the uses and abuses of power. But in any case the principle needs further critical analysis when it is applied to parents who, by definition, have in some way failed to provide a sufficiently safe and healthy environment for their children. The tenor of the guidance on this matter issued in the 1988 and final version of *Working Together* (DHSS, 1988; Home Office *et al.*, 1991) was clear and included specific advice that ACPCs should formally agree 'the principle of including parents and children in all conferences' (Home Office *et al.*, 1991: p. 43, para. 6:14). The tone was set (and the difficult balancing act attempted) in para. 6:11:

'This Guide stresses the need to ensure that the welfare of the children is the overriding factor guiding child protection work. It also emphasises the importance of professionals working in partnership with parents ... and the concept of parental responsibility.'

(Home Office *et al.*, 1991: p. 43, para. 6:11)

Although the guidance was explicit that this concept involves every stage and process of the work, the conference, as a key part of the process, assumed considerable significance in the discussion at local level and was the subject of considerable research and academic comment. A discrete event which symbolised the principle of partnership, the conference has proved a useful focus for the wider debate. Whilst professionals from other agencies expressed some doubts and anxieties about parental participation and were in some instances given insufficient opportunity by social services to air these feelings, research has by and large confirmed that parental attendance was generally accepted by those present and was not seen to pose insurmountable difficulties (Stevenson, 1995).

However, the research leaves many unanswered questions concerning the conduct of the conferences, the context in which they occur and the impact on the parents. In line with the purposes of this chapter, we need to ask whether there is any evidence that the quality of interprofessional communication has been impeded by parental presence. Whilst this has not been documented empirically, it is of concern to many professionals who may have been afraid to speak out in the light of a (mistaken?) perception of what was acceptable. That my personal observation and experience is not idiosyncratic is confirmed by the following comment in the government consultative document (DoH, 1998):

> 'Partnership with parents must be central to the child protection process. But it is also important that there is an opportunity for separate discussion to take place between professionals so that there is an opportunity for the sharing and analysis of key information about the children's safety and welfare. Evidence from the field indicates that partnership with parents has been interpreted to mean that professionals should never engage in analysis of a child's situation without the parents present. This was never the intention.'

(DoH, 1998: p. 49, para. 6:8)

Whether or not it was ever 'the intention', the 1991 guidance gave no advice on appropriate structures for such discussions to take place and there was undoubtedly a feeling abroad that it would be, somehow, 'naughty' and against the spirit of the times to hold them. In fact, as the quotation above indicates, there can be a valid distinction between those occasions when specific decisions must be taken about children's futures and plans made for their protection, including registration, in which parents arguably have a right to be present, and those which facilitate serious exchanges and reflection between professionals about their concerns. It is, of course, possible for such meetings to be 'gossipy' or for them to be used to 'stitch up' plans before parents are present. But this is a misuse and can be prevented by informed and skilled chairing. Without such opportunities, there is a danger that professional assessments will not be founded on a shared search for the meaning and significance of the behaviour which is of concern. A recent small-scale action research (Glennie *et al.*, 1998) in which I have been involved, where workers were together engaged, with facilitation, in the search for understanding of neglectful families, showed powerfully the value to them (and hence to the families) of thoughtful reflection. For example, the significance of a very dirty house or of appalling personal hygiene was seen to differ in different families. This in turn may lead to different strategies for intervention. Ironically, perhaps workers have found discussion of 'neglect' with parents more difficult than other more specific types of abuse.

The general issue of partnership then, illustrates the ways in which principles of central importance can become distorted. It also illustrates that, because of the complexity of local interagency relationships and the lead role assigned to Social Service Departments, apparent consensus can be achieved which may prove in the longer run to be, in some ways, counter-productive.

A further example of interagency work which tests cooperation to the limit lies in the arrangements for examination of child deaths and serious injuries. The 1973 Maria Colwell inquiry provided a model for national and semi-public inquiry into these tragedies and was quickly followed by a number of highly publicised (and very critical) reports. As the consultative paper (DoH, 1998) comments:

> 'while such inquiries helped to raise public awareness of child maltreatment and highlighted the importance of better interagency cooperation, it was doubtful whether their findings made a lasting impact for better day-to-day practice. It was also argued that public inquiries encouraged a defensive and bureaucratic approach to an area of work which inevitably involves difficult judgements of risk.'

(DoH, 1998: p. 57)

From 1991, therefore, a system of local case reviews was set up, coordinated by ACPCs. Whilst some of these resulted in extensive publicity, local and national, they were conducted within local agencies by local staff, brought together by the ACPC, and considered for their lessons for better practice. At their best, they have been models of honest candour to appraise the quality of service offered; however, it is clear that the process is much affected by the management ethos, the commitment of staff to 'learning lessons' and the openness of relationships between agencies. Furthermore, if the focus, however well intentioned, is solely on procedural matters, fundamental questions with implications for practice and training may go undetected.

It is clear from the consultative document (DoH, 1998) that the Government is not satisfied with the present arrangement and that changes are envisaged. Essentially, the most important questions about such reviews which are raised in the document concern the desirability of a greater degree of independence in the conduct of inquiries from local relationships, and more effort in promulgating findings nationally. Underlying this, however, it is also important to ask how and in what ways standards of case reviews can be improved to avoid repetitive mechanistic exercises. What kinds of questions should we ask that are not at present asked? Should the review seek to elicit more information on the exercise of professional judgements and of the context in which particular events unfolded, rather than concentrating on procedural matters? How are the implications of the reviews to be taken into the existing systems to improve practice? Even if external advice and influences are brought into play to improve case reviews, it is essential that changes are 'owned' by the local agencies.

The future

What then, is the future for these evolving, complicated but crucially important relationships between agencies and between professionals? The consultative paper (DoH, 1998) strongly indicates that the intention is to build upon present structures and there will be a continuing role for bodies such as Area Child Protection Committees. Obviously, however, they have to be connected to, and a part of, the wider local systems emerging for child welfare, embodied in Children's Service Plans. ACPCs also have to define the parameters within which 'child protection' is to be located. Thus, for example, the term 'prevention' and the extent to which preventative activities will be seen as part of child protection must be debated. So must the way of constructing effective bridges between the wider systems for children 'in need' and those specifically for protection, both at policy and practice levels. This is especially important in the area of neglect and emotional abuse, in which families may move between the two systems at points in time.

The questions we must ask at this stage are stark but fundamental. There is no doubt that the drive to build these bridges, to improve cooperative working, was given huge impetus by the anxiety which child abuse created in the minds and hearts of those engaged in child protection. Will we be prepared to put similar effort and commitment into work for children in need which is no less necessary but is less dramatic and carries less onerous consequences for the professionals? And if the willingness of individuals to cooperate can be assured, is there also a will to remove bureaucratic obstacles to effective coordination?

Another, no less important, question concerns the maintenance of the drive to improve cooperation in the narrower sphere of child protection. The attractions of the 'refocusing debate' to a number of the professionals are considerable. Is there a danger that this will distract us from the darker, bleaker side of the work? There are certain developments which make this unlikely, notably the implications of the Sex Offenders Act 1997 and of the Utting report *People like us* (1997) concerning abuse in residential and foster care. We have been increasingly made aware of new dimensions of risk and of the need for cooperative activity. Indeed, the years since the Colwell inquiry have revealed many aspects of cooperation, previously unrecognised, and have frequently resulted in effective action at national and local level. For example, issues concerning young people who abuse other young people, domestic violence, child prostitution, have all necessitated interagency debate. Leaving aside the impetus given to cooperation by particular events or legislation, it seems clear that the next wave of energy can profitably be focused on relationships between children's and adult services, across agencies. Structural obstacles and professional blinkers have recreated or hardened problems so that family difficulties may be compartmentalised, with insufficient understanding of their interactive effects. There is always more to do!

References

Birchall, E. & Hallett, C. (1995) *Working Together in Child Protection.* HMSO, London.

Butler-Sloss, Lord Justice E. (1988) *Report of the inquiry into child abuse in Cleveland 1987.* Cmnd 412, HMSO, London.

Corby, B. (1995) Interprofessional cooperation and interagency coordination. In *The Child Protection Handbook* (eds K. Wilson & A. James), pp. 211–26. Baillière Tindall, London.

Curtis Committee (1946) *Report of the Care of Children Committees.* Cmnd. 6922, HMSO, London.

Department of Health (1998) *Working Together to Safeguard Children.* Consultation Paper. HMSO, London.

Department of Health and Social Security (1974a) *Report of the Committee of Inquiry into the Care and Supervision Provided in Relation to Maria Colwell.* HMSO, London.

Department of Health and Social Security (1974b) *Non-accidental injury to children,* LASSL (73) 14.

Department of Health and Social Security (1988) *Working Together: a guide to arrangements for interagency cooperation for the protection from abuse.* HMSO, London.

Glennie, S. & Hendry, E. (1996) *Promoting Quality: Standards for Interagency Training.* PIAT/NSPCC, London.

Glennie, S., Cruden, B. & Thorn, J. (1998) *Neglected Children: Maintaining hope, optimism and direction.* Notts County and City Area Child Protection Committees.

Griffiths & Moynahan (1963) Multiple epiphyseal injuries in babies ('battered baby syndrome'). *British Medical Journal,* December, 1560.

Hallett, C. (1995a) *Interagency Coordination in Child Protection.* HMSO, London.

Hallett, C. (1995b) Taking stock: past developments and future direction in child protection. In *The Child Protection Handbook* (eds K. Wilson & A. James). Balliere Tindall, London.

Hallett, C. & Stevenson, O. (1980) *Child Abuse: abuse of interprofessional cooperation.* Allen & Unwin, London.

Home Office (1945) *Report by Sir Walter Monckton on Dennis and Terence O'Neill.* Cmnd 6636, HMSO, London.

Home Office (1950) *Children neglected or ill-treated in their own homes.* Joint circular with the Ministry of Health and the Ministry of Education. HMSO, London.

Home Office *et al.* (1991) *Working Together under the Children Act 1989.* HMSO, London.

Lampo, A. and Marneffe, C. (1993) Prevention of child abuse and neglect: child protection or mere registration. *4th European Conference on Child Abuse and Neglect,* Padua, Italy.

Parton, N. (1985) *The Politics of Child Abuse*. Macmillan, Basingstoke.

Petrie, S. & James, A. (1995) Partnership with parents. In *The Child Protection Handbook* (eds K. Wilson & A. James), pp. 313–33, Bailliere Tindall, London.

Sanders, R. & Thomas, N. (1997) *Area Child Protection Committees*. Ashgate, Aldershot.

Secretary of State for Scotland (1992) *The report on the inquiry into the removal of children in Orkney in February 1991*. HMSO, London.

Stevenson, O. (1963) Coordination reviewed. In *Case conference Vol. IX, No. 8, 1967*, reprinted in *Social Work and Social Values* (ed. E. Younghusband), pp. 113–20. Allen and Unwin, London.

Stevenson, O. (1995) *Case conferences in child protection*. In *The Child Protection Handbook* (eds K. Wilson & A. Janes), pp. 313–33, Bailliere Tindall, London.

Stevenson, O. (1998) *Neglected Children; Issues and Dilemmas*. Blackwell Science, Oxford.

Utting, W. (1997) *People like us*. HMSO, London.

Chapter 7

Trends in Foster Care and Adoption

June Thoburn

Adoption and foster care: rarely the twain shall meet

Dennis O'Neill died after experiencing cruelty and maltreatment in a foster home. Despite this, the Curtis Committee (1946) placed adoption and foster care at the top of the hierarchy of desirable options for children who could not live at home. The emphasis for the first child care officers was so heavily on family placement that they were frequently referred to as 'boarding-out officers'. At the same time the Children Act 1948 emphasised the importance of *birth families* and the desirability of children returning to their parents at the first opportunity. Foster family placement was thus officially viewed as an essentially temporary measure. However, early research studies such as those of Gray & Parr (1957) and Trasler (1960) showed that not only did the numbers placed in foster homes increase (from 55 000 in 1949 to 64 800 in 1952 according to Packman, 1975), but that many children were spending large proportions of their childhood in care. 'Temporary' foster placements could, and often did, last for years.

Home Office and then Department of Health statistics charted the steady rise in absolute numbers of children placed with foster families as well as the proportion of those in care who were so placed. In 1949 35% of the 55 250 children in care were 'boarded-out'; by 1956, 45% of 62 347 children in care were in foster homes (Heywood, 1959).

Adoption, on the other hand, though located by the Curtis Committee at the top of the hierarchy of placements, received little further attention. It was rarely considered for children in *either* voluntary *or* compulsory care, and was essentially reserved for white babies with no major health problems whose parents requested it. It was sanctioned by separate legislation and most adoption work was undertaken by specialist adoption agencies or by the voluntary child care agencies who would sometimes place children who had medical problems initially as foster children, with a view to adoption at a later stage (Raynor, 1980).

Thus, in law, theory and practice, foster care was seen as a *supplementary* placement with the child care officer and the birth parents having continuing roles to play. The reality was that for many children the foster parents became *substitute* parents as their birth parents receded into the background (Rowe & Lambert, 1973; Rowe *et al.*, 1984; Millham *et al.*, 1986; Masson *et al.*, 1997).

Although a distinction was made in the Home Office boarding-out regulations (Home Office, 1955) between short-term placements (lasting up to two months), and long-term placements, little note is taken either in the practice or research literature of the different purposes of foster family placement. In particular, the early studies reviewing foster care stability and placement breakdown made no differentiation between children who were expected to return to their birth families, those who were intended to remain with the same foster family for several years, and those likely to remain permanently with the foster family.

This situation of two distinct models of family placement – adoption for the healthy white infant whose parent requested it and foster care for those received or taken into care, or those infants seen as 'unadoptable' – continued throughout the 1950s and 1960s. It was reinforced by the Children and Young Persons Act 1963 (section 1) which stressed again the importance of preventing children leaving home in the first place and their being restored as quickly as possible to their families of origin. During this period, early research studies and Home Office statistics began to reveal a picture of movement between foster homes and residential placements, and the first breakdown statistics began to appear.

The 'cracks' in the foster care service begin to appear: permanence policies emerge

The documentation of instability in the lives of children in foster care coincided in the early 1970s with some much publicised accounts of 'tug-of-love' cases, in which children who had grown up since infancy with foster parents were 'reclaimed' by their natural parents in their teens. The death of Maria Colwell, who was returned from foster placement with relatives to maltreatment and death at the hands of her mother and stepfather, provided a major impetus for the move, which was already happening, against prevention and family rehabilitation and towards planning for permanent placement with *substitute* families. The wide dissemination of the research of Rowe & Lambert (1973) (which indicated that a considerable number of children had been long in care and were unlikely to return home) gave a substantial push to the changes brought in by the Children Act 1975 which made it more possible to curtail parental rights, and to place more children for adoption against the wishes of their parents. It was in this period between 1975 and 1980 that the terms 'permanence' and 'permanence policies' were imported from US child welfare and adoption agencies (Jewett, 1978; Churchill, 1979), and adoption began to be seen as a possible placement for *any* child coming into care who was unlikely to return to the natural family. Over the next 20 years adoption without parental consent moved from being a very rare event to being more likely than consensual adoption. From a placement which almost always started by a child being placed in voluntary care or directly with adopters, the 'norm' became an application for a care order or parental right resolution prior to adoption, and the consequent increase in conflict.

These moves did not go unchallenged. Holman (1975) introduced the language of inclusiveness and exclusiveness when studying the attitudes of foster parents to children's families of origin and his arguments were used in the British Association of Social Workers' opposition to those clauses in the Children Act 1975 which curtailed the rights of parents to remove their children from voluntary care after two years had elapsed and made it more possible for the local authority to assume their parental rights. Although the 1975 Act was hailed as a piece of legislation which tipped the balance away from parental rights and towards children's rights, in effect the shift was towards increased powers for *local authorities* and *long-term foster and prospective adoptive families*.

Striking the balance: the rehabilitation of foster care

From 1975 the debate has continued amongst practitioners, in the academic and professional literature, and in the popular press about the balance to be struck between the rights, needs and wishes of children, parents, carers, and local authorities. Its most recent manifestation took the form of a BBC *Today* programme interview with the sociologist, Janet Morgan, who claims that children left in unplanned care are being prevented by left-leaning social workers from being happily looked after in adoptive families. The post-Children Act 1989 research now beginning to appear shows otherwise (Hunt *et al.*, forthcoming; Brandon *et al.*, forthcoming). Children of all ages are still being placed for adoption against the wishes of parents and relatives, and the majority of children in care in need of permanent placement are older and have the sort of problems which would place considerable stress on the most competent of families. The Children Act 1989, in particular the emphasis placed on the early involvement of guardians *ad litem* and children's solicitors, perhaps for the first time placed the rights and needs of *children* above those of either their birth parents or their prospective adopters or foster parents.

Throughout these years, official guidance, starting with the DHSS *Foster Care: A Guide to Practice* (DHSS, 1976) continued to spell out the importance of balancing the needs of all those involved and therefore continuing to work towards the inclusion of families of origin in all except a minority of cases where this was clearly not in the child's interest. In 1984 the House of Commons' Social Services Committee (HMSO, 1984) (usually referred to as the Short Committee) welcomed 'a trend towards more adoptions from care' but added: 'we must sound some notes of warning. There is some danger that a new bandwagon is rolling connecting adoption with the idea of permanence' and stressed that 'adoption is only one eventual outcome amongst many'.

Articles were written in the professional journals emphasising the importance of services for children balancing the needs and wishes of all those involved. Two articles by Rowe (1977, 1983) on *Fostering in the Seventies* and *Fostering in the Eighties*, and articles in the influential journal *Adoption and Fostering* by Stevenson (1980) and Jordan (1981) made important contributions to the debate. However, a sense of hopelessness about the value particularly of long-term foster placement appeared to pervade child placement social work in the late 1970s and 1980s as workers became familiar with the high breakdown rates reported in earlier studies, and the words 'drift' and 'languish' were routinely linked with the words 'foster care' as if they were inevitable. The National Foster Care Association emphasised the *caring* in foster caring and discouraged the use of the term 'foster *parenting*'.

Increasingly, the emphasis in foster care literature and research was on the task-centred nature of such placements. Hazel (1981) brought back from Scandinavia the model of task-centred foster placement for teenagers; here the energies of the most experienced child placement workers tended to be located either in the special permanent placement units emphasising adoption (or occasionally permanent fostering as very much second best), or in the provision of task-centred placements for teenagers. What Rowe *et al.* (1989: p. 79) have described as the 'bread and butter of fostering', the placement of younger children, usually for brief periods, received, and still receives, very little attention in the professional literature as pointed out by Berridge & Cleaver (1987), Sellick (1992), Stone (1995), Triseliotis *et al.* (1995) and Berridge (1996), who have recently tried to redress the balance.

This lack of attention resulted in the 1980s in a vicious circle of failure to meet the needs of the majority of children going into 'ordinary' foster homes, as documented particularly by Millham and colleagues (1986), and Berridge & Cleaver (1987). The children who benefited from either placement for adoption or from placement in the high status task-centred units were a tiny minority. Although in their different ways both the specialist permanence agencies and the task-centred fostering units greatly benefited both child care practice and the children placed, research began to document that their efforts were not without problems. Children placed in task-centred families tended, at best, to put down roots, but, rather than being welcomed, this tended to be disapproved of and equated with 'failure' on the grounds that, if the young people remained, the valuable resource of the specialist carers would be lost (Shaw & Hipgrave, 1983, 1989). Breakdown rates, as we shall see in the next section, were quite high in adoptive placements of children with special needs. Stein & Carey (1986) in the meantime catalogued the despair of young people moving out of either temporary or task-centred placements, sometimes following the breakdown of an adoptive placement which was intended to be permanent.

Other writers who researched young people's careers through the care system noted that many did remain with their foster families, whether these had initially been task-centred carers with whom the children had been placed quite late or de facto adoption (Berridge & Cleaver, 1987; Rowe *et al.*, 1984, 1989; Thoburn, 1990). However, foster care's successes remained 'unsung'. The lack of confidence in the value of short-term placements led to rigid policies which kept out of care children who would have benefited from them, and to Packman and colleagues' (1986) conclusion that children's suffering in care was greatly increased by the precipitate way in which they left their families: 'Admission was sometimes almost unthinkable until it became too late to think at all. "Last resorts" are, after all, seldom desirable or constructive places to be.'

To bring this overview up to date, 50 years after the Children Act 1948, and ten years after the passing of the Children Act 1989, is a period when the continuities can be seen alongside the swings, fashions and bandwagons. A series of research and policy reports in 1997 (ADSS, 1997; Waterhouse, 1997) has re-emphasised the importance of foster care for children of all ages, though Utting (1997) and an earlier survey of the opinions of young people in care (Fletcher, 1993) also look at the problems and still see a place for high quality residential care. Permanence panels are beginning to look for long-term foster placements as placements of first choice for some children since it is recognised that adoption is not the appropriate option for all who cannot return home. (Indeed, Thoburn (1990), Fratter *et al.* (1991) and Thoburn *et al.* (1997) demonstrated that throughout the time when the rhetoric was that 'permanence equals adoption', 'permanent' foster placements were made in not insignificant numbers.)

The importance of links with the family of origin is increasingly recognised by the placement of larger proportions of children both for temporary and longer-term stays with members of the extended family, including grandparents, and a plan for some form of contact is increasingly a part of the care plan for children who cannot return to their families of origin, including those placed for adoption (Fratter *et al.*, 1991; E. Neil (unpublished paper); Thoburn *et al.*, 1997). There are signs, therefore, that the family placement service at the end of the 1990s is closer than it has been since 1948 to attempting to meet the needs and draw on the strengths of birth families, children and carers, rather than, as has been the case for much of the previous 50 years, pushing them into conflict.

The difference between 1948 and 1998 is that the full range of placements, from adoption to respite care, is being considered in terms of the extent to which it can meet the needs of *each particular child and family*. The assumption is no longer made that *only adoption* is appropriate in certain sorts of cases, and *only foster care* in others. The increased complexity of the decision-making and planning process, therefore, makes more complex demands on those who work in the family placement service. The four main aspects of this service in the late 1990s will now be considered:

- making decisions about which placement for which child
- assessing, recruiting and training foster carers and adopters
- matching children and families
- support, help and therapy to children, birth relatives and carers.

Making decisions

In the 1950s and 1960s the range of placements to be considered was seen as uncomplicated. If parents did not request or consent to adoption then foster care would be the only placement considered. Children who had disabilities or may have had health problems, or were of minority ethnic origin, or beyond infancy, were not considered for adoption although they might be placed in foster care with a view to adoption. Most foster placements were seen as short-term as the aim was to return children to their families as soon as possible. There was a presumption that children would stay in touch with their birth parents, but little was done to achieve this and planning for contact was not an important part of the early decision-making process. As the philosophy of child placement moved away from prevention and rehabilitation and towards permanence, this oversimplified way of approaching child placement decision-making continued. 'Permanence' must now be considered for all children who could not be returned home within a reasonably short period of time, interpreted by some as six months, but the only 'permanence' model given serious consideration was a closed model of adoption where all contact with the birth parents, and also often the siblings, would end. (For an example of this model see Hussell & Monaghan, 1982.)

Assessing needs and preparing the care plan

More recently, following the wide dissemination of the findings on the outcomes of child placement during the period leading up to the Children Act 1989 in the two key Department of Health overviews –

Social Work Decisions in Child Care (1985) and *Patterns and Out-comes in Child Placement* (1991) – a more complex model for decision-making emerged. My own work suggests the questions to be asked as:

- If the child needs to leave home, are there more suitable alternatives to being looked after by the local authority, such as placement with relatives, possibly supported by section 17 money, and possibly formalised by the use of a section 8 residence order?
- If being looked after by the local authority is necessary, what legal route is appropriate?
- Which placement will best meet the needs of the child, and if long-term provision may be needed, is a 'bridge' or 'assessment' place-ment necessary in the first instance?
- What might be appropriate in the longer-term?
- What should be the nature of contact between the child, the birth parents, relatives or previous carers and how is the placement and social work service to facilitate such contact?
- What is the nature of the social work and other services to be offered to the child, the birth parents or relatives, the previous carers and the new carers?
- What practical and financial support will be needed to maximise the chance that the placement will meet the needs of the child?

(Adapted from Thoburn, 1994: p. 47)

Research studies are now available which can help social workers to choose the most appropriate placement and to answer these questions in the light of the assessed needs of each particular child. Prompted by the guardians *ad litem*, the majority of whom see it as an imperative that they should be familiar with the research, Courts increasingly require the social work care plan to weigh the chances of success of the different alternatives for the child, both in terms of placement and in terms of the nature of contact with members of the birth family. Courts will also increasingly want to know about the support and therapy likely to be made available.

For a small number of children placed in foster care or for adoption, such as those placed for short periods of respite with the agreement of their parents, or infants placed for adoption at the request of a parent, the issues are comparatively straightforward. However, most children needing family placement have led complex lives and have very com-plex needs, any one of which may be very difficult to meet. Rowe *et al.* (1984, 1989) note that children being placed in 1984 had considerably more difficulties than those placed when the first research was under-taken on foster care by Trasler (1960) and George (1970). Placement guidelines and regulations have always required that for short- as well as for long-term placements a statement about the needs of the child and how the proposed carers will meet those needs should be recorded on file; a regulation which researchers and social services inspectors over the years have found rarely followed except in adoption (where the recommendation about 'matching' is a major role of the statutory adoption panel).

The importance of a full assessment of the child's strengths, aptitudes, problems and disabilities has been increasingly recognised and formalised by the use of the *Looking After Children* materials (Ward, 1996). These tools for good practice for children already looked after also suggest the key dimensions for assessment of a child's needs prior to placement. These are: health, education, identity, family and social relationships, social presentation, emotional and behavioural development, and self-care skills. The nature of the child's attachments to parents, siblings and close relatives, and to other carers, and (for older children) relationships with friends, teachers and community links, is also recognised as important (Berridge & Cleaver, 1987). The child's opinion and wishes about alternative placements have now by law to be ascertained and given due consideration, and research has indicated (Fitzgerald, 1983; Thoburn, 1990) that failure to do so in the past was associated with placement breakdown.

What works in foster care and adoption?

Finally, the decision-maker must appraise the likelihood of success of the alternative options. How likely is it that a placement able to meet all the child's needs as identified by the assessment can be found in an appropriate time-scale? If this is unlikely, which of the needs can be met in some other way and which are so important that they must be given priority? The importance of being placed with, or keeping links with, a sibling is usually recognised, but children's needs to stay in touch with birth parents when placed with substitute families have often been given low priority on the grounds that it would not be possible to find adopters who would welcome continuing contact, although some agencies have found that they were able to recruit such families (Thoburn *et al.*, 1986; Thoburn, 1990; Fratter *et al.*, 1991). Differences in the proportion of children placed with adoptive families are to some extent accounted for by the fact that those agencies who value parental contact highly are more likely to place children with long-term foster families, than those who see the achieving of the legal status of adoption as being more important than continuing family links.

The importance of placing a child with a family of a similar ethnic and cultural background is accorded weight in the Children Act 1989. Research shows that, over the years, higher priority has been given to this aspect of a child's needs and it is now less usual for a child to be placed with a family of a totally different ethnic background (Barn *et al.*, 1997).

A somewhat surprising aspect of permanence policies, which is only now becoming clearer in the light of hindsight, was that, in their determination to provide children with attachments to new psychological parents, some of the early 'permanence' agencies paid scant regard to existing attachments. Although the enthusiasts of 'permanence' (including Goldstein *et al.*, 1973; and Fahlberg, 1988) stressed the importance of existing attachments, whether with present carers or parents, the 'no child is unadoptable' enthusiasm led many practitioners to be overconfident that any harm from separation and the loss of early attachments could be repaid by high quality parenting. The debate about the reversibility, or otherwise, of harm resulting from separation and loss, which, through the works of Bowlby (1951, 1988), Winnicott (1965) and Rutter (1972), had a formative influence on the first child care officers, went underground in family placement circles and is only now re-emerging and catching up with the large volume of developmental psychology research (Howe, 1995, 1996).

As a result, more careful consideration is given to placing children permanently (or leaving them) with relatives or foster carers when they are already attached, providing these carers are willing to provide a home until the child grows up.

All studies of child placement show an increased use of placement with relatives, either for short-term, intermediate or permanent placements, and indeed this was encouraged by the Children Act. The incorporation into British practice of family group conferences is likely to increase the trend towards more family placements with relatives. Another trend is for combinations of placements, especially for children with serious behavioural problems who may attend boarding schools but look upon their long-term foster parents or adopters as their 'families for life'. As more children with serious difficulties are placed in families, it becomes more necessary to provide respite placements in boarding-school or with other carers in order to maintain the placement.

As well as being aware of the likelihood of successfully finding foster carers or adopters to meet a child's needs, those making decisions about placement have to consider the chances of successful outcomes to the placement. A series of research studies has provided information about breakdown rates, although less information is available on other measures of success such as satisfaction of the different parties, and different aspects of well-being. Sellick & Thoburn (1996) have summarised the research on outcomes for the full range of family placements. In broad terms the research has indicated that some groups of children are difficult to find families for, but once placed appear to have a reasonable good chance of a positive outcome. Family placement for children who have learning or physical disabilities, whether on a short-term or long-term basis, appears to be reasonably successful in that families can be found, and the placements appear to have a good chance of lasting as long as needed, and into adult life if return home is not possible. Older children, and those who are behaviourally or emotionally disturbed, are both hard to find families for, and hard to parent (Fratter *et al.*, 1991).

Rowe *et al.* (1989) found that the main aim at the start of most placements (39%) was temporary care followed by 34% who were in 'task-centred' placements, whose aims could be categorised as assessment, treatment, bridge to independence, or preparation for long-term placement. A further 12% were emergency placements. In reviewing placement outcomes, this group are taken together as 'task-centred' or 'bridge' placements. Thirteen per cent of the placements, including children in all age groups, had as their aim 'care and upbringing' in that the children were expected to remain for three or more years, and a further 2% were placed for adoption. The authors were surprised to find that almost 50% of those placed for 'care and upbringing' were adolescents, with a very small number of these older children being placed with the aim of adoption. Two hundred and twenty-one of the 261 children placed with the aim of adoption were under the age of four, and 32 were aged five or over.

Berridge (1996) provides an overview of the research on foster care and Triseliotis *et al.* (1997) do likewise for adoption. Sellick & Thoburn (1996) divide the studies into those of short-term or task-centred placements and those of permanent placements. They provide a framework for understanding outcome studies and note the many difficulties of researching 'what works':

'The long-term outcomes of adoption of infants are measured 20 or more years after the child was placed, and the practice leading to these outcomes will have moved on in the intervening periods ... The task of evaluating child placement practice is made especially difficult because of the many discrete but interacting components of the effort put into trying to make any one placement successful. The efforts to be evaluated are those of a team of workers using different styles of practice at different times, and of the parents, the children and the carers themselves. It is more possible to evaluate a short episode of care which has a clear purpose, such as a series of short breaks to provide respite, or a single placement to hold a troubled adolescent in caring surroundings until a court hearing, than it is to evaluate all that happens when a three-year-old abused child is placed for adoption.'

(Sellick & Thoburn, 1996: p. 11)

The characteristics of the child needing placement will have an impact on success rates. A six-week-old baby will usually be placed before he or she has had too many damaging experiences. Teenagers are often 'on the move' even in 'ordinary families', and most studies of teenage placements show high rates of breakdown.

The definition of 'success' is also problematic. Most researchers use placement breakdown as an indicator of failure and this is often the only outcome measure in larger-scale surveys, which have sufficient numbers to hold different variables constant. Qualitative studies usually include measures of well-being and satisfaction. Sellick & Thoburn (1996) divide studies into two categories. First, those which use *client outcome* measures such as:

- Was the adopted adult of average well-being?
- Was the adopter generally satisfied with the adoptive experience?

Second, those which use *service outcome* measures such as:

- What proportion of those referred were placed?
- Did the placement last as long as planned?
- Were post-placement services provided?

Outcomes of task-centred placements

Turning to short-term or task-centred placements, the outcome measure most often used is whether the placement broke down. Vernon & Fruin (1986) and Rowe *et al.* (1989) noted that some placements lasted too long (15% of all foster placements in the Rowe *et al.* (1989) study compared with 26% which did not last as long as planned). Berridge & Cleaver (1987) found that 10% of 156 planned short-term placements broke down within a two-month period. However, they also noted that some of the 58 placements which lasted significantly longer than anticipated ended in breakdown, and when these are included, 19% of planned short-term placements broke down. Amongst those which lasted, they concluded that 18% were unsatisfactory in some respect. In attempting to understand factors related to breakdown, they concluded that, in 30% of cases, breakdown was the result of child-focused factors such as the child's behaviour. In 37% of the cases, placement-related problems appeared to be associated with breakdown (such as the marital problems or other difficulties of the foster parents). Almost a quarter broke down in circumstances where both child- and placement-related variables appeared to be involved. In only 3% did the birth parent appear to play some part in the disruption, and in none of these cases was behaviour of the natural parent on its own associated with breakdown. Yet case studies showed that all too often, when stresses in the placement become apparent, contact with the birth parents was curtailed or terminated as a 'solution' to the problem which rarely prevented breakdown.

Most of the research on short-term or intermediate-term placements has been conducted in the context of specialist teenage placement teams. Hazel (1981) and Shaw & Hipgrave (1983, 1989) give indications of high satisfaction rates for young people and the specialist carers recruited to take teenagers. Less is known about the reactions of the birth parents. Aldgate *et al.* (forthcoming) describe generally positive outcomes for respite care services for children whose parents are under stress, as do Robinson (1987) and Stalker (1990) for children with disabilities. However, in these placements the children themselves are most likely to express concern and worry about being placed away from home. These authors give pointers to how this discomfort can be minimised.

Most studies concentrate on *process* and on *service* outcome measures, such as the proportions placed in foster care, or the types of foster carers recruited. Stone (1995) studied a cohort of 183 children placed with short-term foster carers and identified two distinct groups. The majority were aged under nine years and were mostly voluntarily accommodated and returned to their families in less than three months; the minority of often older children required more specialist and longer-term placements. Waterhouse (1996) conducted a major survey on behalf of the National Foster Care Association and the Department of Health into the organisation and delivery of fostering services, and established a database showing the range and variety of fostering service models. Evaluative studies of foster care for black children tend to be restricted to studies of the success of recruiting families from different ethnic groups. The latest of these (Barn *et al.*, 1997) indicates that a larger proportion of children are now placed with families of similar ethnic origin than was the case in earlier studies (Barn, 1993).

How successful are 'permanent' placements?

Turning to long-term or 'permanent' foster family placement or adoption, the clear conclusion from a much more extensive volume of research is that being older at placement and having behavioural or emotional difficulties are highly predictive of placement breakdown. Placement with relatives is generally more successful than placement with families not previously known to the child, as is remaining with a foster family to whom the child is already well-attached on a permanent basis, either as an adopted or long-term foster child. In broad outline, somewhere around 5% of infants placed in adoptive families will experience placement breakdown before they reach adulthood, and in around 80% of adoptive families the adopters and the adopted young people will be generally satisfied with the experience. However, in an unknown proportion of generally satisfactory cases, the adopted adult will feel some sense of unease around issues of identity, loss and biography, which can have a debilitating effect.

For the birth parents, however, the adoption story has few positives. Because of the secrecy which has been seen as a necessary part of the modern adoption process, it is not known what proportion of parents who place a child for adoption are harmed by having done so. However, biography and research studies suggest that there are long-term negative consequences for a substantial proportion of young women who give up their babies for adoption or have children removed by the Courts and for many this will be associated with long-term mental ill health. Even less is known about fathers, but the sense of loss experienced by grandparents is beginning to be acknowledged (Grandparents' Federation, 1996; Tunnard & Thoburn, 1997). Studies beginning to appear suggest that those who retain some form of contact with a child who has been adopted, fare better than those whose child is placed in a 'total severance' model of adoptive placement (Fratter, 1996; Logan, 1996).

When older children or those with disabilities or behavioural or emotional difficulties are placed with permanent substitute families, breakdown rates are broadly similar, irrespective of whether the placement is for adoption or with a foster family, once age at placement is held constant. Around 20% of children placed from care with permanent substitute families will experience breakdown and this rises to almost 50% for those placed around 11 or 12 years of age (Fratter *et al.*, 1991). When well-being as well as disruption is taken into account, Berridge & Cleaver (1987) found of long-term foster children, and Thoburn *et al.* (1997) of children placed with a permanent foster or adoptive family, that some of those placed when *between the ages of five and ten* were experiencing serious difficulties, and assessed as of low well-being even though the placement had not broken down.

Outcomes for children of minority ethnic origin

Much of the practice literature (though little of the UK *research* literature) concerns the placement of children of minority ethnic origin. They appear to experience similar rates of breakdown to white children, although there is some evidence that transracially adopted children are over-represented amongst clinical populations (Howe, 1997; Rushton & Minnis, 1997). Some studies indicate that children of *mixed* ethnic origin are over-represented amongst children being placed with substitute families, and are most likely to experience breakdown. Thoburn & Rowe (in Fratter *et al.*, 1991) and Thoburn *et al.* (1997) found differences between the types of placements chosen for children with one white and one black parent, and those with two black parents. Those with two parents of minority ethnic origin were more likely to be placed with a sibling, to retain contact with birth parents, and to be placed in permanent foster care as opposed to adoption than was the case for those with one ethnic minority parent and one white parent, or those with two white parents.

A more recent study (Thoburn *et al.*, 1997) traced 297 children of minority ethnic origin placed for adoption or permanent fostering between 1980 and 1984 (part of a cohort of 1165 children reported in Fratter *et al.*, 1991) for as long as records were available.

Although almost three-quarters of the children were placed (as was most frequently the case in the early 1980s) in families where both parents or the single parent were white, there was a statistically significant difference in this respect between the children, both of whose parents were of minority ethnic origin, and those of mixed race parentage. Forty-seven per cent of those with two parents of minority ethnic origin, but only 12% of the children of mixed race parentage, were placed with families where either one or both foster or adoptive parents were of minority ethnic origin.

When age at placement was held constant, there was no statistically significant difference in breakdown rates between those placed for long-term or permanent foster care, and those placed for adoption; nor between those placed with two (or a single) white parent, and those where at least one parent was of the same ethnic background as the child.

The researchers supplemented this qualitative data by interviewing 38 of the adoptive or foster parents of 51 of the young people (now aged between 15 and 30). This purposive sample was selected to include roughly equal numbers placed in 'matched' and 'transracial' placements. From these interviews the researchers conclude (and indeed are supported in this conclusion by all but a tiny minority of the white and black parents and by young people placed transracially or in racially matched placements), that there are strong reasons to support Department of Health guidance that, wherever possible, children should join new families of similar ethnic backgrounds, culture and religion. This is not to say, however, that families of a different ethnic origin cannot successfully parent a child whose ethnic origins are different from their own, if the circumstances of the particular case make this appropriate. The birth parents or, indeed, the young person who is well-settled with a white foster parent and has comfortable contact with birth relatives may request that he or she remain there rather than being moved on to a new family they do not know. A cooperative relationship between the two sets of parents can ensure that the birth parent or extended family is able to help the child develop skills to deal effectively with racism and to develop a sense of pride as a member of a particular ethnic group. In other cases a complex cluster of problems, perhaps including disabilities which require very special treatment, may mean that there is a very restricted choice of carer with those particular skills. Again, if this necessitates a transracial placement, care must be taken to ensure that there is good contact with role models of the same ethnic group, and continuing family contact may again have an important part to play in meeting those needs which arise from membership of a particular cultural, religious or ethnic group.

As more children are placed in matched *temporary* foster homes, transracial permanent placements occur less often in circumstances where a further move is judged inappropriate. However, the conclusion from our own and other studies in the UK and the USA, summarised most recently by Bagley (1993), Rushton & Minnis (1997), and Triseliotis *et al.* (1997), who have followed cohorts of children into adulthood, is that some foster or adoptive parents can successfully nurture children of a different ethnic origin and help them to grow up with a strong sense of pride in their ethnic and cultural heritage. Even if policies to recruit families from the range of ethnic backgrounds represented in our multiracial society are vigorously pursued, as I believe they should be, and it is then rarely necessary to make transracial placements, they will still occur not least because *transnational* adoption is likely to be here to stay and many of these placements are *trans-racial*. (The subject of transnational adoption is not covered in any detail in this chapter, since it is the subject of neither the 1948 nor the 1989 Act. It has had a major impact on proposals for adoption reform and will be referred to in the conclusion. Selman & White (1994) provide an overview and references.)

Finding, assessing and preparing the families

Over the last 50 years there have been many changes to the way in which adoptive and foster families have been recruited, approved, trained and supported, reimbursed for their expenses, rewarded for their efforts, and had their performance in their role as foster carers reviewed and evaluated. Stroud (1960) gives a child care officer's fictionalised account of these early years and there are many autobiographical accounts of those on the receiving end of the results. In the early days, any family willing to take on the task was quickly approved to do so, and the main defence against incompetence or cruelty appears to have been that if carers were only barely compensated for the costs, the wrong people would not put themselves forward because it would not be seen as an income-generating proposition.

Very quickly, however, the recruitment of foster carers received attention in the professional literature and professional training. The main job of child care officers was to 'board-out' children in care and consequently practice in recruitment and support of foster carers was emphasised in the specialist university child care officer courses. The task emphasised was the professional one of assessing (or 'vetting' as it was usually known). As the research began to appear about high rates of breakdown, child care officers and their managers and educators gave more attention to the information which should be obtained about prospective foster carers in order to try to reduce the incidence of breakdown. All the child care texts in the 1960s and 1970s had sections on foster home recruitment and approval. The DHSS guidance, *Foster*

Care: A Guide to Practice, published in 1976 following the Maria Colwell inquiry, provides an excellent summary of the theory of foster care practice at that time (DHSS, 1976).

In this early writing the emphasis was on the values and special understanding and skills needed by those who cared for *someone else's child*, and indeed this was the title of one of the earlier texts written for foster parents but widely read also by social workers (Stevenson, 1965). The theme is repeated in all the early child care officer training material and the articles in *Accord*, the journal of The Association of Child Care Officers (for example, Pugh, 1968; Tod, 1968 in respect of foster care; and Kirk, 1964, and Tod, 1971 in respect of adoption). This literature stressed that some children would need long-term foster families. Even after the tide had begun to turn away from the provision of support to birth families in their attempt to retain contact with their children following the Colwell case, *Foster Care: A Guide to Practice* (DHSS, 1976: p. 7) states:

'Whilst some foster children may be adopted into their foster families, most remain in the care of the agency until they return home or reach adulthood. Where children remain in foster care, the extent of parental contact varies considerably. In some cases they continue to feel part of their natural family. In others there may be little parental contact, and especially where children were placed at a young age, they may come to look upon their foster family as their own. The foster parents in their turn then see themselves more as parents than as participating in an agency caring role.'

Elsewhere (p. 9) the members of the Working Party note:

'In fostering there is a long continuum of types of placement ranging from the short through long stay, with or without rehabilitation, on to near adoption. In all stages of this continuum there may be elements which actually overlap. It is important that the practitioner is able to differentiate between these various stages and to apply the appropriate practice skills.'

Rowe (1977) made a similar point:

'The concepts of biological and psychological parenting are basic to any study of fostering relationships ... a foster parent's role must always depend on what aspects of the parental role are still being exercised by the natural parents.'

(Theories of psychological and biological parenting as they have developed in the foster care and adoption literature are further explored by Thoburn (1996) who argues that a model of long-term 'dual' or even 'multiple' psychological parenting will best meet the needs of some children looked after away from home, as it does in the context of marital separation.)

Recruitment campaigns in the years after the Children Act 1948 was implemented, encouraged those coming forward to think about foster care as 'shared parenting'. Other than this, the aim for those 'vetting' families was to 'weed out' those who were unsuitable and a model of a 'normal, middle-of-the-road' family, with or without children, but almost certainly married, preferably only once, appeared to be in their minds. Any 'deviation' from the 'norm' must be carefully explained to the children's officer or council subcommittee which finally approved foster parent applications.

The guidance and training texts of the 1960s and 1970s depict the child care officer's task at the *assessment stage* as providing information to the potential foster carers or adopters, seeking information from them about their inter- and intrapersonal lives and their reactions to what they have been told about the foster care task or about parenting by adoption. Equipped with this information, their task was to make judgements about whether this particular family was likely to be a successful short- or long-term carer or parent, and for what sort of child. As time went on, practice developed and it became quite common to work in pairs on this task. Preparation groups were also introduced both at the assessment and the post-approval stages.

Once placed, training did not figure highly on the agenda. Foster parents and adopters learned as they went along. They were selected because of their perceived ability to be 'good parents', and the local authorities' duty to be a good parent to children in care was delegated to them on a day-to-day basis. Distinctions were made at the approval stage between the tasks of short-term carers and long-term foster parents or adopters, but the training of long-term foster parents often took the form of trying it out first with one or two short-term children. This practice fell out of favour in the mid-1970s for two reasons.

First, as has already been noted, long-term fostering went out of fashion until the present time (and it probably still is in many authorities). Long-term placements continued to be made, but they were made despite agency guidance and the practice theory of the day. Thus, the development of theory and practice wisdom on the recruitment and training of long-term foster parents went into abeyance.

Second, anecdotal evidence of child care officers pointed to the fact that fostering was being seen as a back-door into adoption as the supply of 'perfect' babies dried up. Those who really wanted a foster child to be a full member of their family on a permanent basis tended to be unwelcoming to parents and to fail to work towards rehabilitation of the child. This suspicion was confirmed by research summarised in the influential Department of Health publication *Social Work Decisions in Child Care* (DoH, 1985). Thoburn (1980), Millham *et al.* (1986), and Vernon & Fruin (1986) provided evidence that plans for rehabilitation changed simply because short-term foster carers ceased to work towards rehabilitation and, by their unwelcoming behaviour, made it difficult for parents to stay in touch with their children.

The move in the mid-1970s away from long-term placement and towards either short-term task-centred caring or permanent caring, preferably through adoption, led to significant shifts in practice, training, approval and matching stages. These new theories for practice borrowed heavily from developments in Scandinavia in respect of short-term or task-centred caring (Hazel, 1981; Shaw & Hipgrave, 1983) and from the USA in respect of adoption and what came to be recognised as 'permanent fostering' (Thoburn *et al.*, 1986). Although there was now a clear differentiation between the role and task of short-term *carers* and substitute *parents*, there were marked similarities in the recommendations for practice.

Researchers, theorists and practitioners advocated a more equal partnership at all stages of the work between the specialist child placement social worker and the foster or adoptive parents. The term 'vetting' was replaced by the term 'home study'. Emphasis was placed on the potential carers as learners and on self-assessment rather than on the ability of the social workers to detect possible problems and weaknesses. Experienced foster parents and adopters were increasingly involved in the recruitment and assessment process. *Choosing to Foster*, a training pack based on the original American version, became increasingly a part of the assessment process (National Foster Care Association, 1994). Self-assessment tools were developed both for task-centred and permanent carers. The term 'professional foster carer' came into use particularly for those who were specially recruited for specific tasks such as preparation for independence or remand placements for teenagers, or the preparation of younger children who were to move into substitute families. In the course of my research I was frequently told (though I cannot locate it in print) that it was not 'ordinary families' that were needed, but those who were different, enjoyed a challenge or even 'slightly mad' to want to take on such a task. As a result, not only was no child seen as 'unadoptable' but no family size, shape, gender, sexual orientation, ability or disability ruled out potential adoptive or foster parents.

In the opinion of some commentators, once those who were clearly unsuitable had been screened out following the taking up of police checks and references, there was little place for the professional judgement of the social worker. When fully informed about the nature of the tasks and the skills and values required of them, foster carers or adopters would be able to either rule themselves out or include themselves in and decide best about the sort of child who would fit with their families (Hazel, 1981; Shaw & Hipgrave, 1983).

The major difference in the recruitment and training stage between the work with *adopters or foster parents taking on a long-term, substitute parenting role*, and *task-centred foster carers* was that for the latter, the importance of working with birth parents was still stressed. However, for adopters and long-term foster carers, and indeed those foster parents who were preparing children to move into substitute families, little emphasis was placed on links with birth families. Indeed, some task-centred foster carers (often referred to as 'bridge families') saw their job as caring for the child whilst contact with the family of origin was terminated so that he or she could be delivered, freed from the burdens of their past lives, to their adopters who would continue the process of repairing past damage. Even task-centred carers for teenagers tended to concentrate on helping the child to move into independence rather than on keeping alive links with members of the birth family, and building bridges for a possible reunion and ongoing birth family support for the young adult care-leaver. Even during the earlier period when best practice required social workers and foster families to seek to maintain links between parents and their children, research showed that they faced an uphill task. Millham *et al.* (1986) showed how this change in practice accelerated the speed with which children lost touch with their birth families, even in those cases where no plan was made to place them with substitute parents, or plans failed to materialise.

The influence of the research already summarised, which revealed a higher than expected breakdown rate for older children placed, led to new thinking, especially about the role of foster parents and thus the recruitment, assessment and training task. The nature of 'best practice' is well documented in the guidance to the Children Act 1989. The balance tipped back towards the importance of the social worker's assessment role, to some extent as a result of allegations (some substantiated, some not) of abuse by foster parents. The many gains in practice methods were retained, but the crucial social work role of making sure that everything possible was done to recruit and approve those most likely to succeed in these difficult tasks was again emphasised.

Matching children with families

For short or task-centred placements the homefinder's task at this stage is to match the skills of the carers to the needs of the child and the parents for whom a service is to be provided. This obvious fact led those who write about practice to down-grade the importance of the social worker's matching role and see this as essentially in the domain of the foster carers who will know best what sort of child requiring their particular skills will fit with their particular family at that particular time (Hazel, 1981). The recognition by practitioners and researchers that in permanent placements 'chemistry' might be as important as more tangible attributes also led to an increased role for the potential adopters in choosing the child who might most easily fit. *Blind viewings* (where the adopters get a sight of the child without the child knowing that this is happening), adoption parties, exchange of life books between the child and the potential adopters, videos made by each of them to be seen by the other, are all ways in which the choice of parents may be narrowed down to only those where the 'chemistry' has a reasonable chance of working (Thoburn *et al.*, 1986).

As with recruitment and approval, at the matching stage also, awareness of high breakdown rates has led to emphasis again being placed on the professional role and the knowledge and skills of the child's social worker and the family's support worker. I have argued elsewhere (Thoburn, 1994, 1995) that the art of child placement lies in being clear about what each family is looking for in terms of rewards and what they want and are able to give to the child; and matching them with a child who is likely to be able to give what they hope to receive, and to take from them what they hope to give. Recent research studies (Berridge, 1996; Sellick & Thoburn, 1996) have re-emphasised the importance of the work undertaken at the home study stage. If this has been well-done and well-recorded, in partnership with the potential adopters or long-term foster parents, and if the child's needs and potential have also been properly assessed and documented, a good match is more likely to occur. Thus the motivation of carers, expressed in terms of their skills, attitudes and hoped-for rewards, has re-emerged as important.

Apart from the consistent finding that breakdown is more likely if a child of the family is younger and close in age to the placed child, research gives clues which should aid the matching process, but is inconclusive. A combination of self-directed and altruistic motives has been reported as most likely to be related to more successful placement. Since birth family contact has been identified by some studies as a protective factor even when children cannot return home, and is clearly associated with the child's safe and speedy return home where this is appropriate, emphasis is placed at the matching stage on the ability of the foster parents or adopters to empathise with the birth parents, and to facilitate appropriate levels of contact. Early work by E. Neil (unpublished paper), in a longitudinal study of contact after adoption for children placed when under the age of four, is indicating that those who can empathise with birth parents, including those who have maltreated the child, and can see the value of continuing contact at a level judged to be appropriate for that particular child, are more likely to be placed at the head of the queue of adopters.

Three models of family placement practice in the 1990s

As we move into the next century, there are three common patterns of family placement practice which can be related to supply and demand as well as to developments in practice wisdom and theory.

Model 1

Home-finding or area team social workers use a 'vetting' process (though no longer using the terminology), but adopt some of the practice methods developed from the specialist adoption and teenage placement schemes. They are essentially recruiting task-centred carers but their resources for undertaking this work are limited. Although most foster placements come into this category, the work is generally underfunded and undervalued. As Sellick (1992, 1996) points out, the work has been poorly researched and ill-documented. In a study of foster carers at the time of the implementation of the Children Act 1989, Waterhouse comments:

> 'Foster carers perceived themselves as having low status and little information or influence; many respondents did not perceive themselves as part of an active team working together with social workers and parents to find a satisfactory outcome for a child. This was borne out in the way contact plans and decisions were made by the agencies with little involvement and nurturing of the foster carers.'

> (Waterhouse, 1992: p. 43)

Careful matching rarely happens. Stone (1995) raised concerns about the number of children who were placed with short-term foster carers in emergency situations without any statement that this placement was appropriate to the needs of this particular child. Although in short supply, and with a high drop-out rate after a comparatively small number of placements, potential foster families have continued to come forward and to be approved. Anecdotal evidence suggests that, at the first reviews of their performance required by the Children Act 1989, a sizeable minority of short-term foster parents lacked essential skills and espoused values which did not accord with the aims of the Act, particularly in respect of parental contact. However, deregistrations have not been common. Instead authorities are attempting to use training to move all their foster carers towards what is now recognised as 'best practice' in the specialist units. This is evidenced also in the increased willingness of local authorities and voluntary agencies to pay a reward for service in exchange for the foster parents being more accountable for the work they do, and undertaking additional training.

Model 2

In contrast, what is now recognised as 'best practice' for all foster parents and fostering team workers, has been developing over the past 20 years or so in specialist units providing longer or short-term placements for children whose special needs have been recognised. Starting with adolescents, these schemes have developed to provide: respite care for children with disabilities, or for those whose parents are under stress; adoption or long-term fostering for children with special needs or who have been long in care; and a full family assessment for younger children who may need long-term placement. There is almost always a reward element in the payment, arrangements for insurance and compensation for any damage or loss incurred, training, high levels of support, and well-developed patterns of practice for all the stages of the work (Sellick, 1992; Triseliotis et al., 1995). Increasingly, these specialist units are provided within the context of a 'mixed economy' of child welfare, by local authorities, not-for-profit agencies or private agencies. Some provide education and therapy and all social work services as well as high quality parenting.

Model 3

The third model of family placement practice still obtains where supply is in excess of demand, that is in the placement for adoption of infants. Here, until recently, rationing devices have been part of the recruitment process, as when those over a certain age, those who have health problems or are judged to be overweight, have not been allowed to join the queue. The 'vetting' model of assessment is still dominant, although techniques have been borrowed from the specialist agencies. However, with the government requirement for local authorities to provide an assessment service for those who are willing and have the financial means to seek a baby overseas, rationing devices which are not validated by research findings on outcome, are no longer acceptable. Whilst the supply of infants in the UK is low, sadly there are many abandoned babies available for adoption in the poorest countries of the world.

Support, help and therapy to children, birth parents, foster carers and adopters

Stevenson (Chapter 5) and also in Neglected Children: Issues and Dilemmas (1998) writes about changes in social work practice, especially in working directly with children. Steady progress has been made in the development of methods for working directly with children in need of placement at the preparation, matching and post-placement stages. The problem here is not that knowledge and skills are lacking, but rather the lack of trained and experienced workers to put this knowledge and skill into practice. Outside the specialist agencies, it is recognised that many children looked after by the local authority are receiving inadequate social work help by inadequately trained workers. Indeed, an unacceptably high proportion of children looked after do not have an allocated social worker (Murch et al., forthcoming). The major difference between practice with children in task-centred placements and those who are permanently placed is not in the nature of the work, but in who does it. When a child is in a temporary placement, the argument for a longer-term relationship-based service provided by a social worker allocated specifically to the child is unassailable, and has been made most recently by the Utting Report (Utting, 1997). Others may be called in to undertake pieces of work in partnership with the allocated worker, but continuity of relationship is essential. The thread of this argument runs throughout the literature on child placement, from the debate in *New Society* (Stevenson, 1963) and the work of Claire Winnicott (1994), through the recommendations of *Foster Care: A Guide to Practice*:

> 'Communication can only be established within a relationship of trust and for this to develop it is essential for a foster child to get to know his social worker ... Communicating with children in such circumstances is not easy and the social worker will need to seek contact with the suffering part of each child, because locked up in the suffering is each one's potential for living and for relating to the world. To help children to put painful feelings into words imposes a strain on social workers, for it arouses painful memories of distress that each has experienced and that belong to living. If they are not careful they can find themselves avoiding this essential aspect of their work.'

> (DHSS, 1976: pp. 70–71)

The trend over the years is for increasingly well-trained foster parents to take on important aspects of working directly with the child after placement, especially if their task specifically includes the provision of an assessment or therapeutic service, help to renew links between child and members of the birth family, or foster links with a substitute family.

However, when the child is placed with long-term foster parents or adopters, with the hope that these will become the child's 'psychological parents', most researchers and practitioners have concluded that it is most appropriate for the long-term support of the placement to be undertaken by the specialist social worker who undertook the home study and approval. He or she will concentrate on supporting the family as a whole, and not singling-out the placed child for attention at the time when the prime agenda is to help the new family to knit together. Many children placed for adoption or long-term foster care have talked to researchers about their nervousness when visited by the child's social worker, especially if frequent moves have resulted in anxiety that a visit from the worker may signal another move. Thus, the child's worker is best seen as a caring presence in the background who arrives at the time when the placement is reviewed, but otherwise leaves the support to the new family's worker. He or she may undertake an agreed piece of work at the request of the child, the new family or the support worker, but this is most likely to be needed not so much in the early years but when the family has 'gelled' as well as it is going to.

In a study of permanent placements (Thoburn, 1990) it was found that therapeutic intervention in the early years when the child was settling in was rarely appropriate, although a continuation of the life-story work, often undertaken jointly by the new family's social worker and a new parent (and, where there was continuing contact, a birth parent or relative) could be particularly helpful. The time when therapeutic intervention, either by a therapist skilled and knowledgeable about child placement, or by the family's support worker, was most appropriate was three or four years after placement. Indeed, at this time it may become very necessary, and families have complained to researchers about the difficulties of finding high quality therapy for their children. Occasionally, family therapy techniques with the whole family are appropriate, but more often parents and children are looking for separate help with their different perspectives on the situation. All commentators, especially the Post Adoption Centre writers, Howe & Hinings (1989), and Howe (1997), argue strongly that therapists must address themselves to the very special nature of adoptive family life. In the most complex cases, respite with other foster carers, or longer-term 'supplementary' care in a group care setting or boarding-school, is the only step which can keep long-term relationships alive and prevent total breakdown.

Those requiring specialist *therapeutic* input are, however, in a minority. For most, a range of support services is needed, including practical and financial help. The introduction of adoption allowances has been widely welcomed (Hill *et al.*, 1989; Millham *et al.*, 1989). Murch et al. (forthcoming) make a strong case for their wider availability in the case of older children adopted from care. The fact that Residence Order allowances are generally lower and only discretionary may be regarded as a disincentive to use this legal status when it might be more appropriate than adoption (Grandparents' Federation, 1997; Social Services Inspectorate, 1996).

Help in maintaining long-term links with family members is seen as necessary in some cases, and the possibility of a short piece of 'trouble-shooting' type intervention when needed is valued by the majority of long-term foster parents or adopters. Others prefer to gain their support from those caring for children with similar needs. The Lothian Adopters Group was one of the earliest to have its work recognised by the meeting of some of its secretarial and administrative costs by a local authority (Argent, 1988).

Perhaps most progress has been made in the provision of support for task-centred and short-term foster carers. The development of the role of the foster care support worker has been detailed by Triseliotis *et al.* (1995). From the mid-1970s onwards it has been increasingly recognised that foster carers need their own support worker who provides continuity when children and their workers change, and helps them to develop in their foster care careers. This role was firmed-up by the Guidance and Regulations of the Children Act 1989 in that all foster parents must now have an annual review which combines evaluation of their role with a structured discussion about whether their needs for support are being met, and what changes they would like to see. Authorities which provide payments for service on top of maintenance payments often combine this annual review with a discussion as to whether the foster parent is being adequately rewarded for increased skills. Whilst there are few authorities which do not now regularly allocate foster care support workers to all carers, there are also signs that the role of support workers is being undervalued and skills inadequately recognised. In particular, the work has often been allocated to unqualified workers who may have had experience in residential care work, but who have not received training in child and family law and social work practice. There is a risk that those who have not experienced the full range of child and family social work duties will take a somewhat limited view of their role and have a tendency to take the side of the foster parents, the child, or, less frequently, the birth parents, rather than understanding the crucial importance of supporting the foster or prospective adoptive family whilst keeping all aspects of the placement situation in mind.

If work with the child and the foster parents or adopters is sometimes inadequately resourced, work with the birth parents is recognised by researchers and the Social Services Inspectorate to be even more starved of resources and of a generally poor quality (Social Services Inspectorate, 1997). The Children Act 1989 guidance has attempted to remedy the situation in respect of children in foster care by strengthening the part to be played by birth parents in the review process. Farmer & Parker (1991) and Bullock *et al.* (1993) have detailed the extensive work which has to be undertaken when children return home from care and Aldgate *et al.* (forthcoming) have written about social work practice with parents whose children are having regular respite care. Despite the research studies (Thoburn, 1980; Fisher *et al.*, 1986; Millham *et al.*, 1986; Packman *et al.*, 1986) there is evidence that work with birth parents is the weakest link in post-placement practice. This is even more so when children remain long in care. Usually from the time when the case is reallocated or when the first worker leaves, no further work is undertaken with the families of origin (Masson *et al.*, 1997; Social Services Inspectorate, 1997). Mason & Selman (1997) and Lindley (1998) have described the type of work which is welcomed by birth parents.

As with adopters and children, this work changes as time goes on, and the numbness or pain of separation eases. At around the time of placement and during Court proceedings, especially if parents are opposing the adoptive placement or disputing contact arrangements, what is needed most is an advocacy, networking and befriending service. Counselling may be acceptable at the same time, provided that the parents have choice about who is to provide it. Sometimes they will be willing and indeed wish to work with the same social worker who has removed their child, or has responded to their request for placement, but often they will have lost trust in this worker and will require the local authority to fulfil its obligations to them by paying for a counselling service from another source. Once the placement has settled down, they may need help and support in making sure that they play their part in contact arrangements, whether these are through 'letter-box' arrangements or direct contact. At this stage they may also be in need of and more willing to accept counselling or therapy to help them to make sense of the loss of their day-to-day parenting role, and find a way forward as a visiting parent or a 'parent without a child'.

Organisation and management

From 1948 to date, local authorities and voluntary agencies have developed systems in response to changing perspectives on children's, parents', carers' and agencies' needs, wishes rights and responsibilities. The provisions of the Children Act 1989, the Guidance and Regulations and the *Looking After Children* materials encourage child placement practice which provides appropriate safeguards to birth parents, children and adopters or foster carers. There is still need to strengthen the rights which go along with responsibilities for long-term foster parents, possibly by strengthening the residence order or introducing *inter vivos* guardianship provisions, as suggested by the Adoption Law Review Working Group (DoH, 1993; Ball, 1996). The biggest need now is for guidance to local authorities about how to *organise* their services so that parents, children, families and those who care for them, are given a higher priority than is often the case. Numbers in care at any one time are smaller than in earlier years, especially when seen in the context of the vast array of children 'in need'. However, there can be little doubt that unless children looked after by local authorities are provided with appropriate placements and services, they are (in the language of the 1989 Act) '*the most likely* to be *the most significantly* harmed of all children brought to the attention of Social Services Departments'. Specialist family placement teams are essential, and within those teams specialist expertise in task-centred work and permanent placement work is also essential. Although skills are transferable between the different parts of the family placement task, the knowledge requirements are different and practice wisdom acquired in temporary family placement work is not always relevant to work with substitute families.

Some agencies now have 'permanence panels' which make decisions about children to be placed either with long-term foster parents or adopters, depending on the needs of the child, and foster care panels for the approval of task-centred carers. Others have adapted and extended the benefits of their specialist teenage or disability placement work to all their short-term foster carers. A method for allocating and prioritising work which is based less on 'happenstance' is now needed. The research is now available on which to base models of 'best practice' and organisation which are appropriate in different geographical areas. Starting from where they are now, and using available knowledge about organisation and practice, it is possible to move forward in an 'organic' way without the disruption of large-scale reorganisation and loss of valued relationships which always occurs with large-scale reorganisation (Rowe's overview of research in *Patterns and Outcomes in Child Placement*, DoH 1991).

Conclusion

Given the many changes that have occurred since 1948, the shape of child placement practice and the values which inform it are remarkably similar in the late 1990s to the pattern of practice in the late 1950s and early 1960s when the benefits of post 1948 Children Act training were beginning to show through. There are three important differences.

There have been important developments in practice theory, methods and techniques for working with children and adults. In particular, the contribution of foster parents and adopters is now more fully recognised by financial rewards for the services they provide or the continuation (as with adoption payments) of a realistic compensation for the cost of parenting a child with special needs.

Second, the full range of placements from respite care through to adoption is considered for *all* children in the light of their assessed needs. Long-term foster care is again on the list of possible placements for children of all ages, and the contribution of relatives to the short- and long-term care of children is being reassessed. Whilst occasionally the 'total severance' model of adoption is the placement of choice, more often there will be some element of direct or indirect contact with members of the birth family, even of infants whose parents request adoption.

The third and most significant shift results from the change in society's attitude towards parenthood outside marriage, which is now so widespread as to be seen as a different rather than a deviant form of family life. The most obvious result, as the adoption statistics graphically show, is that single mothers have turned away from adoption as a 'solution' to unplanned pregnancy. In the 1940s, adoption and to a lesser extent long-term fostering, were perceived as meeting the needs of birth parents, potential parents (most often those with fertility problems), the children themselves, the local authorities and adoption agencies. In the light of hindsight it has become clear that it rarely met the complex needs of birth parents. There is evidence that in the short and long term it significantly harmed many of those who voluntarily placed their children, and even more so those whose children were placed against their wishes. Though the knowledge and skills are there to help birth parents when placement *is* necessary to safeguard the child's welfare, or when the birth parent really does see this as the best or the only alternative, it should be a cause for concern that the provision of resources is no more a priority now than it was in 1948, and arguably even less so.

Turning to the children, short-term and respite placements generally achieve their aims, but there is still room for improvement which will not happen unless there is greater choice, better matching, and more skilled social work service. With an expanding economy and fewer women choosing to stay at home with their children, there is a crisis in the recruitment of foster carers which will only be addressed by financial recognition and higher status for those who chose this highly skilled work.

Well-planned and supported adoption or permanent fostering with substitute parents who can empathise with the child's pre-placement story and cultural needs, and meet any special needs of those with disabilities or who are of minority ethnic origin, is more often than not successful in providing both a sense of continuity and permanence and a sense of identity for children of all ages who cannot remain with their parents. When researchers return to adoptive families when the children are grown up, they find that roughly equal proportions of adopters and adoptees (around 80%) involved in infant adoptions report themselves to be 'satisfied' or 'very satisfied' with the experience. However, with the placement of children past infancy, higher proportions of adopted young people express satisfaction with their growing-up experience than is the case for the adopters. As the sad stories in the media sometimes tell us, some adopters of older children are so dissatisfied that they seek to 'divorce' their adopted children.

However, the generally favourable results for long-term foster care or adoption lead to the conclusion that permanent family placement will continue to be used by local authorities to discharge their obligations to provide good parenting for an important minority of the children they look after. Between 10 and 15% of those starting to be looked after will be placed with permanent substitute families and around 80% of them will be successfully placed. But the research-literate Director of Social Services will know that adoption does not 'get them off the books'. The price of providing a post-adoption service will have to be paid if the level of breakdown is to be tackled. Included in these costs must be post-placement contact services, from helping with travel costs so that adopters and birth parents can make their own arrangements, 'postbox' services, and providing supportive and supervised contact facilities.

However, for the group who arguably benefited most from adoption 50 years ago, i.e. people with fertility problems, infant adoption plays a very small part indeed in fulfilling their wishes to become parents. Assisted reproduction (with its own complex implications for the future identity needs of the children) has become the main way in which those who are infertile are enabled to become parents. Alongside these new methods of family formation, transnational adoption (which is often also transracial) is growing, though less so in the UK than in other parts of the 'developed' world. The international profession of social work, led by International Social Service workers, has sought to provide maximum protection for children from the dangers consequent on being a much sought-after commodity. Without these social workers, the safeguards in the UN Convention on the Rights of the Child and the Hague Convention on International Adoption would have been considerably weaker.

The issues around intercountry adoption are more complex than sometimes implied. Without doubt, some children have been saved from death or acute deprivation, but their numbers are tiny in the context of the far greater numbers who remain at risk. There is some evidence that the adoption market impedes the development of in-country fostering and adoption services. In Britain, the 'sharp elbows' of those who wrote to their MPs to insist on their 'right' as they saw it, to adopt a child, if necessary from abroad, without 'interference' from social workers, had an impact on the debate about new adoption legislation. There was a danger, which appears to have been headed-off, that adoption would move back from being first and foremost a service for children to become primarily a service for would-be parents.

This brings me, in a roundabout way, to the last 'brick' in the legislative programme necessary to provide a framework for child placement practice after the millennium. In Scotland the Children Act 1995 included changes in adoption law to bring it into line with developments in child care law. In England and Wales, an adoption bill, which, with a little tweaking at the edges, will command widespread support from all who have an interest in making adoption a truly responsive service for children who need it, has not yet found a place in the legislative programme. This is highly regrettable, as there are important differences in the philosophies underpinning the Adoption Act 1976 (conceived in the 'no child is unadoptable' era) and the Children Act 1989 with its welfare check-list, emphasis on consulting the wishes and feelings of children, parents and relatives, and on facilitating contact when this is not contrary to the welfare of the child. It seems likely that a bill will be introduced to allow the UK Government to ratify the Hague Convention, and will be limited to transnational adoption. This will be a lost opportunity to improve in-country adoption, and may, as is the way with 'tinkering' measures, have unanticipated consequences for the placement of British children from care. This will be especially so if scarce resources of skilled social workers are taken away from finding families for vulnerable looked-after children, or providing support to their first and new families, and redeployed to undertake home studies for parents seeking children from overseas.

To end on a more optimistic note, the Children Act 1989 and its accompanying guidance (see especially DoH, 1989), built as they were on practice-based research and the advice of practitioners in local authorities and the Social Services Inspectorate, provide appropriate frameworks for high quality practice. The broad parameters of the way forward are clear, though there are still gaps in our knowledge which researchers must address. Increasing the range of situations when family contact continues after adoption may help with children's and young adults' problems around identity, but may bring other problems in their wake and these must be carefully researched. The impact of sexual abuse and young abusers on the lives of foster and adoptive families and their children is as yet far from fully understood. A major challenge for child placement and child protection agencies is to find ways of investigating allegations made against foster parents, which protect the children without destroying the often fragile relationships within the family and precipitating unnecessary moves.

Others would have chosen to make this contribution as two separate chapters. In deciding to write an integrated review of fostering and adoption, I make a statement of what I believe to be the way forward. Children who, whether for short periods or until they grow up, are unable to live with the parents to whom they were born, have special needs and are especially vulnerable. Fostering and adoption provide different experiences from parenting by birth, which bring their own very special rewards to those who are temperamentally equipped for the task and have the appropriate skills and value-base. Those able to successfully provide this service may be older or younger, able-bodied or disabled, with or without children, homosexual or heterosexual, with or without partners, but will have in common a love of children; an enjoyment in being with them and seeing them grow and develop, and an ability to understand and empathise with the other part of their lives, including their families of origin. For shorter or longer periods they provide resources to be used or sometimes sadly rejected by children, and by the members of their birth families. In very few cases will the child to be placed go through life without some further contact with a mother, a father, a grandparent, or a sibling, which may be continuous, or may happen after a gap of many years.

The range of placements now available to social workers is greater than it was in 1948. For some children, and for some substitute parents, only adoption, or only foster care, will be appropriate. For others, the legal status is unimportant provided the 'fit', the 'chemistry', are right and the necessary skills are there to meet the needs of this particular child.

As we move into the next millennium, much research and practice wisdom has built on the sound foundations of the Children Act 1948. But child placement in the 1990s remains an art. In every case, when the child's needs have been assessed, and the range of possible placements reviewed, an 'imaginative leap' is needed if the right package of decisions and services for each child is to emerge from the conscious and unconscious messages of child, birth parents and potential carers. It seems appropriate to leave the last word with a young person who grew up in a loving adoptive family. The placement was successful in many respects, but the note of ambiguity seemed an appropriate one on which to end this story of the ups and downs of 50 years of family placement:

> 'Personally, I'm not too bothered about finding my birth mother because I'm happy now. Years ago when I was younger I used to cry for her. But now it's more curiosity than anything else. She might accept me. She might not accept me. I do love her because I have good memories of her. But I don't know her.'

References

Aldgate, J., Bradley, M. & Hawley, T. (forthcoming) *The Use of Short-term Accommodation under the Children Act 1989.* HMSO, London.

Argent, H. (1988) *Keeping the Doors Open.* BAAF, London.

Association of Directors of Social Services (1997) *The Foster Care Market: A national perspective.* ADSS, London.

Bagley, C. (1993) Trans-racial adoption in Britain. *Child Welfare* 72 (3), 258–99.

Ball, C. (1996) Adoption: a service for children? *Adoption and Fostering* 20 (2), 27–31.

Barn, R. (1993) Black and white child carers: a different reality. In *Prevention and Reunification in Child Care* (eds P. Marsh & J. Triseliotis). Batsford, London.

Barn, R., Sinclair, R. & Ferdinand, D. (1997) *Acting on Principles: An examination of race and ethnicity in social service provision for children and families.* BAAF, London.

Berridge, D. (1996) *Foster Care: A research review.* HMSO, London.

Berridge, D. & Cleaver, H. (1987) *Foster Home Breakdown.* Basil Blackwell, Oxford.

Bowlby, J. (1951) *Maternal Care and Mental Health.* World Health Organisation, Geneva.

Bowlby, J. (1988) *A Secure Base.* Tavistock, London.

Brandon, M., Lewis, A., Thoburn, J. & Way, A. (forthcoming) *Safeguarding Children with the Children Act 1989.* HMSO, London.

Bullock, R., Little, M. & Millham, S. (1993) *Going Home: the return of children separated from their families*. Dartmouth, Aldershot.

Churchill, S.R. (1979) *No Child is Unadoptable*. Sage, Beverley Hills.

Curtis Committee (1946) *Report of the Care of Children Committee*. Cmd 6922, HMSO, London.

Department of Health (1985) *Social Work Decisions in Child Care*. HMSO, London.

Department of Health (1989) *Principles and Practice in Regulations and Guidance*. HMSO, London.

Department of Health (1991) *Patterns and Outcomes in Child Placement*. HMSO, London.

Department of Health (1993) *Adoption: The Future*. HMSO, London.

Department of Health and Social Security (1976) *Foster Care: A Guide to Practice*. HMSO, London.

Fahlberg, V. (1988) *Fitting the Pieces Together*. BAAF, London.

Farmer, E. and Parker, R.A. (1991) *Trials and Tribulations*. HMSO, London.

Fisher, M., Marsh, P., Phillips, D. & Sainsbury, E. (1986) *In and Out of Care: The Experiences of Children, Parents and Social Workers*. Batsford/BAAF, London.

Fitzgerald, J. (1983) *Understanding Disruption*. BAAF, London.

Fletcher, B. (1993) *What's in a name?* (written for the National Consumer Council and the Who Cares? Trust). National Consumer Council, London.

Fratter, J. (1996) *Perspectives on Adoption with Contact*, BAAF, London.

Fratter, J., Rowe, J., Sapsford, D. & Thoburn, J. (1991) *Permanent Family Placement: A Decade of Experience*. BAAF, London.

George, V. (1970) *Foster Care*. Routledge and Kegan Paul, London.

Goldstein, J., Freud, A. & Solnit, A. (1973) *Beyond the Best Interest of the Child*. Free Press, New York.

Grandparents' Federation (1996) *What's in it for Grandparents?* Grandparents' Federation, Harlow.

Grandparents' Federation (1997) *Residence Order Allowance Survey*. Grandparents' Federation, Harlow.

Gray, P.G. & Parr, E. (1957) *Children in Care and the Recruitment of Foster Parents*. Environment Social Survey.

Hazel, N. (1981) *A Bridge to Independence*. Blackwell Science, Oxford.

Home Office (1955) *The Boarding Out of Children Regulations and Explanatory Memorandum*. HMSO, London.

HMSO (1984) House of Commons Social Services Committee (The Short Committee) *Report on Children in Care*. HMSO, London.

Heywood, J. (1959) *Children in Care*. Routledge and Kegan Paul, London.

Hill, M., Lambert, L. & Triseliotis, J. (1989) *Achieving Adoption with Love and Money*. National Children's Bureau, London.

Holman, R. (1975) The place of fostering in social work. *British Journal of Social Work* 5 (1), 3–29.

Howe, D. (1995) *Attachment Theory for Social Work Practice*. Macmillan, Basingstoke.

Howe, D. (1996) *Attachment and Loss in Child and Family Social Work*. Avebury, Aldershot.

Howe, D. (1997) *Patterns of Adoption: nature, nurture and psychosocial development*. Blackwell Science, Oxford.

Howe, D. & Hinings, D. (1989) *The Post Adoption Centre: The first three years*. UEA, Norwich.

Hunt, J., McLeod, A., Freeman, P. & Thomas, C. (forthcoming) *Statutory Intervention in Children's Lives*. HMSO, London.

Hussell, C. & Monaghan, B. (1982) Child care planning in Lambeth. *Adoption and Fostering* **6** (2), 21–25.

Jewett, C.L. (1978) *Adopting the Older Child*. The Harvard Common Press, Harvard.

Jordan, B. (1981) Prevention. *Adoption and Fostering* **5** (3), 20–22.

Kirk, D. (1964) *Shared Fate: A theory of adoption and mental health*. Free Press, New York.

Lindley, B. (1998) *Secrets or Links*. Family Rights Group, London.

Logan, J. (1996) *Post-adoption Arrangements for Openness and Contact*. University of Manchester, Department of Social Policy and Social Work, Manchester.

Mason, K. & Selman, P. (1997) Birth parents: experiences of contested adoption. *Adoption and Fostering* **21** (1), 21–28.

Masson, J., Harrison, C. & Pavlovic, A. (1997) *Working with Children of 'Lost' Parents*. Rowntree, York.

Millham, S., Bullock, R., Hosie, K. & Haak, M. (1986) *Lost in Care: the family contacts of children in care*. Gower, Aldershot.

Millham, S., Bullock, R., Hosie, K. & Little, M. (1989) *Access Disputes in Child-care*. Gower, Aldershot.

Murch, M., Lowe, N., Beckford, V., Borkowski, M. & Thomas, C. (forthcoming) *A Study of the Adoption Process*. University of Cardiff, Cardiff.

National Foster Care Association (1994) *Choosing to Foster*. NFCA, London.

Packman, J. (1975) *The Child's Generation*. Blackwell Science, Oxford.

Packman, J., Randall, J. & Jacques, N. (1986) *Who Needs Care? Social Work Decisions About Children*. Blackwell Science, Oxford.

Pugh, E. (1968) *Social Work in Child Care*. Routledge and Kegan Paul, London.

Raynor, L. (1980) *The Adopted Child Comes of Age*. Allen and Unwin, London.

Robinson, C. (1987) Key issues for social workers placing children for family based respite care. *British Journal of Social Work* **17** (3), 25–84.

Rowe, J. (1977) Fostering in the seventies. *Adoption and Fostering* **1** (4), 15–20.

Rowe, J. (1983) *Fostering in the Eighties*. BAAF, London.

Rowe, J. & Lambert, L. (1973) *Children Who Wait*. Association of British Adoption and Fostering Agencies, London.

Rowe, J., Cain, H., Hundleby, M. & Keane, A. (1984) *Long-term Foster Care*. Batsford, London.

Rowe, J., Hundleby, M. & Garnett, L. (1989) *Child Care Now – A survey of placement patterns*. BAAF, London.

Rushton, A. & Minnis, H. (1997) Annotation: Transracial family placements. *Journal of Child Psychology and Psychiatry* **38** (2) 147–59.

Rutter, M. (1972) *Maternal Deprivation Reassessed*. Penguin, Harmondsworth.

Sellick, C. (1992) *Supporting Short-term Foster Carers*. Avebury, Aldershot.

Sellick, C. (1996) Short-term foster care. In *Child Welfare Services: Develop-*

ments in Law, Policy, Practice and Research (eds M. Hill & J. Aldgate). Jessica Kingsley Publications, London.

Sellick, C. & Thoburn, J. (1996) *What Works in Family Placement?* Barnardos, Barkingside.

Selman, P. & White, J. (1994) Mediation and the role of 'accredited bodies' in intercountry adoption. *Adoption and Fostering* 18 (2), 7–13.

Shaw, M. & Hipgrave, T. (1983) *Specialist Fostering*. Batsford, London.

Shaw, M. & Hipgrave, T. (1989) Specialist fostering 1988: a research report. *Adoption and Fostering* 13 (3), 17–21.

Stalker, K. (1990) *Share the Care: an evaluation of a family based respite care service*. Jessica Kingsley Publications, London.

Stein, M. & Carey, K. (1986) *Leaving Care*. Basil Blackwell, Oxford.

Stevenson, O. (1963) The understanding caseworker. *New Society* August 1, 84–96.

Stevenson, O. (1965) *Someone Else's Child*. Routledge and Kegan Paul, London.

Stevenson, O. (1980) Family problems and patterns in the 1980s. *Adoption and Fostering* 4 (2), 20–24.

Stevenson, O. (1998) *Neglected Children: Issues and Dilemmas*. Blackwell Science, Oxford.

Social Services Inspectorate (1995) *Residence Orders Study. A study of the experiences of local authorities of public law residence orders*. Department of Health, London.

Social Services Inspectorate (1996, 1997) *For Children's Sake: An inspection of Local Authority post-placement and post-adoption*, Vols 1 and 2. Department of Health, London.

Stone, J. (1995) *Making Positive Moves: Developing Short-term Fostering Services*. BAAF, London.

Stroud, J. (1960) *The Shorn Lamb*. Longman, London.

Thoburn, J. (1980) *Captive Clients*. Routledge, London.

Thoburn, J. (1990) *Success and Failure in Permanent Family Placement*. Gower/Avebury, Aldershot.

Thoburn, J. (1994) *Child Placement: Principles and Practice*. Arena, Aldershot.

Thoburn, J. (1995) Out of home care for the abused or neglected child: research, planning and practice. In *Child Abuse: A Reader for Practitoners* (eds A. James & K. Wilson). Ballière Tindall, London.

Thoburn, J. (1996) Psychological parenting and child placement. In *Attachment and Loss in Child and Family Social Work* (ed. D. Howe). Avebury, Aldershot.

Thoburn, J., Murcoch, A. & O'Brien, A. (1986) *Permanence in Child Care*. Basil Blackwell, Oxford.

Thoburn, J., Norford, C. & Rashid, S. (1997) *Permanent family placement for children of minority ethnic origin: A report to the Department of Health*. University of East Anglia, Norwich.

Tod, R.J.N. (ed.) (1968) *Children in Care*. Longman, London.

Tod, R.J.N. (ed.) (1971) *Social Work in Adoption*. Longman, London.

Trasler, G. (1960) *In Place of Parents*. Routledge and Kegan Paul, London.

Triseliotis, J., Sellick, C. & Short, R. (1995) *Foster Care: Theory and Practice*. Batsford, London.

Triseliotis, J., Shireman, J. & Hundleby, M. (1997) *Adoption Theory, Policy and Practice*. Cassell, London.

Tunnard, J. & Thoburn, J. (1997) *The Grandparents' Supporters Project: An Independent Evaluation*. University of East Anglia/Grandparents' Federation, Norwich.

Utting, W. (1997) *People Like Us: The Report of the review of the safeguards for children living away from home*. HMSO, London.

Vernon, J. & Fruin, D. (1986) *In Care: A Study of Social Work Decision-Making*. National Children's Bureau, London.

Ward, H. (1996) *Looking after Children: Research into Practice*. HMSO, London.

Waterhouse, S. (1992) How foster carers view contact. *Adoption and Fostering* **16** (2), 42–47.

Waterhouse, S. (1996) *The Organisation of Fostering Services: An Investigation of the Structural Arrangements for the Delivery of Fostering Services by Local Authorities in England*. HMSO, London.

Waterhouse, S. (1997) *The Organising of Fostering Services*. NFCA, London.

Winnicott, C. (1994) *Casework in the Child Care Services*. Codicote Press, Hitchin.

Winnicott, D.W. (1965) *The Family and Individual Development*. Tavistock, London.

Chapter 8

The Children Act 1948: residential care

Roger Bullock

Introduction

Residential care has an ambivalent place in the Children Act 1948. Although the quality of care in much of the existing provision had excited stricture, the focus of the new legislation was more on establishing a comprehensive service for the care of children deprived of a normal home life than on scrutinising a particular sector.

There were mixed feelings about residential care, particularly as the enforced foster care of Second World War evacuees had, in some ways, worked well. The Public Assistance workhouse institutions clearly alarmed members of the influential Curtis Committee (1946) while the approved schools, which in subsequent years were to be rocked by a series of scandals, were seen as 'well-conducted in a humane and experimental spirit' (para. 499). The clear preference in the 1948 Act was to foster (or board out) children who could not live at home and, although residential care was viewed as an important part of child care provision, its role was perceived as residual.

However, the 1948 Act devoted several sections to residential care. Local authorities were given a duty to provide, equip and maintain homes for the accommodation of children in their care (s.15.1) and the Secretary of State could make regulations concerning medical care, religious upbringing, the use and design of buildings, the appointment of officers in charge and the length of time that children might spend in reception centres. Hostels were also to be made available for older teenagers and some after-care was envisaged.

In addition to this 'in-house' provision, much of the 1948 Act sought to regulate the plethora of voluntary homes which then existed. These posed a problem for the Government as there were literally hundreds of them, each of varying size and quality. Some were run by powerful charities, such as Barnardos, an organisation that won the Curtis Committee's approval, but others were the responsibility of small associations whose performance was castigated. Their children were, in the view of Lady Allen of Hurtwood (Allen, 1944), overwhelmed by precisely the sort of stigma that the Children Act of 1948 sought to abolish. In 1945, 33 000 children were being cared for by voluntary bodies although not all of them were placed residentially. The Act offered a compromise by which registration and inspection were seen as sufficient to ensure good standards without reproach or undermining the work of the better homes.

The Curtis Committee and Children Act legislators viewed residential care as significant rather than central to their thinking. The main emphasis in the legislation, as Stevenson (Chapter 5) discusses, was the creation of a unified administrative structure, with regulatory powers, for children deprived of an ordinary home life. By the standards of today, there were glaring omissions. For example, there was no consideration of the merits of local authorities assuming parental rights, of having separate institutions for young offenders, or of the need to consider the child's wishes. Also, there was little consideration of prevention, although the legislation emphasised the need to avoid reception into care wherever possible, a provision which quickly assumed importance in the work of child care officers.

The social and political context with regard to residential care in 1948

It is well-known that several events were cogent in the framing of legislation. The wartime evacuation of children from cities and coastal areas to safe rural locations, the death of Dennis O'Neill from physical abuse suffered in a farmhouse 90 miles from home, the campaign led by Lady Allen and her famous letter to *The Times* of 15 July 1944 (Allen, 1944), the disturbing deficiencies highlighted in the Curtis Committee report and the desire of the new Labour Government to develop a comprehensive welfare state, were all clearly important in their own way. It is easy to interpret these events as a causal chain in which one thing led to another but Parker (1983) urges caution about simple explanations. The Curtis Committee, for example, was set up before the O'Neill tragedy, not in response to it; the Poor Law was already seen as inadequate to deal with the widespread homelessness that was expected to follow the end of the Second World War, not just as an inappropriate administration for the care of children. In their own ways, each of these events fuelled a desire for reform, leading to the widespread consensus and the auspicious political context that is necessary for major legislative change (Hall *et al.*, 1975).

Cretney, in his unpublished paper *The State as Parent: The Children Act 1948 in Retrospect*, suggests four major influences on the Act, one of which concerns residential care. First was the problem of homeless evacuees. Following the outbreak of war, over a million children were moved to the countryside. This was organised by transporting whole school groups to new locations but the placement of individual children was still very much a question of carers being told to go to the railway station and 'pick one'. This, in addition to separation and movement to a strange area, proved to be a traumatic event for some children and there are heart-rending accounts of the misery experienced by young-sters, such as the handicapped and physically unattractive children whom nobody chose. There was also concern, largely misplaced, that many children would not get back home as many houses had been destroyed and marriages dissolved.

The *History of the Second World War* (Titmuss, 1976) records the number of unsuccessful reunions as tiny but a whole generation knew the true heartaches of separations and damaged relationships. Never-theless, some benefits accrued from the exodus from the cities. Middle-class England was alerted to the poor physical condition and quality of life of many urban children thus creating a climate sympathetic to welfare reform. It also gave valuable experience to a group of eva-cuation officers who, once the war was over, moved into child care work and further illustrious careers. Lucy Faithfull ended her career as a social services advocate in the House of Lords; the seven-year-old Spencer Millham and his fellow pupils were greeted at Pontllanfraith station by a young welfare worker, George Thomas, who later became Speaker of the House of Commons.

Two forces for change, already alluded to, were: the need to replace the Poor Law, which in 1944 cared for 27 000 children, with a single well-qualified and sympathetic administration; and the activities of Lady Allen who led a relentless campaign, often using her personal friendships with top politicians to further her cause. She was particu-larly perplexed by the administrative confusion surrounding residential care and irritated by the lack of concern about children's health and education in government proposals of the time. She describes in her memoirs (Allen & Nicholson, 1975) how children from Poor Law institutions are always noticeable by their 'fat, flabby and listless appearance and by their heavy ill-fitting clothes and boots, so heavy that they could only shuffle along.'

The fourth influence stemmed specifically from worries about resi-dential care. In November 1944, John Watson, a well-respected juvenile court magistrate, criticised a London County Council remand home and in particular the placement of a seven-year-old girl with 43 adolescents whose criminal and sexual behaviour were causing con-cern. (In his book, *Which is the Justice?* (Watson, 1969), he described the home as 'a grim, soulless place where girls have little to occupy their time and had scarcely any outdoor exercise because of the danger of their scaling the walls and running away.') A report, *London County Council Remand Homes* (London County Council, 1945), soon fol-lowed Watson's attack, but this tended to criticise Watson for abusing his position rather than lambast the LCC for poor child care practice.

The raising of these issues by such a prominent person meant that a committee of inquiry, or something similar to it, was inevitable.

Several other factors have to be acknowledged in this attempt to understand the context in which in the 1948 Act was conceived and the place of residential care in this process. The backlash against fostering that some professionals had expected after the O'Neill death, never materialised, and residential care avoided universal condemnation, maintaining a firm place in the continuum of provision. However, improvements in practice proved difficult to achieve; for example, while the 1948 Act facilitated child care training, this was orientated to boarding-out officers rather than residential workers despite the fact that the latter were in short supply. The 'First World War spinsters', who had served residential care so well in the past, were beginning to retire. In addition, until the 1950s there was a serious shortage of building materials and the few resources that were available went into the housing effort. Much residential stock had been neglected and damaged in the 1940s – indeed many homes and schools had been occupied for military purposes – and opportunities for refurbishment and new building were severely limited. Residential care was held back somewhat as the newly-established Children's Departments began their work and many smaller voluntary establishments went to the wall. Expansion came later in more prosperous times.

In addition to the restrictions imposed by post-war austerity, there was a growing intellectual concern about the effects of long stays in residential institutions. These criticisms were to flourish in the early 1960s after Goffman (1961) published *Asylums*, Vaizey (1959) wrote *Scenes from Institutional Life*, and Barton (1959) defined the syndrome of institutional neurosis; but disquiet was already being expressed by 1945. No research was commissioned for the Curtis inquiry and empirical evidence was patchy even though the investigating team did visit 451 residential establishments. However, the insights of clinicians such as Bowlby, Isaacs, Winnicott and Britton were influential and it was soon clear to everyone that the effects of long stays in poor quality homes could be devastating for children. Indeed, the description in the Curtis Report (Curtis Committee, 1946: para. 144) of a mentally defective eight-year-old girl living in the children's ward of a work-house remains one of the most horrific accounts in all child care literature, although sadly it was to be almost equalled by Oswin's (1978) descriptions of hospitals for severely handicapped children in the 1970s, indicating how slow change was in some service sectors.

Psychiatrists, too, noted the predominance of affectionless person-alities, attention-seeking and touch-hungry behaviour among the residentially placed children whom they treated, raising serious doubts about the suitability of such environments for children's healthy psychosocial development. It was for these reasons that the 1948 Act's embrace of residential care can at best be described as lukewarm and that its implementation was followed by widespread closures of residential nurseries for very young children. In addition, the disruption and separation of wartime were still keenly remembered; lonely barracks, lost letters and the power of distant decision-makers were all so familiar, and resented, that a change of attitude towards those in state care was inevitable.

This then was the context in which residential care was placed. The next section examines the different traditions and approaches which informed child care services and the ways in which they developed in the years that followed. The perspective of the institutional solution, and the three major traditions which underpinned it, will be described.

Institutional solutions

A distinguishing feature of residential institutions is their varied use in different countries. It is noticeable how some countries have a much greater institutional heritage than others. England, for example, has more residential establishments than Wales and Scotland, while some countries appear never to have adopted institutional responses to social or educational problems. Any generalisation is dangerous but it seems that Catholic and Communist countries have traditionally preferred residential care to fostering and adoption for deprived young people. Pressing socialisation functions might also explain the high use of residential education in countries such as England and Israel. The point is not to prove a cultural or historical thesis but to consider why residence is seen as a solution to child care problems at certain times and not others. Why, for example, was there such a boom in all sorts of residential provision in mid-Victorian England? Is it related to the roles people are expected to fulfil in society, to available wealth or patronage, to religious or political fervour, to perceived improvements in the quality of life within institutional walls, or to the strength of the family *vis-à-vis* the State? Probably the answer is a mixture that varies for different groups of children as well as for social classes, cultures and countries.

Lambert *et al.* (1975) noted that in England there is selective use in that residential experiences are confined to children of the very rich or the very poor. The former go to boarding schools at least in part because of their educational excellence and their supposed character-forming benefits, while the latter are placed by the State residentially for their own good, usually against their and their parents' wishes.

This 'residential' solution, to borrow Davis's (1981) term, certainly applied to much child care policy that preceded the 1948 Act but, somewhat surprisingly, was neither reinforced nor challenged by the new legislation. Although that Act can be considered radical in its condemnation of Poor Law institutional approaches, in its desire to raise standards and its challenge to the rescue philosophy of child care, it was fundamentally conservative in that it did not question the ability of the State to parent, nor the policy of voluntary societies which continued through emigration to the colonies to sever children's parental links. Residential services kept their place as a legitimate child care service but no indication was given about whom they should serve, how big the sector should be, what staff training was needed and what sorts of relationships separated children should enjoy with their families. Although the greater flexibility in the use and style of residential care introduced 40 years later, by the Children Act 1989, was probably laid down in 1948, the interim has seen little direction in the services provided. Services have been characterised by limited appreciation of the relationship between residential care and other provision, some unnecessary expansion and in recent years considerable contraction in the numbers sheltered. It has taken a long time for the ideology of the 'institutional solution', and the endless concern with the mechanics of running them, to decline (Jones & Fowles, 1984).

In reviewing changes in residential care, it is important to view developments in the context of social attitudes to residential living generally. Since the 1960s, there has been a noticeable decline in all sorts of residential life; students prefer their own flats to halls of residence, soldiers and sailors rush home at weekends, monasteries are short of novices and residential 'living in' is decreasingly attractive to staff. It would be misleading to impute changes in residential child care solely to professional policy and practice as there are wider forces at work.

These points make it easier to avoid the trap of imposing 1997 ideas on post-war thinking. It is hard today to understand why the Curtis Committee was not more shocked by what they saw in the 1940s. For example, corporal punishment in approved schools was dealt with uncritically and perfunctorily, yet its misuse led to a criticism of the system in 1968. Similarly, many institutional practices that horrify us today may have seemed acceptable at the time. In one of her articles in the *News of the World*, Lady Allen described a large voluntary association which 'admitted only the illegitimate, allowed no parental contact, and rebaptised and renamed the children'. At one of the country's leading preparatory schools, there were five types of caning: a whip, a whop, a whip-whop, a sizzler, and an arse blaster, all devised and administered by a clergyman headmaster with a first-class degree.

These practices might seem incomprehensible in the present climate of abuse inquiries, evidence-based practice and respect for users' rights, but this reflects contemporary frames of reference. It has to be remembered just how poor many families were before the rehousing programme and economic boom of the 1960s. Children often shared beds, so a lack of privacy was not an issue for them; similarly, the policy of severing children's family links was seen as a 'fresh start', designed to aid their escape to a better world. The ever-present threat of infection and malnutrition necessitated institutional rituals of ablutions, intimate physical examinations and obsession about diet. Religious instruction was also perceived as a key component of children's welfare in a way which may surprise us today.

What types of residential accommodation were important in 1948?

Existing provision at the time of the 1948 Act

It is difficult to know just how much residential provision existed in 1948 and who lived and worked in it. The large number of voluntary homes had confounded the Curtis Committee and it was not until 1971 that a reliable census of all residential placements was undertaken. This census showed (Moss, 1975) that each day some 235 850 children aged 0–19 sat down to an institutional breakfast. The majority (60%) were in boarding schools with some 14% in child care accommodation, 4% in approved schools and remand homes, 9% in special schools for the handicapped, 6% in provision for mental handicap or mental illness, 7% in hospital and 1% in Borstal or prison. Little was known about the detail in each category; indeed, the first study of the regimes of children's homes and the characteristics of the resident children did not appear until 1985 (Berridge, 1985) and there still has been no robust follow-up study of leavers from special schools with the exception of that undertaken at the Caldecott Community (Little & Kelly, 1995).

In the boarding school sector, knowledge was equally sparse and Lambert (1965) found all sorts of establishments, such as state boarding schools, that had developed from earlier 'camp' and 'delicate' schools often located miles away from the education authorities that ran them. There were schools for the sons and daughters of naval ratings, distressed gentlefolk, and so on. Some of these have survived but most disappeared with the comprehensive reorganisation of state education in the 1960s and 1970s. Similar continuities could be found in the child care field. For example, the Brixham Boys' Home for the orphans of seafarers had its own band that marched through the town on church parade each Sunday until well into the 1980s.

Thus, the Children Act 1948 was enacted in a context of varied residential provision crossing many administrative boundaries. It did little to challenge the status quo and, as has been explained, saw registration and inspection as the answer to quality control. The challenge to residential care came more from the social work profession established by the 1948 Act and the ideas it came to espouse. Before examining these changes and the reasons for them, it is helpful to review the intellectual traditions that underpinned contemporary provision and practice.

Child care establishments

The Curtis Committee vividly portrayed some of the residential provision in which children lived and, as has been said, the picture was very varied. The growth of family group homes and reception centres that followed the Act was a big improvement on what had existed before. In the family group homes a married couple lived with a small group of children and acted as responsible parents. The Curtis Committee report saw the resulting affection and personal interest, stability, opportunity to make the best of abilities and aptitudes, and participation in a common life as the key benefits for children. Another set of establishments was to specialise in reception and assessment, while others offered nursery provision for babies and infants although, as has been explained, numbers cared for in these places quickly declined from 5000 in 1954 to 2500 in 1970. A weakness in the Curtis recommendations was the low standard of training set for residential staff compared with that envisaged for boarding-out officers. While graduates were sought for the latter posts, 'non-technical instruction in child development and elementary lectures in social conditions and social services' were deemed sufficient for the former, a status difference that has bedevilled the service ever since.

There was no doubt that the development of these new style homes marked a new era (Packman, 1975). However, establishing a system of residential care that avoided the large impersonal 'institutional' style was not always easy. Costs, difficulties in recruiting suitable staff, and the incubus of existing physical plant, all militated against change; nevertheless, the growth of professional knowledge based on sound child care principles eventually won through. Thus, Packman concludes optimistically that the transformation of residential care was concerned with much more than the externals of smaller buildings, better equipment, pastel paint and pictures, however limited it might have appeared at the time.

Approved schools and remand homes

As indicated previously, approved schools and remand homes were untouched by the 1948 Act and, given the impetus of a treatment philosophy and generous Home Office funding, expanded throughout the 1950s. Most approved schools were relatively large (70–100 pupils) and were run by voluntary or charity organisations. They were single sex and often located in remote rural areas. Regimes were firm and brisk and the curriculum was centred on classroom work and trade training; hence many staff were teachers or, in the intermediate and senior schools, tradesmen. In 1948, most were 'block' establishments in that pupils did everything together but smaller house units were encouraged in the 1950s. Young people were isolated from home and community; only 18 days home leave were allowed; absconding was dealt with severely, including prosecution for those who harboured them; and boys were set a battery of tests at classifying centres to see which regime would suit them best.

In this context, a healthy body of research, much of it encouraged by the Home Office, meant that more was known about this sector of child care than any other. There were numerous comparisons of delinquents with control groups outside, and attempts to assess the effects of different regimes. The only randomised control allocation to contrasting regimes ever undertaken in residential child care was conducted in an approved school (Cornish & Clarke, 1975). The problem was that the messages from this research were not particularly encouraging. Reoffending rates increased relentlessly, regimes seemed to make little difference to outcomes, and studies of children's backgrounds showed that many young offenders were also very deprived. It was not surprising that child care thinking became increasingly unsympathetic to the approved school methods and supported a more general welfare approach for all young people, whether 'delinquent' or 'deprived' (Millham *et al.*, 1975). An attempt was made to set a new standard with the government publication *Care and Treatment in a Planned Environment* (Advisory Council on Child Care, 1970) and the reorganisation of three show schools by the Home Office Development Group, but further administrative change was necessary as the schools had become increasingly marginalised. In 1974, they were incorporated into general social services' provision for all children in need, after which most of them were closed or radically altered.

Provision for children with special needs

Progress in special education was much less than in other areas of residential care. In a study published in 1971, 23 years after the 1948 Act, Tizard (1975) concluded:

> 'most severely retarded children live in conditions which compare very unfavourably with those which govern the lives of ordinary children brought up away from parents in long-stay residential nurseries and children's homes.'

His study with King & Raynes (King *et al.*, 1973) revealed a varied picture but with very poor standards at the lower end. The key variable was the manner of child management. In long-stay hospitals it tended to be rigid and inflexible, with self-expression and privacy discouraged and staff interactions with children formal. In children's homes and mental subnormality hostels, regimes were far more child-focused. Individuality was respected, children were given choice, interactions were friendly, and privacy and possessions were encouraged. Staff roles and staff performance accounted for most of the variation, the attitude of the unit head and the extent of his or her child care training being especially important.

From this discussion, it can be seen that the impact of the 1948 Act on residential child care was significant but that it was more marked and more rapid in some areas than others. As the child care profession grew stronger, the clearer became the underlying principles, reaching their full flower much later on, in the legislation of 1989. The next section discusses some of the other residential traditions, those outside child care, in order to chart the full context in which the 1948 Act was conceived and enacted.

Public schools

At first sight, the English public schools seem to have little relevance to the Children Act 1948; however, they are important for two reasons. First, they provided the most well-developed model of boarding education, features of which were aped by many less prestigious establishments. Second, they had been the educational experience of most senior civil servants and administrators and thus provided them with a blueprint, a model for residential care. Naturally, these sentiments were rarely echoed by social workers, not just for ideological reasons but because the approach of those former pupils was viewed as irrelevant to the needs of deprived children. As one children's officer commented at the 1966 officers' annual conference, 'few children in care have the stamina to survive such an experience'.

Although public schools are now associated with wealthy families, many had begun as charities and had admitted working class boys. Spinley (1953), in a fascinating but now forgotten study, found that fee-paying and charity pupils sometimes had in common high levels of emotional deprivation. Lambert (1969) described certain features of the public school ethos which can be seen to have influenced attitudes towards residential care. There was an assumption that a 'total' environment which met all of a child's needs was beneficial in that it freed the child from the distracting influences of home and community. Isolation also produced high dependency on the institution which was a potent influence on values and behaviour. In organisational terms, the division of large establishments into smaller groups, the allocation of pastoral roles to key staff, the opportunity to achieve status and esteem in a number of areas, not just the academic, and the security offered by clear structures seemed to many observers just what deprived youngsters needed. In addition, many children's idealised expectations of residential care came from reading Billy Bunter and Stalky & Co., books now as extinct as the dodo.

Again, it is important to appreciate the values of the time and the fact that most adults had been in the armed services during the war and were all too familiar with institutional living. The influence of public school methods on child care practice was modest but could be observed in the changes introduced into approved schools, the special boarding schools and larger establishments, such as remand homes, in the two decades following the Act. Later on, the Public Schools Commission of 1968 seriously considered allocating a proportion of places in public boarding schools to children in need but by this time the idea was virtually redundant and few children's officers could see much benefit in this.

The major public schools continue to thrive but have changed radically in the last few years. Even though they are far more benevolent and sensitive to children's needs than before, they have little influence on current child care thinking. There has been considerable contraction in numbers of children boarding and some less prestigious establishments have closed, especially those at junior level, in preparatory schools, and those educating girls. However, boarding schools still shelter many children with serious problems and do much to meet middle-class need. Little is known about this contribution but it is probably much greater than realised.

Progressive schools

A small set of boarding schools stood apart from mainstream education. These were the self-styled progressive schools which grew up in the 1930s and 1940s, gathered together in a loose confederation. Their approach was fashioned to contrast with the traditional public school and attracted interest and sponsorship from many avant-garde intellectuals of the time. Their message was highly relevant to child care thinking, not just in residential education and schools, but by its child-centred approach, its tolerance and acceptance.

Children were to be treated as individuals, the environment was to be comfortable and the regime benign. As children develop at different rates, the curriculum should be designed to follow them, not the reverse. Coeducation was to be real, not a frigid charade, both at child and staff levels, manifest in living arrangements, staff appointments, pastoral roles and decision-making. Hierarchies were to be avoided, as was formality in relationships, dogmatic religious education and compulsory games. Children were given powers to make decisions, even on matters such as whether to go to classes and whether community meetings should take precedence over everything else. Sexual and emotional feelings were to be discussed openly and displayed, even paraded, without embarrassment.

Sadly, nearly all of these schools struggled financially. They lacked endowment and were at the mercy of fashion. Some achieved a reputation for crankiness, 'full of vegetarian pacifists' as one eminent bishop retorted, in a phrase guaranteed to alienate a generation that had endured meat rationing and fought a war. Nevertheless, the progressive movement was led by some impressive charismatics; even Bertrand Russell tried his hand. Figures such as Neill (Summerhill) and Curry (Dartington Hall) seemed to offer a genuine alternative to public school 'thuggery and buggery' and a quite different philosophy from 'a healthy mind in a healthy body'.

Each of the progressive schools was different in its own way and generalisation is difficult (Ash, 1969; Bridgeland, 1971). However, there did seem to be a model for child care to follow, even though some schools, it has to be said, were more interested in children disturbed by the artistic temperaments of their well-heeled liberal parents rather than in the needs of the 'great unwashed'. This twentieth century application of Rousseau's *Émile* had some intellectual support, from education-alists abroad, such as Homer Lane and Bettelheim in the USA, and psychiatrists at home, such as Winnicott and Bowlby, both of whom had won the nation's respect for their work on the wartime evacuees. However, there was little evidence that 'progressive' education pro-duced more adjusted or creative people (Hudson, 1969), indeed some research suggested that children failed to reach either their academic or their social potential (Punch, 1977). Nevertheless, the approach seemed right and its influence soon became apparent in some special schools and therapeutic communities. As a result, the early progressives were joined by people such as Lyward, Lenhoff, Rendell, Barnes, Balbernie and Rose, who in their own way sought to provide a therapeutic resi-dential refuge for troubled and troublesome children (Wills, 1971; Little & Kelly, 1995; Rose, 1997).

The faults of these new establishments were depressingly familiar; they could still be considered 'total' institutions because of their over-whelming belief systems. Behaviour and belief were imposed on each other by all the members of the community, not just those with formal power. But the child-centred approach, the respect for individuals, the cultivated ambience, the open emotional warmth and the partisan stance taken by staff on behalf of children were particularly attractive to the 'treatment' approach that was being developed by the emerging child guidance movement. Particularly important were ideas that childhood and adolescence were states to be enjoyed in their own right and were not to be viewed as a preparation for adult roles. Often the coeducational style adopted was enlightened.

In their detail, these residential approaches do not differ much from the practice encouraged in the Volume Four Guidance and Regulations on residential care that accompany the Children Act 1989. While the majority of schools tried hard with increasingly difficult children, some failed to protect them; indeed, a few special schools have been at the centre of recent serious abuse revelations. Ironically enough, while the special school system flourished, the progressive schools on which they were modelled ran into difficulties. Many closed as their founders retired, others became less fashionable and economically vulnerable, particularly as state education embraced progressive ideas about wider curricula, close staff–pupil relationships and acceptance of adolescent roles and sexual behaviour. A few even survived by becoming more respectable and orthodox.

The role and context of residential care since 1948

Although residential care has always been viewed as an important part of the services for children in need, its uses have changed considerably since the 1948 legislation. The most notable feature is a marked decline. The numbers of young people under the age of 18 living in residential establishments at any one time for welfare, criminal or special education reasons fell in England and Wales by 47% in the 20 years between 1971 and 1991, the dates of two accurate surveys by Moss (1975) and Gooch (1996). The figure is now less than 30 000. The drop in annual throughput of children, however, may be less as fewer young people enter residential care before the age of 11, hence the chances of a long stay are much reduced. Indeed, a sizeable proportion of adolescents who are looked after away from home are still likely to have a residential experience. But even here, there have been practice changes over the last decade and the present figure is considerably less than the 80% found 15 years ago for those admitted to care over the age of ten (Millham *et al.*, 1986); it is probably nearer 60% (Bullock *et al.*, 1998).

The continuing importance of residential care for adolescents is demonstrated by two examples. Cliffe & Berridge (1992) showed that those local authorities that have stopped providing children's residential care, such as Solihull and Warwickshire, have found that for a proportion of adolescents (some 10–15%) there is no viable alternative to residential placement. Similarly, an analysis of referrals to several Social Services Departments using the planning tool *Matching Needs and Services* (Dartington Social Research Unit, 1995), identified a small number of children whose needs were best met by residential care, although not always of the type available. However, despite this continuing demand, further decline seems likely as discriminating purchasers seek value for money and cheaper alternatives. What are the reasons for this decline? Several factors are important, the overwhelming one of which is a declining belief.

The decline of belief in residential care

Several concerns, shortly to be discussed, swiftly challenged the heady beliefs in the therapeutic qualities of residential care prevalent in the immediate post-war decade. Benefits were difficult to demonstrate and today there is a more jaundiced view of the possibilities of residential interventions than that envisaged in the *Care and Treatment in a Planned Environment* blueprint of 1970 (Advisory Council on Child Care, 1970). Other factors, such as a growing awareness of the intractability of some children's problems, respect for consumers' rights, diminished public funding and disappointing research results have all fuelled this scepticism.

In addition to these rather underlying factors, the image of residential care has been severely dented by the revelations of child abuse inquiries. Scandals in residential settings are not new and, throughout the nineteenth century Parliament endlessly debated riots, suspicious deaths and acts of violence in residential institutions. Physical assault, neglect and occasional sexual abuse seem to have been almost an expectation of residential life. The establishment of Children's Departments in 1948 raised standards in children's homes but the violent undercurrent survived in some larger establishments, such as approved schools, until the 1970s when tolerance decreased and suspicions of abuse were confirmed by independent scrutiny. Several sexual abuse scandals not only became public but were also followed by judicial inquiries, closures and criminal prosecutions. The shock produced by these investigations resulted not just from the sordid detail but also the fact that abuse seemed to occur in all kinds of establishment, even some small children's homes, and that it was often accompanied by repressive regimes which discouraged innocent observers, let alone victims, from speaking out. Moreover, the abuse was often found to be perpetrated by individuals who moved round the child care system and were known to one other. Two recent reports, *Choosing with Care* (DoH, 1992) and *People Like Us* (Department of Health, 1997) have made recommendations to ensure children's safety more effectively.

But perhaps the most problematic changes have been the weakening of the traditional links between residential care and occupational outlets and the challenges to the cultural values that supported these disposals. The idea of preparing young people for employment and creating the bridges necessary to facilitate their transitions to independence was for centuries a common aspect of residential care and helped it work smoothly; it was not until the 1970s that widespread youth unemployment and cultural diversity among residents necessitated a complete rethink of aims and methods.

This tension is further illustrated by the debate about residential treatment and its alternatives during the 1960s. The term 'treatment' was favoured by those who adopted a psychological position and viewed problem behaviours as springing from adverse childhood experience, faulty learning or trauma. This view encouraged a search for causes, evidence-based treatments and the holy grail of the significant causal variable. Social workers, however, were increasingly attracted to a sociological perspective that emphasised the fact that people with problems were usually orthodox in most other respects and that most deviance was contextual. These beliefs stressed sub-cultures, blocked aspirations, identity and career and condemned the labelling and isolation associated with residential approaches – experiences that were seen as exacerbating young people's already difficult situations and deviant identities.

As a result of these and other pressures arising from increasing costs and administrative changes during the 1970s, the approved schools closed and similar run-downs occurred in large mental hospitals and children's homes. For the first time, viable alternatives to residential care seemed possible for the majority of children. This change was aided by the creation of local authority Social Services Departments in 1971 which brought together aspects of juvenile justice, mental health and social services under a single administration, so facilitating flexibility and planning.

Nevertheless, it was becoming increasingly clear that for a small number of difficult young people, sophisticated treatment was not only necessary but could best be delivered residentially. As a result, specialist residential 'treatment' approaches were extended for a minority of those in need. There was a growth in secure accommodation (none of the approved schools had been secure and some Borstals had been open) and new therapeutic communities were founded at places such as Peper Harow and the Cotswold Community, both former approved schools. Initiatives based on behaviourist theories were developed at Aycliffe and Chelfham Mill. The most ambitious development of all was the setting up of two Youth Treatment Centres at St Charles and Glenthorne in the late 1960s and the stated intention (never implemented) to open three more.

While this institutional diversity was welcomed by professionals seeking placement options, it did little to mollify critics of the 'treatment' approach. Welfare economists questioned the evidence to justify the considerable expenditure these new developments required. Therapists argued about what precisely constituted treatment; for example, did simply keeping an adolescent safe qualify? Social workers expressed concern that the secondary effects of residence, such as withering links with home and local community, could aggravate young people's difficulties, while lawyers agonised over whether treatment could be enforced on grounds of welfare. The new interest in organisational management highlighted the tendency for residential institutions to be readily filled, and questioned whether services were provision-led rather than 'needs'-led. Treatment was thus criticised by the 'left' and the 'right' of the political spectrum. Much of the policy since the mid-1970s, of diversion, opening up residential units and making life in them as normal as possible, reflects attempts to reconcile these differences in professional and political opinion.

How these changes have affected what happens in residential care

Caution must be taken when generalising about residential services. Any search for single-issue explanations of developments must account for the revival in usage in the 1970s as well as the decline of the 1980s. Neither should the fact that children in residential care undoubtedly have complex needs, be confused with myths that they are all delinquent or are all victims of sexual abuse. Nonetheless, at least a dozen separate recent trends within the residential sector as a whole can be identified. These are:

- the replacement of single-sex establishments by ones that are coeducational but which, in practice, are dominated by boys
- the increasing age of residents at entry
- more young people with health problems, behaviour disorders and disabilities
- greater racial and ethnic mix
- larger catchment areas which create problems for children's educational continuity and contact with home
- more provision by private agencies
- less specialisation by sector with a resulting mix of needs in each establishment
- assessment by need criteria rather than social role categories, such as disabled or special educational needs
- a more generalist service
- shorter stays
- rising cost
- more concerns about rights and child protection
- further reductions in the size of units and in the numbers accommodated.

Paradoxically, among children placed residentially there is now a larger proportion of children in secure accommodation or other specialist centres such as therapeutic communities.

Naturally, the factors that explain changes in the use of private boarding schools, schools for children with special educational needs and penal institutions are likely to be different from those that affect child care establishments but the common feature is that in all of these sectors viable alternatives have been created. Even in interventions with delinquent and disruptive adolescents, the emergence of a more coherent juvenile justice system has been of major importance, although there is still considerable reliance on residence as a last resort.

Despite the important functions served by residential care, the Children Act 1989 echoes previous attempts to shed the 'last resort' image of residential care and ensure that it is integral to children's services. It should be used as a 'positive choice' whenever needed and should be sufficiently attractive to young people for them to request it. The strengths of the best residential approaches have been identified (Bullock *et al.*, 1993) and it is encouraging that recent research studies of teenagers in community homes have found that many young people speak favourably about their experiences (Sinclair & Gibbs, 1998). Sadly, some residential care falls short of the ideal but, as recent studies show, some works well.

Of particular importance has been the preparedness of social workers to eschew a 'for' or 'against' view of residential care for one that perceives it in the wider context of the young person's needs and the services that are most appropriate. A package of services is usually needed to help difficult adolescents and, if separation is required, continuities in the young person's life should be cherished. It has become increasingly clear that the needs of young people and their families cannot be fragmented and an undue emphasis on one problem can lead to other aspects of the young person's needs being ignored. The philosophy underpinning the Children Act 1989, echoes many of the principles expounded 50 years earlier but ties them into a stronger framework and body of research evidence. It thus facilitates both the focused approach that seems to work best and the wider strategies for helping children and families that research suggests are needed.

When the Curtis Committee reported in 1946, its members would not have envisaged the growth of the child care services they called into being or the problems, such as child maltreatment, drug abuse, adolescent homelessness and alienation, that the services would have to tackle. Nevertheless, the principles behind the Children Act 1948, explored and extended in 1963, 1969 and 1989, have stood the test of time and served our children well.

References

Advisory Council on Child Care (1970) *Care and Treatment in a Planned Environment.* Advisory Council on Child Care, London.
Allen (Lady Allen of Hurtwood) (1944) *The Times*, 15 July.
Allen, M. & Nicholson, M. (1975) *Memoirs of an Uneducated Lady.* Thames and Hudson, London.
Ash, M. (1969) *Who are the Progressives Now?* Routledge and Kegan Paul, London.
Barton, R. (1959) *Institutional Neurosis.* Wright, London.
Berridge, D. (1985) *Children's Homes.* Blackwell Science, Oxford.
Berridge, D. & Brodie, I. (1997) *Children's Homes Revisited.* Jessica Kingsley, London.
Bridgeland, M. (1971) *Pioneer Work with Maladjusted Children: A study of the development of therapeutic education.* Staples Press, London.
Bullock, R., Little, M. & Millham, S. (1993) *Residential Care: The research reviewed.* HMSO, London.

Bullock, R., Gooch, D. & Little, M. (1998) *Children Going Home: The reunification of families*. Ashgate, Aldershot.
Cliffe, D. & Berridge, D. (1992) *Closing Children's Homes*. National Children's Bureau, London.
Cornish, D. & Clarke, R. (1975) *Residential Care and its Effects on Delinquency*. HMSO, London.
Curtis Committee (1946) *Report of the Care of Children Committee*. Cmd 6922, HMSO, London.
Dartington Social Research Unit (1995) *Matching Needs and Services: The audit of local authority provision for looked after children*. Dartington Social Research Unit, Dartington.
Davis, A. (1981) *The Residential Solution*. Tavistock, London.
Department of Health (1992) *Choosing with Care*. HMSO, London.
Department of Health (1997) *People Like Us: The Report of the Review of the Safeguards for Children Living Away from Home*. The Stationery Office, London.
Goffman, E. (1961) *Asylums*. Doubleday, New York.
Gooch, D. (1996) Home and away: the residential care, education and control of children in historical and political context. *Child and Family Social Work* I, 19–32.
Hall, P., Land, H., Parker, R. & Webb, A. (1975) *Change, Choice and Conflict in Social Policy*. Heinemann, London.
Hudson, L. (1969) Lieben und arbeiten – a case of cake and eat it. In *Who are the Progressives Now?* (ed. M. Ash), pp. 171–80. Routledge and Kegan Paul, London.
Jones, K. & Fowles, A. (1984) *Ideas on Institutions: Analysing the literature on long-term care and custody*. Routledge and Kegan Paul, London.
King, R., Raynes, N. & Tizard, J. (1973) *Patterns of Residential Care*. Routledge and Kegan Paul, London.
Lambert, R. (1965) *The State and Boarding Education*. Methuen, London.
Lambert, R., Hipkin, J. & Stagg, S. (1969) *New Wine in Old Bottles*. Bell, London.
Lambert, R., Millham, S. & Bullock, R. (1975) *The Chance of a Lifetime? A study of boarding education*. Weidenfeld and Nicolson, London.
Little, M. & Kelly, S. (1995) *A Life without Problems: The achievements of a therapeutic community*. Arena, Aldershot.
London County Council (1945) *London County Council Remand Homes*. LCC, London.
Millham, S., Bullock, R. & Cherrett, P. (1975) *After Grace-Teeth: A comparative study of the residential experience of boys in approved schools*. Human Context Books, London.
Millham, S., Bullock, R., Hosie, K. & Haak, M. (1986) *Lost in Care: The Problems of Maintaining Links between Children in Care and their Families*. Bower, Aldershot.
Moss, P. (1975) Residential care of children: a general view. In *Varieties of Residential Experience* (eds. J. Tizard, I. Sinclair & R. Clark), pp. 17–51. Routledge and Kegan Paul, London.
Oswin, M. (1978) *Children Living in Long Stay Hospitals*. London Spastics International Medical Publications, London.

Packman, J. (1975) *The Child's Generation: Child care policy from Curtis to Houghton*. Blackwell Science, Oxford.

Parker, R. (1983) The gestation of reform: the Children Act 1948. In *Approaches to Welfare* (eds. P. Bean & S. Macpherson), Routledge and Kegan Paul, London. pp. 196–217.

Parker, R. (1988) Children. In *Residential Care: The research reviewed*, pp. 57–124. HMSO, London.

Parker, R. (1990) *Away from Home: A history of child care*. Barnardos, Barkingside.

Punch, M. (1977) *Progressive Retreat: A sociological study of Dartington Hall School and some of its pupils*. University Press, Cambridge.

Rose, M. (1997) *Transforming Hate to Love: An outcome study of the Peper Harow treatment process for adolescents*. Routledge, London.

Sinclair, I., Parker, R., Leat, D. & Williams, J. (1990) *The Kaleidoscope of Care: A review of research on welfare provision for elderly people*, pp. 5–22. HMSO, London.

Sinclair, I. & Gibbs, I. (1998) *The Quality of Care in Children's Homes*. Wiley, Chichester.

Spinley, M. (1953) *The Deprived and Privileged*. Routledge and Kegan Paul, London.

Titmuss, R. (1976) *History of the Second World War*. HMSO, London.

Tizard, J. (1975) Quality of residential care for retarded children. In *Varieties of Residential Experience* (eds. J. Tizard, I. Sinclair & R. Clarke), pp. 52–68. Routledge and Kegan Paul, London.

Vaizey, J. (1959) *Scenes from Institutional Life*. Faber and Faber, London.

Watson, J. (1969) *Which is the Justice?* George Allen and Unwin, London.

Wills, D. (1971) *Spare the Child*. Penguin, Harmondsworth.

Chapter 9

Leaving Care: reflections and challenges

Mike Stein

Introduction

Young people leaving care are first and foremost *young people* and as such their destiny is in part shaped by the opportunities, policies and attitudes that are common to all young people. Indeed, their high degree of vulnerability, to unemployment and homelessness, for example, has in recent years been an indicator of major structural and social policy changes affecting young people more generally in society. These wider contextual influences and constraints have interacted with a more parochial child welfare agenda, and the agency and actions of many, including young people themselves, in the making of leaving care policy. This chapter tells the story of the main developments in leaving care policy and practice between the Children Act 1948 and 1998. It is a story which will be told in three main parts: After-care and Children's Departments 1948–1971; Social services and leaving care 1971–1989; and the Children Act 1989 and continuing care? 1989–1998.

After-care and Children's Departments 1948–1971

The Children Act 1948, based upon the recommendations of the Curtis Committee, created the new Children's Departments. A single Committee and Department was, for the first time, to have the responsibility for the continuous care of all children deprived of a normal home life. The reforming spirit of 1945 and Labour's social democratic politics provided the ideological climate for the acceptance of welfare policies which reflected a more humane and liberal approach. In keeping with this, section 12 of the 1948 Act finally broke with the poor law status of 'less eligibility' for children in care. Local authorities now had a duty to:

> further best interests ... and afford opportunities for proper development of character and abilities ... and make such use of

facilities and service available for children in the care of their own parents.'

(The Children Act, 1948: section 12(1) and (2))

The responsibilities introduced in respect of the after-care of children formerly in the care of local authorities or voluntary organisations were consistent with this new thinking and in laying down a legal framework of powers and duties which still remains largely intact today. By section 13(4) of the Act 'young people over compulsory school age [but] who have not attained the age of 21 ... may be accommodated and maintained in any hostel.' Section 20(1) (2) (3) of the Act empowered local authorities to give, to young people between the ages of 18 and 21 who have ceased to be in their care, financial assistance towards the costs of accommodation and maintenance and connected with their receiving suitable education and training, grants in respect of education and training continuing until completion of the course. Section 34(1) of the Act made it a duty of local authorities to 'advise and befriend' a child in their area who is under the age of 18 and who passed out of the care of a local authority or voluntary agency after reaching school-leaving age, unless 'the authority is satisfied that the welfare of the child does not require it' or that there are effective arrangements for the voluntary organisation to do so. Under section 34(2) of the Act, local authorities had a duty to inform other local authorities if a young person who is over compulsory school leaving age, or one whom they have been advising and befriending, proposes to transfer or has transferred residence to the area of another local authority.

In contrast to a rich history on many areas of the work of Children's Departments (see, for example, Heywood, 1978; Packman, 1981), very little is known about after-care policy and practice, including the fate of care leavers, during this period. We do know that the economic context, particularly from the 1950s to the mid-1970s, was very favourable. After World War II, and following a period of post-war austerity, the economy moved into its boom years – Modernity's heyday – providing job opportunities for all young people, all be it within a market reflecting and reproducing existing class and gender divisions. There was full youth employment during most of these years. Analysis of data from the National Child Development Study revealed that as late as 1976 most young people left school at the minimum school-leaving age of 16 and nine out of ten had secured employment within six months of leaving (Kiernan, 1992). There were jobs on offer for those living in care and leaving school at 15, and, on the raising of the school leaving age in 1972, at 16. And, indeed, the homes provided for in section 13 of the Act became widely known as 'working boys'' and 'working girls'' hostels. Also, between 1948 and 1962, on leaving care at 18, young men were required to do up to two years National Service, and even until the implementation of the Children and Young Persons Act 1969, in 1971, there were specialist approved schools which trained young men for the services.

Also, a new approach to practice, the child care officer's social casework, developed during this period. As Frost & Stein have commented:

> 'The morality theory of the Charity Organisation Society, religious and biological determinism, condemned the poor and thus these ideas were no longer acceptable in the post-war egalitarian climate.'

> (Frost & Stein, 1989: p. 34)

Social casework, derived from psychoanalytic theory, offered the potential for a new non-coercive response (Donzelot, 1980). The work of the child psychiatrists Anna Freud, Donald Winnicott and John Bowlby was very influential and Bowlby's 'maternal deprivation' theory became the key work in the training of child care officers (Packman, 1981). The message of his research was unequivocal: *a child needs a warm, intimate and continuous relationship with his/her mother or mother substitute.* Consistent with these findings, and their legal embodiment within the 1948 Act, the philosophy and practice was on rescuing children from institutional care by boarding out with foster parents or by returning them to the family home. But the assessment and treatment of the needs of children and young people more *generally* was a foundation stone of the child care officer's new and developing social casework. This casework included practice with children and young people in and after care. Those young people unable to return home normally, remained in care until they were 18 years of age and were ready to leave. Indeed, the age of 18 became accepted as the normal age of leaving care in Children's Departments, being derived from legal authority – the expiry age of parental rights resolutions and fit person orders. In this respect, both the law and child care practice mirrored the accepted age and process of *rite de passage* for most young people at that time. For 18 was the age when apprenticeships ended and adult wages began, when you could be conscripted, and when you could marry without parental consent.

In working boys' and girls' hostels, help was given in preparing them to leave care, through attention to practical and social skills, in finding accommodation and work, and in supporting them after they left care. In some local authorities, child care officers were appointed solely to work with teenagers, including those leaving care. Nationally, designated child care and probation and 'after-care' officers worked specifically with young people returning from approved schools.

The only change to the law in relation to leaving care during this period was as a result of the Children and Young Persons Act 1963. Section 58 of this Act gave local authorities new powers in respect of young people who were in care at 17 years of age (previously it had

been 18) and who left care. This included a new power *to be visited*, as
well as *to be advised and befriended*. The Seebohm Report (House of
Commons, 1968a; Seebohm Committee, 1968), in supporting the
recommendations of the 1968 White Paper *Children in Trouble* (House
of Commons, 1968b), envisaged that a comprehensive aftercare service
could be provided by the new Social Service Departments, but this
would require the transfer of 'many probation and after-care officers
... to the Social Services Department' (para. 265). This was important,
for by 1968 half of the children and young people on licence from
approved schools were supervised by the probation and aftercare service (para. 257).

Social services and leaving care 1971–1989

By the beginning of the 1970s it seemed that social work had developed
a strong professional identity and a clear vision of the future. The
growing influence and power of social work was exemplified by the key
role of child care experts in shaping the Children and Young Persons
Act 1969, and, by its contribution to the Seebohm Report, in determining the future organisation of social services. But at the same time as
the internal dynamic for professional unity and growth was reaching its
peak, the external context was changing. The consensus surrounding
the belief in the good society was evaporating (Pearson, 1975).

The rediscovery of poverty, greater recognition of a range of social
problems including inner-city deprivation, homelessness, ethnic conflict and educational underachievement, combined with challenges to
traditional forms of authority by 'new' pressure groups and social
movements, to point to a far more uncertain future. A professional
culture which had stabilised itself around a psychodynamic world view
and which focused exclusively upon the pathology of the individual, or
family, as both cause and solution, was being challenged. The new
curriculum included anti-psychiatry, deviance theory and Marxism, the
new practice welfare rights, community work and advocacy. The total
equalled radical social work (Frost & Stein, 1989)

More specifically, the reorganisation of the personal social services
and the introduction of the Children and Young Persons Act 1969,
both in 1971, far from leading to a comprehensive after-care service
within the new departments, resulted in the decline of specialist after-
care work in many local authorities. The end of the probation service's
involvement in after-care, with no commensurate transfer of resources
as envisaged by Seebohm, the replacement of approved school orders
with the new all-purpose care orders, and the related redesignation of
approved schools as community homes with education, all contributed
to the demise of the specialist after-care officer. Specialist work with
teenagers, either living in children's homes (now designated community

homes) or after they left care, became a very low priority among the
new front line generic social workers; and many fieldwork practitioners
were new and untrained following the Seebohm bureaucratisation of
social services. Care leavers became a forgotten group. But it was not
too long before their voices were heard. Against the wider background
of the major social changes outlined above, as well as the emergence of
an embryonic children's rights movement, there was a reawakening of
leaving care in the professional and political consciousness.

From as early as 1973 small groups of young people living in care
came together to talk about their experiences of living in children's
homes, of being on 'the receiving end'. Local 'in care' groups, the Who
Cares? project, Black and In Care, and the National Association of
Young People in Care, in different ways began to unlock the feelings
and views of young people about care and in particular the connections
between their lives in care and their lives after care (Stein, 1983; Collins
& Stein, 1989). A major theme that emerged from the voices of young
people was their lack of power over their lives, for example, in relation
to their use of money, their attendance at their own reviews, their
opportunities to shop, cook and generally to participate while in care.
The dependency created by care was related to their fears about leaving
care. Young people who participated in Who Cares? spoke of: constant
years of tight-held hand and dominant guidance ... of being a child
until you are 18 ... of social services planning your life for you ... [and]
... of being kicked out of care. For the first time, through the publication, in September 1997, of *Who Cares? Young People in Care
Speak Out* (Page & Clark, 1997), the words of these young people
received widespread publicity in the national media, including the
popular press and the television programme *World at One*.

Following the tragic death of Maria Colwell in 1973, and media and
government response to it, the Children Act 1975 placed a new duty on
local authorities 'to ascertain as far as is practicable the wishes and
feelings of the child and give due consideration to them' (section 59),
thus providing a legal framework for the consultative rights of young
people living in care, and a momentum for the further development of
the 'in-care rights' movement.

A major gap in our knowledge in the post-war period was the
absence of any research into after-care. But this was beginning to
change from the second half of the 1970s with the publication of
mainly small-scale descriptive studies (Godek, 1976; Mulvey, 1977;
Kahan, 1976; Triseliotis, 1980; Burgess, 1981; Stein & Ellis, 1983;
Lupton, 1985; Morgan-Klein, 1985; Stein & Maynard, 1985; Millham
et al., 1986; Stein & Carey, 1986; First Key, 1987). These studies
highlighted the diversity of the care experience showing that care
leavers were not a homogeneous group in terms of their care experiences, their care histories, their needs and abilities or their cultural and
ethnic backgrounds. Care may have been valued by young people and

helped them but it may have also contributed to other problems. They were likely to have experienced movement and disruption, a weakening of family links and identity confusion stemming from incomplete information, separation and rejection. The research revealed that these feelings could be amplified for black and mixed heritage young people brought up in a predominantly 'white' care system, particularly if they became detached from their families and communities. These early studies also documented the poor educational performance of care leavers, their feelings of being stigmatised by care and their variable preparation for leaving care. Moreover, upon leaving, at between just 16 and 18 years of age, loneliness, isolation, unemployment and 'drift' were likely to feature significantly in many of their lives.

In March 1980 the plight of homeless teenagers first became a headline story following the media take-up of Christian Wolmar's (1980) article 'Out of Care' which appeared in Shelter's magazine *Roof*. The author's combative exposé of ex-care homeless young people in London, drifting from hostels to squats to railway arches, led directly to Shelter setting up Homebase (now First Key) in response to the 'inadequate housing provision being made by local authorities for young people leaving care' (Wolmar, 1980).

The actions and self-organisation of young people themselves, the findings from researchers, the increased awareness by practitioners and managers of the problems faced by care leavers, and the campaigning activities of Shelter and First Key, provided a momentum for a change to the law in relation to leaving care which in sections 27–29 and 69 and 72 of the consolidating Child Care Act 1980 had remained much the same as the 1948 Act. The House of Commons Social Services Committee on Children in Care sitting in 1983 provided an opportunity for evidence which was duly taken up by several organisations including the National Association of Young People in Care. In its 1984 report (known as the Short Report) the Committee noted:

> 'The main cause for concern is the considerable variation in the sort of assistance which can be expected, which is at present unacceptably dependent on geographical happenstance. This wide variation in turn arises from the weak and confused state of the law in this respect ... present legislation on continuing care for young people leaving local authority care is diffuse and misleading, and is by nature discretionary rather than obligatory.'

> (House of Commons, 1984: para. 302, p. 303)

The Short Report recommended strengthening the law in three main areas: by introducing a new duty to prepare young people for leaving, by a stronger and wider duty in respect of after-care support, and by prioritising housing need. But perhaps an opportunity was also lost – to recommend new duties in respect of financial assistance. However, radical change was not on the agenda.

After all the evidence had been considered, and the law reviewed, there was only to be one significant *obligatory* change between the new Children Act 1989 and the old Children Act 1948 – a new duty, under section 24(1) 'to advise, assist and befriend young people who are looked after with a view to promote their welfare when they cease to be looked after.' New *permissive* powers were introduced under section 24 'to advise and befriend other young people under 21 who were cared for away from home', thus widening the target group for after-care support; and under section 27, 'the power to request the help of other local authorities including any local housing authority to enable them to comply with their duties to provide accommodation.' But other than that there is far more of the old than the new in the 1989 Act – the old duty to advise and befriend young people under 21 who were 'looked after' remains, as do the permissive powers to provide financial assistance. In fairness, it could be argued that the 1989 Act introduces a far more progressive legal framework as a general context for care leavers, given the connections between the lives of young people in families, in care and after care. In this sense the new provisions for family support services, for the inclusion of children with disabilities, for the recognition of culture, language, racial origin and religion, for consultative rights, for the accommodation of children in need, and for new rights to complain, are all to be welcomed (Stein, 1991), as is the detailed guidance on after-care (Department of Health, 1991).

However, this should not detract from the way that social work policy and practice failed many of these young people during much of this period. The geographical variations, identified by the Short Report, and the problems experienced by care leavers highlighted in the early research studies, were in part a consequence of these failures. Such findings included the lowering of the age at which young people left care, often as young as 16, and were expected to be independent. Changes in child care law and practice, as a result of the Children and Young Persons Act 1969, contributed to this. The old approved school orders, parental rights resolutions and fit person orders combined legal prescription and high level committee authority with normative expectations, in determining the age of discharge from care. Discretionary welfare, embodied in the new care order, was far more subject to individual social work judgement and external constraint: the latter including pragmatic concerns such as the pressure on residential care places. This was an ironic situation given the hopes riding on the new welfare thinking to contribute to a more needs-led practice. The low priority afforded to these young people in the new generic social service departments has already been commented upon. There was to be little improvement in after-care services during the 1970s and early 1980s, for against a background of successive child abuse inquiries, child protection work increasingly became the main pre-occupation (Parton, 1985). In addition, whereas an emerging welfare model had gone hand in hand with the commitment of the pre-See-bohm child care officer to assist these young people, radical social work and the new curriculum, including the developing children's rights discourse, was a far more contradictory force. As has been argued, this radical social work did provide a climate for the reawakening of leaving care in the political and professional consciousness, particularly through its support for advocacy and in-care groups. But it was a crude practice nourished on a very basic diet of Marxism (Pearson, 1975). It did not want to know about residential care, about more bricks in the wall – and even less about those behind the wall.

Also, subsequent policy developments during this period, however progressive in themselves, did not serve these young people well. The persistence of the institutional critique and the closely linked and enduring popularity of community care, both underpinned by a rare academic and political consensus, the rise of the permanency movement to greatly increase the use of adoption and fostering, and the managerial and professional drive to prevent and divert young people from entering care, all reinforced the same message: residential care is bad. And it was – and a lot worse than was realised given recent revelations of physical and sexual abuse (Stein, 1993). During these years residential care increasingly operated in a climate of denial and welfare planning blight as well as in a philosophical and theoretical void. In this context little thought was given to preparation for leaving or to the type and extent of after-care support needed. Social Service Departments were thus, in the main, unprepared for the major changes in society and in social legislation that were to have such a significant impact upon the lives of care leavers.

From the late 1970s onwards there have been profound economic and social changes, changes described and analysed as post-Fordism and, more recently, by post-modernism (Clarke, 1996). The former captures the processes of economic reorganisation in advanced industrial societies. The latter suggests a new post – or late? – modern era of fundamental and complex transformations in the social, economic, cultural and technological spheres (Giddens, 1991). The decline in traditional industries, the development in new technologies and the dramatic rise in youth unemployment during the 1980s had a major impact upon the lives of many young people (Coles, 1995). In the past, a highly stratified job market had been able to provide opportunities for all, whatever their level of education; later the low levels of educational attainment of most care leavers left them ill-prepared to compete in an increasingly competitive youth labour market (Stein, 1997). As a consequence a high proportion were unemployed and dependent on some form of benefit and therefore living in, or on, the margins of poverty. In 1985 the Government published its Green

Paper *Reform of Social Security* (House of Commons, 1985) upon which the Social Security Acts 1986 and 1988 were based. It argued that families should take greater financial responsibility for their young people and, in keeping with this logic, the Acts ended income support for 16- and 17-year-olds, except in severe hardship, and abolished 'householder status' for under-25s by the introduction of lower rates of income support for this age group. The impact of these changes for care leavers, for many of whom family support is not an option, proved disastrous (Stein, 1990). Although campaigning activity by care leavers resulted in exceptions for care leavers to receive income support at 16 and 17 for limited periods, the differential age rates of income support remained intact, resulting in demands on Social Services to use their discretionary powers to 'top up' benefit payments in order to prevent young people from experiencing extreme poverty, deprivation and homelessness (Stein, 1990). What was a national social security system of entitlement, has, in effect, been replaced by one of local welfare discretion.

This period has also witnessed major changes in the housing market. Following a period of growth in the post-war years, housing finance has, since the late 1970s, borne the brunt of cut-backs in public expenditure. This has resulted in a major decline in house building, particularly of the type of dwellings appropriate for this age group. The situation was made considerably worse by the continued decline in the private rental sector. The housing market has shrunk and thus, as with employment, has become increasingly competitive. In this context, local authority housing departments and housing associations have been the main provider of accommodation for young people leaving care. Access to council accommodation has been dependent upon local agreements, particularly in respect of young people being defined as 'vulnerable' under the Housing (Homeless Persons) Act and its successor legislation, the Housing Act 1985, and its related code of guidance. Housing Associations have pioneered many imaginative housing-plus-support schemes for this group of young people, often in conjunction with Social Services (Stein, 1997). However, their availability is subject to considerable variation. Indeed, the overall national picture is one of great variation, which, combined with the rise in youth unemployment among care leavers and dependency on benefits, has contributed to the rise in homelessness during this period. Following Christian Wolmar's 1980 revelations of homelessness among care leavers, two studies, published in 1981, both showed that over a third of single homeless people had experienced local authority care (DoE, 1981; SCSH, 1981). In 1988, Centrepoint Soho, a night shelter for young people in London, found that 23% of young people who referred themselves had lived in children's homes, and the percentage had risen to 41% in 1989 (Randall, 1988; 1989).

The Children Act 1989 and continuing care? 1989–1998

The Children Act 1989, described as 'the most comprehensive and far-reaching reform of child care law which has come before Parliament in living memory', was introduced in October 1991 (Smith, 1989). However, it could not have been implemented at a more difficult time for care leavers, who were having to face the virtual end of the traditional job market, shrinking housing options, major cuts in welfare benefits, and reduced expenditure on public services.

From the mid-1980s, in response to the increasingly desperate situation facing many young people leaving care, some voluntary organisations and local authorities – but by no means all – pioneered specialist leaving care schemes and projects (Bonnerjea, 1990; Stone, 1990). Indeed, planning for the new Act raised the profile and awareness of leaving care within many authorities and the introduction of specialist schemes was seen by social services as a way of meeting their new legal responsibilities under the Children Act 1989 (Biehal *et al.*, 1995). For some local authorities the Children Act has provided the legislative framework for a comprehensive range of leaving care services, through the provision of specialist leaving care schemes, integrated within an overall general child care strategy linking care and after-care. However, the more general picture in England and Wales is of great variation in the resourcing, range and quality of service provision (Broad, 1998). The problem of 'geographical happenstance', identified by the Short Report, or what might more appropriately be called territorial injustice, both within and between local authority areas, remains a major cause for concern.

An important developmental initiative in response to such variations in service has been the National Standards Working Group convened by First Key. The purpose of standards is to make explicit the quality of performance an agency should achieve and to facilitate the measurement and evaluation of current services as well as the development of future services. The 17 standards proposed by the working group were derived from current legislation, regulations and guidance and informed by research findings and professional experience (First Key, 1996).

As already suggested, the introduction of specialist schemes and services represented the main development in leaving care policy and practice from the mid-1980s. However, this was a rediscovery rather than an innovation; for, as we have seen, working boys' and working girls' hostels, and designated after-care probation and children's officers, were in existence between 1948 and 1971. It was after 1971 that the needs of care leavers were increasingly neglected in many authorities, until the rediscovery of specialist responses during the 1980s. The consensus that was emerging in both the voluntary and statutory sector at this time was that the aim of leaving care policy should be to prepare

young people for independent living from 16 years of age. As Stein &
Carey, writing at the time, argued, support for the independence
philosophy was strong in that it united a number of different ideas:

'These include the voiced opinions of young people themselves
highlighting the overprotective aspects of care ... the sociological
critique of institutions ... the current disillusionment with "welfare"
and "treatment" models ... cuts in capital and revenue expenditure
"relieving" social services of extended financial commitments and
responsibilities ... and finally the current revival of so-called Victorian values – after all, self-help equals managing on your own.'

(Stein & Carey, 1986: p. 156)

Many local authorities developed independence units and independence training programmes within their children's homes with the aim
of training young people to manage on their own through instruction in
practical survival skills and in coping with minimum support:

'Some of these units see independence training like a domestic
combat course: young people being marked out of ten on a check-list
for each activity, from opening a tin of baked beans to folding sheets,
and then "passing out" when they have reached the required standard.'

(Stein & Carey, 1986: p. 157)

Research highlighting the loneliness, isolation and high breakdown
rate of such 'independent' 16- and 17-year-old care leavers in their own
accommodation led to the questioning of the Independence approach
and to the development, in some areas, of what have been called Inter-
Dependence models of provision. Their underlying philosophy is that
leaving care is seen as a psychosocial transition, a high priority being
placed on interpersonal skills, developing self-esteem and confidence,
and young people receiving ongoing support. It was this thinking which
lay behind many of the schemes that have developed in response to the
Children Act 1989 and which aimed to meet the core needs of care
leavers – for accommodation, ongoing support, financial assistance and
help with careers. The work of these schemes, post Children Act, has
included: contributing to policy development and the coordination of
leaving-care services within local authority areas; developing a flexible
range of resource options for young people and coordinating access to
them, especially housing and financial support; developing inter-agency
links to ensure an integrated approach; providing advice, information
and consultancy services to young people, social workers and carers –
including assistance with preparation and leaving-care planning; and
offering direct and group-based support to young people including
those both leaving care and those living independently in the community. Although there is evidence that most specialist schemes contribute

to these discrete areas, there is considerable diversity in the types of schemes: in terms of perspective, methods of working and the extent to which their work is young person demand-led or social work planned; in regard to the nature of the providing agency, and in the contribution specialist schemes make to the development of leaving-care policy within their local areas (Biehal *et al.*, 1995).

The same research study also showed that specialist leaving-care schemes made a positive contribution to specific outcomes for care leavers. They worked particularly well in respect of meeting accommodation needs and assisting life skills. However, the development of what is in effect a specialist service within substitute care raises a key policy and practice question: what should the relationship be between specialist leaving-care services and foster and residential carers? Most young people are referred to leaving-care schemes at just 15 or 16 years of age when they are expected to leave their care placement and move on to a specialist project. But, ideally, leaving care should be at one with a common developmental journey, from being a young person to becoming an adult. Assisting adulthood, assisting young people leaving care, should be the role of the substitute carer. The research discussed above showed that specialist schemes had little impact upon other important outcomes. Successful educational outcomes were closely connected to placement stability, more often, although not exclusively, achieved in foster care placements, which provided a supportive and encouraging environment for study. Without such stability, post-16 employment, education and training outcomes were also likely to be very poor. Also, success in social networks, personal relationships and having a positive self-image was closely connected with young people having supportive relationships with family members or former carers. The message is clear: specialist schemes can only build upon what has gone before. Stability, continuity of family and carer links are the foundation stones. Young people should not be expected to leave their settled placements when they reach just 15 or 16 years of age: there should be a more gradual and flexible approach to leaving.

Conclusion

As we approach the millennium the research evidence is convincing that young people leaving care are still a relatively small but highly disadvantaged group. They are likely to have experienced abuse or neglect, or difficulties within their families which has contributed to behavioural problems such as not going to school, running away from home or getting into trouble. For too many, care has been unable to compensate them developmentally, emotionally and educationally, so by the time they leave care their life chances are very poor indeed. On leaving care at between 16 and 18 years of age, paradoxically far younger than their peers leave home, they are far more likely than other young people to be unemployed and be dependent on welfare benefits, to leave school at the minimum age without qualifications, to become young parents, and to experience homelessness and prison. Their journey to adulthood is both compressed and accelerated. Specialist leaving care schemes have been developed during the last ten years to assist these young people and there is evidence that they can help many of them, particularly given their very disadvantaged starting points. However, the availability of such schemes is still very variable. In addition, the very early age at which young people are expected to move on to specialist schemes, and their separation from foster and residential care, often deny young people a foundation of emotional stability and continuity for their transition to adulthood. Good leaving-care policy and practice can only be built upon good quality substitute care.

The Children Act 1948 laid down a legal foundation of duties and powers in regard to after-care which remains largely intact today. However, against a background of territorial injustice, the present legislation – the Children Act 1989 – could serve these young people better if its discretionary powers were replaced by new duties, particularly in respect of financial assistance.

Shifts in leaving care policy and practice, and their ideological underpinning, have been far greater than changes in the legal framework. Following the 1948 Act specialist services developed and practice was increasingly influenced by the rise of the new welfare thinking, embodied in the child care officer's social casework. However, ironically, the zenith of welfarism, represented by the reorganisation of the personal social services and changes in child care law introduced in 1971 led, in effect, to the end of specialist after-care provision. The priority afforded these vulnerable young people lessened, and the age they were expected to leave care reduced. The shifts from a welfare perspective to more radical responses, including advocacy and a practice increasingly influenced by a developing children's rights discourse, proved contradictory. For although supporting the voice and self-organisation of young people in care, it had little interest in care itself or the fate of care leavers: community work, advocacy and prevention was where it was at. More mainstream child care developments – including the prioritisation of child protection work, planning for permanency, and diversion – by and large, ignored care leavers. It was not until the mid- to late 1980s, following sustained campaigning, publicity and research surrounding their plight, that specialist provision developed in many areas.

The present social policy framework, particularly in relation to benefits and housing, is complex, discretionary and, generally, discouraging for care leavers. Securing financial support can involve negotiations with local authority social services, housing and education departments, in addition to the Benefits Agency. The income support system for under-25-year-olds is based on the assumption of parental support – hence the lower levels of benefit for this age group and the 'estrangement' hurdles that 16- and 17-year-olds have to overcome to secure benefits. Access to local authority housing also involves negotiations over 'vulnerability'. For those young people without the assistance of specialist schemes there is evidence of great hardship, including destitution.

Finally, it is to be hoped that the specific needs of this group of highly vulnerable young people will be recognised by the Government's Social Exclusion Unit and the New Deal pilot projects. The costs of continued failure to deny them opportunities to become self-supporting adults is enormous, both to care leavers and to society.

References

Biehal, N., Clayden, J., Stein, M. & Wade, J. (1995) *Moving On: young people and leaving care schemes*. HMSO, London.

Bonnerjea, L., (1990) *Leaving Care in London*. London Boroughs Children's Regional Planning Committee, London.

Broad, B. (1998) *Young People Leaving Care: Life After the Children Act 1989*. Jessica Kingsley, London.

Burgess, C. (1981) *In Care and Into Work*. Tavistock, London.

Clarke, J. (1996) After social work. In *Social Theory, Social Change and Social Work* (ed. N. Parton). Routledge, London.

Coles, B. (1995) *Youth and Social Policy*. UCL Press, London.

Collins, S. & Stein, M. (1989) Users fight back: collectives in social work. In *The Haunt of Misery* (eds C. Rojeck, G. Peacock & S. Collins). Routledge, London.

Department of the Environment (1981) *Single and Homeless*. HMSO, London.

Department of Health (1991) *The Children Act 1989, Guidance and Regulations, Vol. 4*. HMSO, London.

Donzelot, J. (1980) *The Policing of Families*. Hutchinson, London.

First Key (1987) *A Study of Black Young People Leaving Care*. First Key, Leeds.

First Key (1996) *Standards in Leaving Care*. First Key, Leeds.

Frost, N. & Stein, M. (1989) *The Politics of Child Welfare*. Harvester Wheatsheaf, Hemel Hempstead.

Giddens, A. (1991) *Modernity and Self-identity: Self and Society in the Late Modern Age*. Polity Press, Cambridge.

Godek, S. (1976) *Leaving Care*. Barnardos, Barkingside.

Heywood, J. (1978) *Children in Care*. Routledge and Kegan Paul, London.

House of Commons (1968a) *Report of The Committee on Local Authority and Allied Personal Social Services*. Cmnd 9703, HMSO, London.

House of Commons (1968b) *Children in Trouble*. Cmnd 3601. HMSO, London.

House of Commons (1984) *Second Report from the Social Services Committee, Children in Care*. HMSO, London.

House of Commons (1985) *Reform of Social Security*. Cmnd 9517. HMSO, London.

Kahan, B. (1976) *Growing Up in Care*. Blackwell Science, Oxford.

Kiernan, K. (1992) The impact of family disruption in childhood on transitions made in young adult life. *Population Studies* **46**, 213–34.

Lupton, C. (1985) *Moving Out*. Portsmouth Polytechnic, Portsmouth.

Millham, S., Bullock, R., Hosie, K. & Haak, M. (1986) *Lost in Care*. Gower, Aldershot.

Morgan-Klein, B. (1985) *Where Am I Going To Stay?* Scottish Council for Single Homeless, Edinburgh.

Mulvey, T. (1977) After-care – who cares? *Concern* No. 26, National Children's Bureau, London.

Packman, J. (1981) *The Child's Generation*. Blackwell and Robertson, London.

Page, R. & Clark, G. (1997) *Who Cares? Young People in Care Speak Out*. National Children's Bureau, London.

Parton, N. (1985) *The Politics of Child Abuse*. Macmillan, London.

Pearson, G. (1975) *The Deviant Imagination*. Macmillan, London.

Randall, G. (1988) *No Way Home*. Centrepoint, London.

Randall, G. (1989) *Homeless and Hungry*. Centrepoint, London.

Scottish Council for Single Homeless (1981) *Think Single*. SCSH, Edinburgh.

Seebohm Committee (1968) *Report of the Committee on Local Authority and Allied Personal Social Services*. Cmnd 3703, HMSO, London.

Smith, P. (1989) *The Children Act 1989*. Highlight, National Children's Bureau, London.

Stein M. (1983) Protest in care. In *The Political Dimensions of Social Work* (eds B. Jordan & N. Parton). Blackwell Science, Oxford.

Stein, M. (1990) *Living Out of Care*. Barnardos, Barkingside.

Stein, M. (1991) *Leaving Care and the 1989 Children Act, the Agenda*. First Key, Leeds.

Stein, M. (1993) The abuses and uses of residential child care. In *Surviving Childhood Adversity* (eds H. Furguson, R. Gilligan & R. Torode). Social Studies Press, Dublin.

Stein, M. (1997) *What Works in Leaving Care?* Barnardos, Barkingside.

Stein, M. & Carey, K. (1986) *Leaving Care*. Blackwell Science, Oxford.

Stein, M. & Ellis, S. (1983) *Reviews and Young People in Care*. NAYPIC, London.

Stein, M. & Maynard (1985) *I've Never Been so Lonely*. NAYPIC, London.

Stone, M. (1990) *Young People Leaving Care*. RPS, Redhill.

Triseliotis, J. (1980) Growing up in foster care. In *New Developments in Foster Care and Adoption* (ed. J. Triseliotis). Routledge and Kegan Paul, London.

Wolmar, C. (1980) Out of care. *Roof*, March/April, Shelter, London.

Chapter 10

Juvenile Justice in England and Wales and in Scotland Since the Children Act 1948 (Plus Ça Change)

Stewart Asquith

Introduction

With the killing of James Bulger in 1993 by two young boys just around the age of criminal responsibility – ten in England and Wales – fundamental questions were asked, not only about the way in which a society should respond to those children who commit offences, particularly serious offences, but also about the nature of the attitude of society to our children. That a child should die in that way provoked not only a questioning of the very system of juvenile justice and the philosophy on which it is based, but also of the nature of the life experiences we offer to our children which might produce in two young boys the motivation or drive to kill a young child (Asquith, 1996).

Almost 50 years ago, though circumstances themselves were very different, similar questions were asked in the wake of the death of the young boy Dennis O'Neill whilst in care. The Curtis report of 1947 had also addressed the issue of the whole attitude of society to the treatment of children (Curtis Committee, 1947). Having met Tom O'Neill (Dennis's elder brother) in the early 1970s, as he sought a publisher for his manuscript (later published as *A Place Called Hope* (O'Neill, 1981)), I was immensely struck by the emotion of this man seeking to let the world know about his life experiences, about his brother, about his childhood, about his own delinquency and about the people and factors in his life which helped him move on. The death of his brother was, of course, one of the contributory factors leading to the Children Act 1948.

Four points arise from the O'Neill and Bulger episodes. First, the development of policies and practices for children have unfortunately often been in the wake of some tragedy in which children have been the victims, sometimes with horrific and even fatal consequences. This has applied in both the child welfare and offender fields.

Second, though the commitment to prevention, to reducing the risk that children will offend or be in need later in life, has been a constant and recurring theme in many reports from inquiries and commissions, few resources have been devoted to preventative strategies. The focus of attention has often been the need to respond to crises provoked in our systems of child care and juvenile justice by such tragic events as the deaths of Dennis O'Neill and James Bulger. In relation to those children who offend, and in particular those who commit the more serious offences, the reaction to the Bulger case graphically illustrated the continuing uneasy relationship between the wish to protect children on the one hand and the acceptance by many that such children should be the subject of severe, retributive and punitive sanctions. Developments in juvenile justice and delinquency control over the past 50 years reveal the respective sides of the 'angels and devils' debates. Children are either 'angels' in need of care or protection or 'devils' from whom society ought to be protected.

Third, the research literature has increasingly shown that the line between a child being at risk of being in need or of being an offender is very thin indeed and the development of child care and delinquency prevention measures over the past 50 years reflects a continuing convergence of policies and practices in both fields. This is best represented recently in the work of Farrington (1994) and in *Childhood Matters* (the Report of the Commission of Inquiry into the Prevention of Child Abuse (HMSO, 1996)). As Murphy (1992: p. 119) shows, from the 1950s, there had been concern expressed by child care professionals 'that both deprived and delinquent children came from very similar backgrounds, but were treated differently by the mere accident of which law delivered them for public action'. This theme is still a central issue in debates about young offenders and the development of appropriate policies and practices.

Fourth, the question of what kind of process or forum is most appropriate for dealing with offenders depends largely on the way in which offending is explained. Thus, where the line between being 'an offender' or being a child 'in need of care and protection' is drawn very finely, there is less of an argument for distinct forms of proceedings. One of the characteristic features of developments in juvenile justice over the past 50 years in the UK has been the search for a form of proceedings appropriate for dealing with those children who offend. In particular, the relevance of juvenile court structure for dealing with those who offend has been regularly challenged both north and south of the border. Perspectives on the relative merits of a court structure are, of course, inextricably linked to an ideological position on the value of punishment to the individual and as a social deterrent.

The main purpose of this chapter is to explore the evolution of juvenile justice in England and Wales and in Scotland since the 1948 Children Act; to consider the historical development of philosophies

and explanations of offending behaviour of children and the implications of these for policies and practices in the respective jurisdictions.
Particularly serious cases, such as the Bulger case, highlight the inherent
difficulty of seeking to deal with children both as offenders and as
children, and of reconciling the potentially conflicting need to meet the
demands of justice and of welfare. Although the philosophies underpinning the respective systems of justice for children in England and
Wales and in Scotland are relatively similar, the structural arrangements are, and have been for some time, very different.

'Welfare' or 'justice' – common issues

The systems of juvenile justice in Scotland and in England and Wales
both have their roots in the Children Act 1908. In both jurisdictions,
there was an assumption – which was to have important implications –
that juvenile courts had jurisdiction over both civil and criminal matters.
The increasing emphasis on the welfare of children, including those who
had committed offences, meant that delinquent and other children could
be subjected to the same measure and committed to similar institutions.
The Children and Young Persons Act 1933 (followed by the 1937
Children and Young Persons (Scotland) Act) emphasised the requirement of 'having regard to the welfare of the child'.

The tension between welfare and criminal considerations has for
some time been seen (see, for example, Wootton, 1959), and continues
to be seen, as a source of conflict for the development of any system of
juvenile justice. The difficulty of reconciling these is reflected in the
reviews of juvenile justice currently being undertaken in many
countries, particularly in Central and Eastern Europe. It is also a
powerful source of conflict and disagreement in the UK in the 1990s
when children commit particularly serious offences. Are they to be
treated as children first whose welfare we must protect, or as offenders
who have to be dealt with in a way appropriate to what they have
done? Contemporary movements such as the 'abolitionist' movement
in the United States suggest that, though the welfare of all children
(including offenders) is high on contemporary political agenda, some
would argue that children who offend should be dealt with in courts of
criminal law as offenders.

Such current preoccupations are not new; the history of juvenile
justice has been one in which different structural arrangements have
been developed to accommodate changes in philosophy and explanations offered for offending by children and young people. The historical
differences between the respective systems in Scotland and in England
and Wales reflect, first, the contestability of philosophies on which to
base policies and practices, and second, the continual shifts in the
balance between welfare and criminal considerations, in particular

between the relative merits of a 'justice' or a 'welfare' approach or between 'treatment' and 'punishment'. The merits of a 'justice' approach were forcibly put by the 'return to justice' movement in the late 1970s and early 1980s in a reaction to the (then) accepted currency of welfare. However, that movement was only a reflection of the fact that the relationship between justice and welfare philosophies as they apply to children who offend is in a continual state of flux and renegotiation.

The wish to find a different way and avoid the persisting pendulum-like swing between welfare and justice or treatment and punishment (which are in reality not true dichotomies anyway) has prompted a search for a new ideological prescription on which to found our juvenile justice institutions (for example, the discussion of 'restorative justice' (Walgrave, 1995)).

Court or tribunal

Though the Curtis Report (Curtis Committee, 1947) addressed the issue of delinquency, its main recommendations were directed at child care issues, and the Children Act 1948 left the juvenile court system, in operation since the 1933 Children and Young Persons Act, relatively intact. The 1948 Act rested on a philosophy which emphasised the importance of the welfare of the child and in some respects this crystallised further the basic conflict for the juvenile courts, seeking to reconcile the potentially conflicting claims of welfare and judicial considerations. The incompatibility of a conceptual framework underlying notions of welfare and treatment on the one hand and notions of crime and punishment on the other is well reflected in two passages from the reports which were to determine for some time the nature of juvenile justice in England and Wales and in Scotland – the Ingleby (1960) and Kilbrandon (1964) reports:

> 'The court remains a criminal court in the sense that it is a magistrates' court, that it is principally concerned with trying offences, that its procedure is a modified form of ordinary criminal law and that, with a few special provisions, it is governed by the law of evidence in criminal cases. Yet the requirement to have regard to the welfare of the child, and the various ways in which the court may deal with an offender, suggest a jurisdiction that is not criminal. It is not easy to see how these two principles may be reconciled.'

> (Ingleby, 1960: para. 60)

Also, from the Kilbrandon Report (1964: para. 54):

> 'In drawing a contrast between a system resting primarily on ideas of crime, responsibility and punishment and one proceeding primarily

on the principle of prevention, we are not, of course, suggesting that the methods of dealing with adult crime are entirely governed by the first concept or that a working compromise between them is not possible. In practice the present arrangements represent such a compromise, and at any given time and certainly in relation to any individual offender, a balance has to be sought on an empirical basis between the conflicting aims of the two principles.'

The solutions to the basic conflict of the juvenile court offered in two reports, though derived from a common concern, were to determine very different trajectories north and south of the border for the development of juvenile justice. One, which has characterised juvenile justice in England and Wales since the early 1950s, was more incremental in modifying and adapting the juvenile court structure. The other was more radical, based on the assumption that the juvenile court structure was inappropriate both in concept and in practice. It provided the philosophical framework on which is based the unique Scottish Children's Hearings.

England and Wales – Ingleby and after

The Ingleby Committee, set up in 1956, to examine the law in its application to children in England and Wales, did not recommend the abolition of the juvenile court though it did address the potential for conflict between welfare and judicial considerations. The solution offered provided a template for developments in juvenile justice which are mirrored in current arrangements. The committee recommended that the juvenile courts be retained but that it be recognised that they provided a less appropriate forum for dealing with those young children who offended and in respect of whom welfare considerations were more important. Although the welfare of those children who offend was important, there were other issues which had to be taken into consideration, such as the need to protect society and deter would-be offenders:

'Although it may be right for the court's action to be determined primarily by the needs of the particular child before it, the court cannot entirely disregard other considerations such as the need to deter potential offenders. An element of general deterrence must enter into many of the court's decisions and this must make the distinction between treatment and punishment even more difficult to draw.'

(Ingleby Report, 1960: para. 7)

However, for younger offenders, proceedings were to be modified to allow children to be dealt with mainly within a civil jurisdiction, extending the principles on which the 1908 Act was based. Children who were under 12 were to be dealt with as far as possible outside the courts – allowing for a degree of flexibility and demanding an equal degree of cooperation between agencies such as the police and social services. All children under 12 were to be dealt with as in need of care, protection and control (Ingleby Report, 1960: para. 84).

Those between 12 and 17 who had committed offences were to be dealt with by the courts within the (then) prevailing criminal jurisdiction and were to be held responsible for what they had done. They would experience a somewhat modified form of court procedure and could be liable to punishment. The age of responsibility was to be raised to 12. The welfare of such offenders was also to be taken into account though less so than in the case of the younger offender.

Ingleby had in fact recommended a compromise between welfare and justice considerations which recognised the importance of welfare. The report emphasised the significance of age as a factor in a model which was based on the assumption that the older the offender, the greater his/her degree of responsibility. The committee was committed to a court structure for young offenders based on a modified version of the criminal courts as they applied to adults. In 1960, Ingleby made what were in fact very conservative recommendations, and though there were attempts to be more revolutionary in the late 1960s, juvenile justice in England and Wales has continued to operate largely on the basis of the principles on which the Ingleby recommendations were based. The more radical thrust of the Scottish developments ran parallel to debates in that decade south of the border, but the respective systems followed very different courses.

There was some dismay at the conservative nature of the changes proposed in the Ingleby report. Baroness Wootton said:

'We had been hoping for a bold and imaginative reconstruction of the whole system for dealing with unfortunate children in this day and age. What we got was a number of useful technical minor reforms on a system which in the judgement of many of us is already outmoded.'

(Hansard, 1962: CCXL1V, 815)

A number of concerns were voiced in England and Wales which echoed the arguments being made north of the border at that time. These included the need for a whole new form of proceedings, the need to keep as many children as possible out of court and the importance of the family as a focus of intervention in the interest of preventing offending behaviour in the first place, These were themes which were to be picked up and developed in the Labour Party Report (the Longford Committee) in 1964 (the same year as Kilbrandon reported in Scotland) which advocated a family service and a form of proceedings which was outside the courts (Longford Committee, 1964). The White Paper which followed, *The Child, the Family and the Young Offender* (HMSO, 1965), recommended the setting-up of a 'family council' to deal with all cases of delinquency, care, protection and control. Just as the Kilbrandon Committee had recognised non-judicial juvenile panels, the family council was not to be a court of law, though children were to be able to have the facts of the case decided in court.

However, the proposal to abolish the juvenile courts was unacceptable to a number of constituencies in England and Wales and it was the White Paper of 1968, *Children in Trouble* (HMSO, 1968), which provided the basis of the Children and Young Persons Act 1969. The White Paper argued for the retention of the juvenile court but wished to further the protection afforded to younger offenders by confirming that those under the age of criminal responsibility (now ten) would not be subject to criminal proceedings; that in the case of those between 10 and 14 the commission of an offence was not sufficient in itself to warrant proceedings; it had also to be shown that the child was 'not receiving such care, protection and guidance as a good parent may reasonably be expected to give'.

Though there was disagreement reflected through the various reports and White Papers about the most appropriate form of proceedings, a recurrent feature of the discussions of the time was the importance of the family in the causation and prevention of delinquency and the need for an expanded role for integrated social services.

It is impossible to understand the development of delinquency control and juvenile justice in both Scotland and England and Wales without locating it in the context of the reorganisation of social work. Scotland was to take the more radical approach in that respect as well. At the end of the 1960s, England and Wales not only retained the juvenile court but also retained a distinct probation service. In Scotland, a fundamentally different form of juvenile justice was introduced and the probation service, including service to adults, was disbanded with the introduction of generic social work departments.

At the end of the 1960s, a number of principles had been established in England and Wales which apply in the arrangements for juvenile justice to the present day. These include a commitment to non-court-based measures as far as possible; the commitment to the involvement of all concerned – including the families – in the prevention of delinquency; the extreme importance of welfare considerations and the need to address factors in the child's life experience.

However, this commitment to a welfare perspective, albeit within the context of a juvenile court, did not proceed without critical analysis and opposition. Graham (1996) writing of England and Wales, argues:

'In practice the [1969] Act was never fully implemented, and by the end of the 1970s the welfare approach was increasingly being questioned. Arguments prevailed for a return to a "just deserts" model, for proportionality in sentencing, ... for determinate penalties and for greater protection of the legal rights of juveniles. Legislation in the 1980s went some way to achieving these objectives.'

(Graham, 1996: p. 74)

He continues:

'Up to the end of the 1980s, the history of juvenile justice was characterised by contrasting views on the causes of (and hence remedies for) offending. Legislation and criminal justice policy and practice swung towards and then away from a welfare approach to juvenile offenders, at times emphasising the needs of the child, at others the importance of punishment.'

(Graham, 1996: p. 75)

The 'return to justice' movement had argued that those children who offend should be dealt with separately from those children in need of care and protection. Criminal matters should be dealt with in a criminal jurisdiction whereas civil matters should be dealt with in a separate forum altogether. It was this line of thinking which determined, through the Children Act 1989, one of the major changes in juvenile justice in England and Wales – the removal of all civil care proceedings from the juvenile court leaving it to deal only with those children who had offended. The commitment to diverting as many people from the juvenile court system itself also reflected the growing use of diversionary measures for less serious cases. The principle underlying such developments, and which characterises much of current thinking about how to deal with young offenders, is that there is no need for the vast majority of young offenders to appear in court or be caught up in the formal system of control; court appearances and punitive sanctions should be reserved for the more serious cases and more serious and persistent offenders. This was the principle on which the Children's Hearings system in Scotland had been based at its introduction some 20 years earlier.

Many of the present arrangements in England and Wales for dealing with children and young people who offend derive from the Criminal Justice Act 1991. This introduced another major change, with the creation of a new Youth Court based on a commitment to a number of principles which included the wish to divert as many young offenders as possible from the court system and from custody and the greater importance attached to the community, both in terms of preventing delinquency and to the reintegration of young offenders.

As Graham (1996) also points out, in England and Wales in the 1990s there was a growing belief that there should be a twin-track approach to dealing with children and young people who offend. For a minority of serious cases, a court-based structure provides an appropriate means for dealing with young offenders. For the vast majority of young offenders, however, their behaviour is not deemed sufficiently serious to provoke concerns about the need to protect society through a judicial and punitive system; they can be dealt with in the community and in such a way as to emphasise the importance of welfare considerations. What can also be detected is the beginning of an appreciation that juvenile justice and criminal justice systems, in and of themselves, cannot be expected to provide the solutions to the prevention and reduction of offending behaviour by children and young people.

Concern about the adequacy of the system for dealing with those children who commit very serious offences was expressed in the wake of the Bulger case. This was no better expressed than in the oft quoted statement by the (then) Prime Minister that, in the belief that welfare approaches had failed, we should 'condemn more and understand less'. This anticipated a much more punitive reaction towards the control of offending behaviour by the young (Graham, 1996; Asquith & Docherty, forthcoming). It forced a reappraisal of what philosophies were the most appropriate on which to base the treatment of young offenders. At what age should children be criminally responsible? What is the most appropriate form of proceedings for children who offend? What assumptions about children, childhood and the competencies of children are embedded in our key social institutions such as our juvenile justice systems? What does their offending behaviour say about the kind of society in which our children live and the kind of life chances they experience?

The Bulger case also highlighted the significance of much broader social policy concerns such as parenting, childcare, housing policy, poverty and social injustice. Such considerations demand a much wider approach than the conventional crime, responsibility and punishment syndrome. It also suggests that those policies and practices which focus on the welfare of individual children will inevitably be inadequate and reveal considerable shortcomings in as much as they fail to address the wider social context in which children live. In many respects this does not seem so very different from the discussions contained in the Curtis Report some 50 years before.

Scotland – Kilbrandon and after

The Kilbrandon Committee was set up in 1961 to:

> 'consider the provisions of the law of Scotland relating to the treatment of juvenile delinquents and juveniles in need of care and protection or beyond parental control, and in particular, the constitution, powers and procedure of the courts dealing with such juveniles.'

Concerns in Scotland in the years that followed the Children Act 1948 were very similar to those which had prompted the Ingleby Inquiry: the appropriate forum for dealing with children; the relative merits of punishment; and treatment and the increasing commitment to the importance of the welfare of the child.

Though juvenile justice had shared common roots with the system in England and Wales, there were a number of major differences. One was that there had never been in Scotland a uniform juvenile court-based system. Rather there were a number of different types of courts, Sheriff courts, Burgh or police courts, the Justice of the Peace Court and specially constituted juvenile courts. Thus there was never such a powerful and vocal body of juvenile magistrates as in England to defend the merits of the juvenile court structure. This in part accounts for the acceptance of the radical recommendations made by the Kilbrandon Committee in 1964:

> 'What had evolved in Scotland was a system of juvenile justice which, unlike that in England and Wales, lacked any coherence or uniformity, a factor which must surely have contributed to the acceptance of the radical recommendations made by the Kilbrandon Committee.'
>
> (Asquith, 1983: p. 26)

In addition to the more radical recommendations of the Kilbrandon report, two factors have consolidated the present differences between the English and Welsh systems and that in Scotland. First, within four years, the principles of the Kilbrandon report were embodied in legislation in the Social Work (Scotland) Act of 1968.

Second, the Children's Hearings system introduced in 1971 has remained relatively unchanged for more than a quarter of a century and the Kilbrandon philosophy is still considered as relevant today as it was when the report first appeared. Thus there has been a much lengthier period of continuity in juvenile justice in Scotland than in England and Wales where there have been regular changes, some of them major, to the system of justice for children and young people who commit offences.

Ingleby had argued against the abolition of the juvenile courts largely on the grounds of the need for legal and judicial scrutiny of decision-making and of the relevance of factors other than the welfare of the child – the need, for example, to protect society and of the importance of the court appearance itself. The arguments made against the retention of a juvenile court structure by the Kilbrandon Committee were almost the complete opposite. This is what makes a historical comparison of the respective systems of juvenile justice exciting – it is not simply a matter of charting organisational and institutional change. It demands an appreciation of the different values and philosophies embedded in such changes and of the political context of juvenile justice.

Kilbrandon's arguments against the juvenile court can be summed up in the following five ways. First, welfare and criminal considerations rest on very different conceptual frameworks:

'Welfare is, of course, irrelevant to the questions of the determination of innocence or guilt and relates to the second stage of the proceedings, namely the form of treatment appropriate to the case once the facts have been established.'

(Kilbrandon Report, 1964: para. 50)

This was to underpin the radical recommendation the Committee made to separate completely these two functions.

Second, the crime–responsibility–punishment syndrome, south of the border, not only inhibited the determination of welfare measures but also fostered a culture antithetical to the promotion of preventative strategies. Thus, in a court-based structure, not only might the determination of measures to deal with an offender be unduly influenced by the nature of the offence but there would also be ideological forces at work which militated against the development of appropriate preventative measures.

Third, whereas the judiciary had the skills and expertise to determine questions of guilt or innocence or to establish the facts of the case, they were not necessarily the best qualified to make decisions about the welfare needs of the children.

Fourth, the distinction between children who offended and those in need of care and protection was too sharply drawn. Given the commitment to explanations of deprivation and delinquency as having common roots, some means had to be found whereby children could be dealt within a common framework.

Fifth, a juvenile court-based structure, even if modified, is essentially a court of criminal law operating with a high degree of formality and stigma associated with court appearance. Parents as well as children may well be inhibited from discussion and from playing a central role in seeking to meet the needs of their children. The family was considered by Kilbrandon as probably the most important context in which delinquency had to be understood and could be prevented, an approach which was shared in the reports from south of the border but did not lead to the same conclusions.

Given these kinds of concern, it appeared to the Kilbrandon Committee that the solution sought had to be one based on fundamental rather than incremental change since further modification or tinkering with the juvenile court structure would not necessarily make the changes needed nor have the desired effect. The Scottish solution was based on outright rejection of court-based approaches. The Kilbrandon recommendation was:

'to devise a procedure whereby juvenile offenders would in all cases be brought before a specialised agency whose sole concern would be the measures to be applied on what amounts to an agreed referral.'

(Kilbrandon Report, 1964: para. 73)

Although the arguments contained in the Kilbrandon Report reflected many of those made in the Ingleby Report, in the Longford Report, and in the White Paper *The Child, the Family and the Young Offender* (HMSO, 1965), the outcomes were radically different.

With a number of alterations to the recommendations of the report made in the White Paper *Social Work and the Community* (1966), the proposal for the new system of juvenile justice and the reorganisation of social work received legislative backing in the Social Work (Scotland) Act 1968 and the system of the Children's Hearings was introduced three years later (see Martin & Murray, 1976, and Martin *et al.*, 1981 for a fuller description of the Children's Hearings system in theory and in practice). A single piece of legislation introduced such changes in the late 1960s in Scotland, whereas the developments in juvenile justice and in social work in England and Wales took separate paths through the Children and Young Persons Act 1969 and the recommendations of the Seebohm Committee of 1968 (Seebohm Committee, 1968). It is that solution, offered in 1964, which still underpins juvenile justice in Scotland in the late 1990s and has stood the test of time. Recent support by the Secretary of State for Scotland (Secretary of State for Scotland, 1977) for the distinctive Scottish system of justice for children suggests that there will be little change introduced to the system in the near future and that it has the support of the current Government.

The Kilbrandon Report, whilst arguing for the abolition of the juvenile court, had always accepted that there would be a number of offenders who would have to go to court. Although Scotland has a juvenile justice system which deals with the vast majority of those children who offend, a small number of children may be, and indeed are, prosecuted in court each year. Just as the Bulger case in the 1990s forced questions about how to deal with those children who commit serious offences, in the early history of the Children's Hearings system, similar questions were asked in the wake of the case of nine-year-old Mary Cairns who was involved in stabbing one of her friends. Thus:

'It could be argued that whereas the conceptual ambiguity of care and control was resolved (in England and Wales) by the distinction of care and criminal proceedings within the juvenile court structure, the Scottish solution was to separate the two realms of operation.'

(Asquith, 1983: p. 31)

However, this separation did not, and does not to this day, mean that children in Scotland are wholly exempted from prosecution. Kilbrandon was concerned about serious offences and with the need to protect society and recognised that there are categories of children who could be subject to punitive measures. Children may be prosecuted if they have committed a number of stated offences including technical offences such as road traffic offences; offences committed with an older offender; and serious offences including rape, arson and murder. Although the majority of children are dealt with in the Hearing system, the paradox is that the age of criminal responsibility in Scotland remains at 8 though children under 13 may only be prosecuted at the instigation of the Lord Advocate. Less than 200 children a year are prosecuted.

The majority of children who offend may be referred initially to a Reporter whose function is to determine whether the child referred may be in need of compulsory measures of care and consequently whether the child should be referred on to a Children's Hearing. Children's Hearings are not courts of law but administrative tribunals whose only function is to determine the potential need for compulsory measures of care and what form such measures should take. There is no jurisdiction over the question of guilt or innocence and where facts have to be established, the case must be referred to court. Given that children can also be prosecuted, there is in effect a very intricate set of relationships between the Children's Hearings and the courts. A further distinguishing feature of the Children's Hearings is that there is no judiciary involved and the decisions are made by lay members of the public – in as informal a setting and procedures as is possible and involving the family and child.

The Children's Hearings have remained relatively unchanged since their introduction though there have been some incremental modifications. Nevertheless, as Graham (1996) pointed out in reference to England and Wales, recent moves in the wake of the Bulger and other such cases to introduce more severe sanctions, and a more punitive approach to young offenders, have also influenced developments in Scotland. For example, there has clearly been a move towards emphasising the protection of society. Kilbrandon had indeed accepted that this was important, but there has to be some question as to whether recent developments threaten the basis of the philosophy of that report. The Children Act (Scotland) 1995 continues the emphasis on the welfare of the child. However, it also contains a statement that the protection of society from serious harm may overrule the commitment to the child's welfare (see s.16 (5) and s.17 (5) of the 1995 Act). As we have argued elsewhere, using public protection issues to justify measures which are not in the best interests of the child implies that, before such a course of action can be justified and pursued, an assessment of dangerousness must be made (Asquith & Docherty, forthcoming).

The promotion of social protection, alongside proposals to introduce electronic tagging for children, the introduction of curfews for children, and the apparent increase in the fear society has of its children and young people, suggests that the 'angels' and 'devils' debate and the questions of the relationship between welfare or justice are far from over.

Juvenile justice in England and Wales and in Scotland – some general comments

Thus, structural arrangements in juvenile justice and their historical development over the past 50 years, between the two jurisdictions, are different but they represent successive attempts to resolve very similar issues and in particular the basic difficulty of reconciling welfare and criminal considerations. Furthermore, they have been influenced by very similar trends in the philosophies underpinning practices and policies for dealing with young offenders. It is clear that there are a number of current movements which will have to be accommodated further within future policy and practice developments in both juris-dictions. Amongst the most important, and they are all related, would be:

(1) *The development of preventative strategies.* For the past 50 years the development of a preventative framework has been a recom-mendation in a number of reports in the welfare field, not just in relation to children who offend. Nevertheless, there has been a general failure to promote prevention, largely through the lack of resources and political will. The importance of addressing factors early in children's lives, with a view to reducing the risk of them becoming offenders later in life, is now well-documented (Far-rington, 1994; Asquith *et al.*, 1996). A number of implications follow from this, in particular the need for a political mind shift away from a 'crisis response' approach to the allocation of resources; this would enhance the quality of children's life experiences through early intervention and preventative strategies. As stated above, changes in juvenile justice and child care have often followed tragic cases and this militates against the considered development of policies of prevention.

(2) *The development of an integrated policy framework.* Closely related to item (1) is the increasing recognition (reminiscent of the debates in the 1950s and 1960s) of the common life experiences of children who offend and those children who are in need of care and protection. Nor does this apply simply to those children who commit the less serious offences. As Boswell (1995) has shown, even in the case of offenders in England and Wales who have committed the most serious offences including murder, there is

considerable evidence of extreme trauma and negative early life experiences when children. Similarly, the development of a preventative framework for early intervention in the lives of children must include all services and agencies which impact on children.

A glaring omission from a research point of view is the lack of systematic comparative research within the UK in the juvenile justice field. Though a committed European would support the need for European comparative research in this field, this should not be at the exclusion of evaluations of very different forms of juvenile justice within the UK. There is much to be learnt from such comparative work.

(3) *Children's rights*. This issue is discussed more fully by Harding in Chapter 4. The UK is a signatory to the United Nations Convention of the Rights of the Child. The recent Children (Scotland) Act 1995 is explicitly based on the key principles in the UN Convention and there is general agreement that future developments in child-related policies and practices should be governed by, and reflect, a commitment to the importance of children's rights. In relation to juvenile justice, discussions about the rights of children has often been about the rights of those children caught up in the formal systems of social control.

There can be no doubt that the rights of children within systems of juvenile justice are important and should be recognised appropriately. However, the UN Convention promotes more than simply procedural rights: it emphasises the social and economic rights of children. In particular, it emphasises the right of all children to life experiences which promote healthy growth and development. Such rights provide a framework on which to develop an integrated strategy of early intervention in order to enhance the quality of the life experiences of all our children. The potential of the UN Convention on the Rights of the Child to force a consideration of the life opportunities afforded to our children, address shortcomings, and amongst other things to reduce the risk of children becoming offenders in later life, is clear. But, above all, the Convention provides a rights-based framework for the legitimate realisation of the preventative arguments made over the past 50 years. It puts the issues of prevention and the life experiences of our children higher on the political agenda. It raises the possibility that our current policies may in fact be blaming the victims of an inequitable distribution of social and economic life chances.

(4) *The development of a new philosophy of juvenile justice*. As we have seen, over the past 50 years the pendulum has swung between welfare and justice, treatment and punishment. The failure (Walgrave, 1995) of contemporary systems of juvenile justice to achieve an adequate reduction in offending by children

and young people has prompted the search for new forms of justice for children. A notion of justice for children which rests on a concept of juvenile justice, focused on individual children must surely be too narrow and restrictive. If, however, we are truly committed to the notion of justice for children, we have to be much more concerned how social justice for children is to be promoted in our society. Developments in juvenile justice over the past 50 years have only obliquely addressed the need to pay attention to children's life experiences. Developments in policies and practices for those children who offend and those who are in need (and they may well be the same children) have to be articulated directly and explicitly to much broader concerns if we are to halt the endless swinging of the pendulum between welfare and criminal considerations.

References

Asquith, S. & Docherty, M. (forthcoming) Preventing offending by children and young people in Scotland. In *Criminal Justice in Scotland* (eds P. Duff & N. Hutton). Dartmouth Publishing, Dartmouth.

Asquith, S. (1983) *Children and Justice: Decision-making in Children's Hearings and Juvenile Courts*. Edinburgh University Press, Edinburgh.

Asquith S. (1996) Children who kill children. *International Journal of Childhood* 3 (1), 99–116.

Boswell, G. (1995) *Violent Victims: the prevalence of abuse and loss in the lives of section 53 offenders*. The Princes Trust, London.

Curtis Committee (1947), *Report of the Committee on Care of Children*. Cmnd 6922, HMSO, London.

Farrington, D. (1994) Early development prevention of juvenile delinquency. *Journal of the Royal Society for the Promotion of the Arts and Commerce*, November, 22–34.

Graham, J. (1996), The organisation and functioning of juvenile justice in England and Wales. In *Children and Young People in Conflict with the Law, Research Highlights in Social Work 30* (ed. S. Asquith). Jessica Kingsley, London.

Hansard, H.L. (1962) CCXLIV, 815.

HMSO (1965) *The Child, The Family and the Young Offender*. Cmnd 2742, HMSO, London.

HMSO (1968) *Children in Trouble*. Cmnd 3601, HMSO, London.

HMSO (1996) *Childhood Matters: Report of the National Commission of Inquiry into the Prevention of Child Abuse*. HMSO, London.

Ingleby Report (1960) *Report of the Committee on Children and Young Persons*. Cmnd 1191, HMSO, London.

Kilbrandon Report (1964) *Report on Children and Young Persons, Scotland*. Cmnd 2306, HMSO, London.

Longford Committee (1964) *Longford Report. Crime: A Challenge to Us All*. Labour Party, London.

Martin, F. & Murray, K. (1976) *Scottish Juvenile Justice*. Scottish Academic Press, Edinburgh.

Martin, F., Fox, S. & Murray, K. (1981) *Children Out of Court*. Scottish Academic Press, Edinburgh.

Murphy, J. (1992) *British Social Services: The Scottish Dimension*. Scottish Academic Press, Edinburgh.

O'Neill, T. (1981) *A Place Called Hope*. Blackwell Science, Oxford.

Secretary of State for Scotland (1997) Justice for Scotland's Children. *The 3rd Kilbrandon Lecture*, 10 November. University of Glasgow.

Seebohm Committee (1968) *Report of the Committee on Local Authority and Allied Personal Social Services*. Cmnd 3703, HMSO, London.

Social Work and the Community (1966) White Paper. HMSO, London.

Walgrave, L. (1995) Restorative juvenile justice: a way to restore justice in western European systems. In *Children and Young People in Conflict with the Law* (ed. S. Asquith). Jessica Kingsley, London.

Wootton, B. (1959) *Social Science and Social Pathology*. Allen & Unwin, London.

Chapter 11
Concluding Reflections
Olive Stevenson

In this brief concluding chapter, it is important to identify certain issues which it has not been possible to discuss sufficiently within the confines of this book. These are of two kinds: first, what may be described as *substantive* issues, that is, policies and strategies for child welfare; second, there are *process* issues, that is, what happens along the way – factors which come into play which affect policy and practice. In both much can be learnt from the experience of the past 50 years, described in these chapters.

Substantive issues

The place of substitute and complementary care

The time is seriously overdue for comprehensive examination of the place of substitute and complementary care within British child welfare. Chapter 7 by Thoburn and Chapter 8 by Bullock describe many aspects of these services to children which (inevitably) raise wider questions about the way forward.

The Utting report (1997) places on record its conviction that residential care should have a continuing part to play within the spectrum of provision, despite the grave damage done to its image by the scandals to which Bullock refers in Chapter 8. Yet even without those revelations, the history of residential care has been chequered and problematic, for at least two reasons. First, its development has been confused because of uncertainty about its purposes and, hence, about the appropriate models for it. In the years after 1948, once we had disposed of large residential nurseries inappropriate for the care of young children, a restless search began for the type of home which would give children an experience of a kind of family life. Just as Barnado had dreamed of cottage homes, built round a village green, so we dreamt of council houses on housing estates, with housefathers going out to work, housemothers staying at home and small numbers of children of all ages living relatively normal lives. That did not last long; the idealised view of a replica of family life was not sustainable. So, through various experiments, we have moved towards a residential experience which does not pretend to offer 'family life', and in which there are few staff in residence. We were, of course, driven towards change by the changing nature of the clientele. The concentration of adolescent young people in residential care and the very serious problems, often of sexual abuse, which brought them into care or, in the later terminology, to be 'looked after', were not anticipated or effectively addressed. The failure of government at central and local level to take hold of the emerging crisis was woeful, and may have played a part, although indirectly, in allowing a culture to develop within which abuse could thrive. The Utting report (1997) is the last in a long series of reports, spanning many years, which have identified difficulties and deficits but have not resulted in effective reforms. It is devoutly to be hoped that the measures which it recommends will now be given the impetus and resources which they require.

As Bullock describes in Chapter 8, the trends in, and models of, residential care were further confused by the unresolved debate, running from the 1960s onwards, concerning the relationship of care for 'the deprived' on the one hand and 'the depraved' on the other. Asquith, in Chapter 10, shows that this is part of the wider question of distinctions between welfare–treatment and justice–punishment approaches. These arguments are of great significance when they centre on the models of residential care which should be provided for children and young people, most of whom do not fall conveniently into one or other category. Inevitably, they lead back to reflections on the best ways to change the behaviour of young people and to make good some of the deficits in their lives. This requires some coherent theoretical assumptions, which have been sadly lacking in recent years. Bullock refers to the progressive schools of the 1960s and 1970s, which have lost the prestige which they earlier enjoyed. Whether or not one endorses their theoretical rationale, they illustrated a purposeful attempt to give disturbed children meaningful experiences in a carefully planned residential context.

It is significant that, without a vision, residential care has too often failed to provide even those basic elements of good parenting, let alone the more sophisticated treatment which many young people have required. The steps to redress this, through the introduction of the 'looking after children' materials (DoH, 1991) are greatly to be welcomed but can only be effective if they are part of an integrated strategy, crucial elements of which concern the recruitment, selection, training and retention of staff. Perhaps the greatest failure in the past 20 years or so in child welfare services has been in this area; this despite the recommendations of various reports, the most recent of which (DoH, 1992), in the years following its publication, did not receive from government the attention which it deserved.

In this book, to my regret, we have not been able to give adequate consideration to these matters and to some associated important questions, for example, to the similarities and differences in the knowledge base and skills needed for residential and field social work or to the importance of ensuring parity of status between the two. Although the work of caring more adequately and sensitively for disturbed adolescents, including delinquents, will remain at the heart of residential provisions and requires an intense theoretical and practical dialogue, other important functions for residential care should also be addressed concerning provision for children who need various forms of respite care. I shall return to this later.

Thoburn, in Chapter 7, identifies the long-running tension in foster care between a model of 'homely' families offering 'natural care' and specialist foster parents who are part of the therapeutic team. In some ways, this mirrors the tension in residential care, earlier described, between 'happy families' and treatment centres (however inadequately the latter may sometimes have functioned). We have been genuinely uncertain between how to help children: when is the natural, spontaneous care of good people sufficient and when do we need expertise? There are, of course, less altruistic motives for concentrating on the former; expertise, implying as it does, training and improvement payment, pushes the expense ever upward. However, this is a crucial area for policy deliberation, especially in the light of the traumatic experiences (including sexual abuse) of many of those entering foster care, who are exceedingly difficult to care for.

In recent years, it has become clear that many social workers and, indeed, other professionals have become increasingly reluctant to recommend that children enter the care system, even when home circumstances strongly indicate it, because of their doubts about the quality of the 'career in care' which so many children experience. There is thus a 'knock-on' effect on all child welfare work. It comes as a shock to see the numbers of moves and breakdowns which certain children experience; these and the associated delays, sometimes in relation to the court process, can be disastrous for children's well-being. The costs in terms of the children's mental health and associated problems as they grow older are incalculable.

The services which we have been discussing are normally associated with residence, with children living full time away from home. A variant on this is 'respite care' and this has been offered to children in need, especially those who are disabled. However, as Aldgate *et al.* (1996) have discussed, many categories of children in need can be helped by such 'respite' provision. Furthermore, it is not difficult to envisage many variants of this for children whose families have strengths but whose care is deficient in certain ways. For example, the line between 'residence' and day care (or even night care) need not be firmly drawn: there are endless permutations of 'shared care' which could benefit children, especially in those cases where neglect is a significant problem. I have chosen the term 'complementary care' (Stevenson, 1998) to emphasise the great possibilities of such arrangements.

The problem of ethnic minority children in child welfare

Any review of the last 50 years must consider what has been, or ought to have been, learnt about the needs of children from ethnic minorities. Chapter 5 addresses this matter from a particular angle – the impact of the rhetoric of anti-oppressive practice on social work. This is, of course, a partial and very limited exploration. There are two serious deficiencies in current discussion of these issues. The first is that, despite the raft of recent research in child welfare, very few advances have been made in our knowledge of the situations faced by these children, their families and the workers. Part of this can be explained by conventional sampling methods in quantitative research which resulted in small numbers of ethnic minorities in the studies and thus have difficulty in making useful generalisations. This explanation alone, however, is not adequate and raises wider questions about research priorities, and perhaps, about anxious avoidance of contentious areas. A major exception to this is in the as yet unpublished work of Thoburn, Norfork & Rashid at the University of East Anglia, whose research was designed to give an account of the experiences of children from ethnic minorities placed with foster or adoptive families and of their substitute families. As Thoburn, in Chapter 7, shows, this research promises to be of great value in throwing light on vital questions. Hopefully, the next decade will see further research explorations in this field.

A second deficiency, which I have discussed at some length in relation to neglect (Stevenson, 1998) concerns the reluctance of social workers to engage with issues concerning cultural differences rather than racism, in the understanding of practice with ethnic minority families. As Channer & Parton (1990) have argued, there may in fact be latent racism in this. They refer to 'reconstructed racism which leads to a failure to act at all ' (p. 112). Certainly, there is a lack of legitimate curiosity and excitement; perhaps it is stifled by cultural relativism, and the fear of having to distinguish between valid alternative ways of bringing up children and damaging practices. The black novelist, Alice Walker, recently remarked tersely that cultural relativism was 'extremely lazy!' (*The Guardian*, 1998). Such observations suggest that British workers should now move towards a greater sophistication of understanding, fired by the acknowledgement that shamefully little was done to address these complex areas in earlier years.

Prevention and family support

The third crucial substantive issue is that of prevention, discussed by Hardiker in Chapter 3. As she shows, the question is complex, theoretically. It is also one which politicians and senior managers tend to view with suspicion because of the difficulties of demonstrating 'value for money' outputs in terms of conventional research and evaluation. When resources are in chronically short supply, and there are many pressing problems, programmes or aspects of service delivery which cannot prove their short-term effectiveness can easily be pushed aside. Improved mental health and happier families when children become adults may seem a very long way away to politicians and managers with short-term objectives but less so to field workers who see every day the consequences for adults of earlier suffering.

Yet, whilst it is important to be precise in goals and to monitor and evaluate intervention whenever possible, in the end the case for prevention is a moral one, buttressed by well-founded knowledge of the damage inflicted by poor parenting. The aim of preventative work is to diminish actual or likely suffering and to enhance well-being. We may not always know how best to achieve our aims but there are elements in this endeavour which are based on tried and trustworthy assumptions, many of which are connected to what is known about the ingredients for healthy child development. The Government's refocusing initiative ensures a fresh debate on prevention; different levels and spheres will be identified and choices made within the framework of Children's Service Plans, in which Area Child Protection activity will be placed. We have an opportunity to examine policy and practice with rigour but the underlying principles must surely be welcomed.

Process issues

Finally, I wish to draw attention to the dynamic, complex interactions and processes which can be seen in the story of these 50 years. These have affected the direction and outcomes of child welfare services at every turn and in every area. Some of these forces are essentially external, social, political and economic (as discussed by Parton in Chapter 1 and Hardiker in Chapter 3), or arise from developments in other social services (discussed by Bilton in Chapter 2). As such, child welfare workers are at the mercy of matters largely outside their control, except possibly through corporate professional activity. This unfortunately has been little in evidence except for parliamentary activity. Some of the fundamental difficulties, for example in relation to the Central Council for Education and Training in Social Work (CCETSW) and the organisation of Social Service Departments (see Chapter 5), might have been addressed if there had been a more confident and well-founded professional base. If the establishment of a General Social Care Council contributes to a more articulate profession, it will be a great advance. There seem now to be three urgent questions for all concerned in child welfare to reflect upon.

First, how can we change the culture of child welfare work to ensure the *rebalancing* of professional and bureaucratic preoccupations? Such rebalancing would include, for example, the institution of effective professional development programmes for individuals and opportunities for creative consultation.

Second, how can we better manage organisational change to minimise the adverse effects on staff and hence on children and families?

Third, how can we encourage a constructive dialogue between theorists and practitioners so that policy and practice can be better articulated and the dangers of rigid, damaging policy applications avoided?

Unless these issues are comprehensively discussed and policies to address them developed, the early promise of child welfare services will not be fulfilled, despite the commitment and energy of thousands of workers at all levels over 50 years.

References

Aldgate, J., Bradley, M. & Hawley, D. (1996) Respite accommodation: a case study of partnership under the Children Act 1989. In *Child Welfare Services* (eds M. Hill & J. Aldgate), pp. 147–69. Jessica Kingsley, London.

Channer, Y. & Parton, N. (1990) Racism, cultural relativism and child protection. In *Violence against Children Study Group. Taking child abuse seriously*, pp. 105–120. Unwin, London.

Department of Health (1991 *et seq.*) *Looking After Children: Research into Practice*. Department of Health, London.

Department of Health (1992) Choosing with Care (The Warner Report). HMSO, London.

Stevenson, O. (1998) *Neglected Children: issues and dilemmas*. Blackwell Science, Oxford.

Utting, W. (1997) *People Like Us: A review of the safeguards for children living away from home*. Department of Health, London.

Walker, A. (1998) *The Guardian*, 29 April.

Index